Smart Marriage

Smart Marriage

Using Your (Business) Head as Well as
Your Heart to Find Wedded Bliss

Allen M. Parkman

PRAEGER

Westport, Connecticut
London

Library of Congress Cataloging-in-Publication Data

Parkman, Allen M.
    Smart marriage : using your (business) head as well as your heart to find wedded bliss /
Allen M. Parkman.
        p. cm.
    Includes bibliographical references and index.
    ISBN-13: 978-0-275-99455-6 (alk. paper)
    1. Marriage. 2. Decision making. I. Title.
HQ734.P2123   2007
646.7'8—dc22   2007028065

British Library Cataloguing in Publication Data is available.

Library of Congress Catalog Card Number: 2007028065
ISBN-13: 978-0-275-99455-6

First published in 2007

Praeger Publishers, 88 Post Road West, Westport, CT 06881
An imprint of Greenwood Publishing Group, Inc.
www.praeger.com

Printed in the United States of America

The paper used in this book complies with the
Permanent Paper Standard issued by the National
Information Standards Organization (Z39.48-1984).

10 9 8 7 6 5 4 3 2 1

To Amy and for Ian and Andrew

Contents

Preface

I just had to write this book. Having parents who divorced when I was four and yet having been married myself for more than 30 years, the reasons why some marriages fail and others succeed has always intrigued me. To be blunt, I—like many people—would view my life as a failure if I was unable to establish a successful family. In the 1980s, my research interests started to move from traditional economic topics such as regulation and anti-trust to the family. Of particular interest to me was the effect of the shift from the fault to the no-fault grounds for divorce on the decisions being made by married couples. A closer review of those laws suggested that in effect the change was from mutual consent to unilateral action as a basis for the dissolution of marriage. This interest resulted in two books and numerous articles. The central theme in my legal analysis was that unilateral divorce throughout marriage was not a great idea and that mutual consent—rather than fault—would be better for established marriages. The economic analysis provides some evidence that unilateral divorce produced additional incentives for married women to work outside the home. Overall, I concluded that unilateral divorce throughout marriage encourages adults to become more concerned about their own narrowly defined self-interest and less concerned about other family members often to the detriment of their marriage.

This book is the result of my conclusion that unilateral divorce is here to stay, so people have to make good decisions about marriage despite it. People have to work harder to make the kinds of decisions that will continue to make attractive the marriage that they entered into optimistically. While considering why our marriage has succeeded and my parents'—and many other people's—marriages failed, I realized that my education and experience has played a part in our success. Neither my education nor experience has anything to do directly with marriage, as I am an economist/lawyer teaching in a business school. While it is commonly acknowledged that businesses have to make good decisions to survive, seldom has that perspective been applied to marriages. Still, adults have much less guidance than in the past about the decisions that will result in a successful marriage.

This book applies business principles to many of the critical decisions associated with marital success. Initially, it suggests that people should be looking for a business partner as well as a lover. Then, insights from business are applied to decisions about the allocation of responsibilities during marriage, careers and children. A pragmatic approach to marriage is not a substitute for a romantic one, but rather a complement as its goal is to help people establish the successful marriage that most of us want.

This book would not have been possible without the help of numerous people. Most important has been my wife, Amy, who has tolerated my economic perspective on life for all these years. It has also benefited from the research support that I have received from the Anderson Schools of Management at the University of New Mexico over many years. More recently, it has benefited from the diligent efforts of my agent, Jeff Olsen, and my editor at Praeger, Debbie Carvalko.

Introduction

One has to wonder why it is so difficult for people to have a successful marriage, since that goal is usually central to what they perceive to be the good life. When people are asked about their personal goals, it is always at the top of the list. High school seniors consistently rank having a good marriage and family life as their most important goal.[1] It is viewed as more important than making lots of money or saving the planet, for example. Even twice-divorced Donald Trump said that marriage is a great institution—if you get it right.

Marriage is a practical as well as romantic goal for most people. Married people are healthier, wealthier, happier, and have longer lives than single people. Married couples even have better sex. Sociologist Linda Waite and journalist Maggie Gallagher summarize the research on marriage in their book, *The Case for Marriage*.[2] Married couples are better off than other adults in virtually any dimension of life. Benefits accrue to both husbands and wives. They feel healthier than those who are divorced, separated, or widowed. Married couples also have more financial resources. Marriage provides the best environment for raising children. Moreover, women are safer in marriage than in other types of relationships.

While some people dismiss the importance of marriage as a key social institution, less than five percent of people have never married by age seventy-five.[3] The percentage of adults who have married has fallen recently, but in 2005 only 28 percent of men and 22 percent of women had never married. And that, to some extent, is a reflection of people delaying marriage rather than rejecting it.

Even with the increase in the divorce rate, most people marry with the expectation of a long-term, if not life-long, commitment. We do not want to face the pain and frustration associated with divorce. We would prefer to be more successful than Liza Minnelli, who was proud that her marriage to sculptor Mark Gero lasted all of twelve years. While some authors, such as Constance Ahrons in her book, *The Good Divorce*,[4] want to sugarcoat the effects of divorce, every divorce has to be viewed as a failure—certainly relative to the expectations at marriage.

Most couples who are anticipating a long-term relationship marry, but others do not tie the knot for a variety of reasons. For some it is a matter of choice. Kurt Russell and Goldie Hawn have been together for over twenty years without marrying, something Goldie rationalizes by pointing to her two failed marriages before she met Kurt. Others have not married because of the legal restrictions on who can marry. Elton John and David Furnish were a couple for more than ten years before they eventually married, after laws prohibiting same-sex marriage were relaxed. Still, these couples have had to make important decisions about a mate and roles within their relationships just like couples who marry.

Even though easy, unilateral divorce has blurred the distinction between co-habitation and marriage in the eyes of many, marriage still serves an important, symbolic purpose: No matter how much people say that they are committed to a relationship, the commitment is suspect without a willingness to marry. Sure it may just mean a wedding ceremony and a ring, but the act of marrying is still a very important symbol of commitment.

You probably want to marry–or stay married–and you want to do it right the first time. Yet, many people fail to attain those goals. Essentially, all couples enter marriage optimistically with the expectation that they will have a better life as a result. Unfortunately, approximately half of those couples will eventually conclude that they were so wrong that the only solution is to dissolve their marriage. While the divorce rate peaked in the early 1980s, it is still much higher than in any other period in American history.[5] Other married couples do not divorce, but they conclude that their marriage has not lived up to their expectations. Even among couples that stay married, the level of satisfaction with their marriage has been declining.[6]

A SMART MARRIAGE

The goal of a Smart Marriage is to solve the puzzle associated with marriage. For most people, nothing is more important for their long-term happiness than a successful marriage. They marry optimistically in pursuit of that goal–and yet many people are incapable of establishing the marriage that they anticipated. You will have a Smart Marriage if you can solve this puzzle by choosing the right person to marry and then by both you and your spouse continuing to agree that it is a success. You cannot have a successful marriage just because you want it. Sure, luck has a role in marital success, but bad luck can, too often, be traced to poor decisions.

Creating a Smart Marriage requires you to use your head as well as your heart to make critical decisions before and during marriage. Some people will make the right decisions and others will not. This book will help you make better decisions and give you a good shot at long-term marital bliss.

Why do people have such a difficult time accomplishing this most fundamental task? After all, most people appear to be capable of accomplishing other strategic goals. If you want to be a lawyer, you go to law school. If you want to live in Southern California, you move there. But you may be much less successful at establishing a successful marriage. How do you improve your ability to accomplish that goal and end up happily married?

First you have to recognize that times have changed. While many people bemoan the decline in the state of families in America—often attributing it to a shift in values toward more self-indulgent behavior—seldom do we appreciate the increase in the complexity of the decisions necessary for a successful marriage. Up until just a few generations ago, essentially all adults wanted to be married and most accomplished that goal. The range of choices that they had before and during marriage was very limited. They chose a spouse (or often one was chosen for them) from within a narrow socioeconomic group and then they assumed socially determined roles— often subtly based on necessity—similar to those of their parents. Having married, they became parents, often having numerous children.

This hardly describes the situation now. All of those choices have changed dramatically. There are critical choices at each step described above. Should you marry? What type of person among the numerous people to which you are exposed should you marry? How should you balance your career and your marriage? How does that balancing affect when you marry? What roles should you assume when you marry and what roles should you expect your spouse to assume? To be blunt, who should wash the dishes? Should you have children? How many should you have? When should you have them? The list goes on and on. You have to make far more decisions than your grandparents made.

Like most adults, my wife, Amy, and I have struggled with all of these decisions. Having a successful marriage and happy family has been important to both of us. In contrast to many people, I can say after over thirty years of marriage that we have been fairly successful at accomplishing those goals. As I reflect on our success, I have developed a deeper appreciation for the benefits of my education and the job that I have had for the last thirty years. No, I am not a successful marriage counselor. Far from it. Neither my education nor my job has anything directly to do with marriage as I am a lawyer/economist who teaches in a business school. However, economics and a business perspective have permitted me to develop valuable insights about the choices that we made that led to a successful marriage. Reflecting back,

I think that most of our decisions were good ones, but often the decisions then did not benefit from the insights that we have now. So, where do you look for guidance for making the best decisions?

A BUSINESS APPROACH TO MARRIAGE

If you want to have a Smart Marriage, you have to make better decisions. In a business setting, people have recognized the importance—if not necessity—of making good decisions. A substantial literature has developed in support of those decisions. This literature has important insights about the choices that people make and how they can improve them.

A pragmatic, business-like approach to marriage is not new. In fact, it has often been the only approach. For most of the history of Europe and the Americas—and still in much of the rest of the world—marriage was viewed as much too important to be trusted to the decisions of the young. In those times and places, romance took a back seat to parents and others who decided who would make the best couples and the roles that they would assume after marriage. Tradition established processes the people felt improved their welfare. On closer examination, these traditions had a business-like goal of attempting to increase societies' production. In times that were much less prosperous than ours, people had to make difficult decisions. Traditional arrangements were viewed as best for providing such things as more food and better shelter.

We all recognize that times have changed. Traditional arrangements and roles have very little influence on decisions about marriage in the United States today, where romance has become the primary basis for marriage. Yet, people still have the same goal of a successful marriage.

A pragmatic perspective on marriage, therefore, is not an alternative to a romantic one based on love and physical attraction. The two approaches are complementary as they both attempt to make a marriage a success. People get married because they are in love, but they stay married because they are satisfied with their marriage. They feel that they are better off in it than in any other arrangement.

While this book uses insights from business to improve decisions affecting marriage, the last thing I want to do is to obscure the importance of love and physical attraction in marriage. That is where all successful marriages (at least in industrial countries) start. But that is not the end. Being somewhat more pragmatic can result in the happy marriage that so many of us desire. We will be discussing concepts such as the potential gains from specialization of labor during marriage as a basis for improving a family's welfare. We will not, however, suggest that marriage is just another business proposition for which the best approach, for example, is a detailed premarital contract specifying the ongoing roles of the spouses.

The first step toward making better decisions consists of having a clearer understanding of what motivates your decisions and what you are attempting to accomplish. Economists observe that people tend to be motivated by their self-interest with the goal of increasing their welfare. So, don't kid yourself. The most important person in your life will always be you. You want to love—and you want to be loved. While profits serve a central role in the welfare of a business, welfare is a much broader concept for individuals. It varies among people based on a range of goals such as happiness, peace of mind, and financial success. For most people, a successful marriage is an important means for accomplishing those goals.

COMMON SENSE

In many areas of everyday life, you have little need for insights from business to provide guidance as to how you can improve your decisions. Common sense has already provided you with guidance. Consider the choices that you make as a consumer or worker.

As a consumer, you have gradually learned how to allocate your limited time and money more efficiently. Initially, you observed others making decisions. You heard your parents debating about how to spend your family's income and allocate their time. Eventually, you may have received an allowance from your parents to cover your recreational expenses. It was apparent then that spending too much on some things like video games left less for others. Gradually, even if you continued to be dependent on your parents, the activities that you were expected to cover with your allowance and earnings expanded to include clothing and meals. Often, going away to college is an important period for people to learn how to better allocate their limited money and time. Finally, you were making your own decisions about the sources of your income and the allocation of your expenditures. Tradeoffs became even clearer. Less attractive alternatives had to be rejected and better alternatives accepted. While you would like a new car, for example, saving up to buy a house may be more important. Making choices can be frustrating, but consumers eventually learn how to improve the satisfaction that they receive from the goods and services that they acquire using their limited resources of income and time.

A similar process leads people to their preferred career. Initially, you observed the world around you and as a result you may have wanted to be an emergency room doctor. Eventually, through courses in school and part-time employment, you developed a clearer sense of potential careers. Again you were faced with tradeoffs among your alternatives. Some jobs are enjoyable but do not pay very much, while others pay better, but are less enjoyable. You become aware that jobs in a field that you thought that you would enjoy would require you to relocate, sacrificing friends and family relationships. Again, you were faced with more tradeoffs. There is substantial job mobility by young workers as they search for a preferred career. Eventually, people decide on a career and employer and job mobility is much less common among older workers. At this point, some people even find economics interesting as a career. Few jobs will be perfect, but people learn to appreciate the tradeoffs among positions, finding the combination of attributes in one that they find most appealing.

Common sense, however, may not provide adequate guidance for making the best decisions about marriage. Then you need a more structured approach that can be provided by a business-like framework. While the marital decisions suggested by a business framework may be subtle and sometimes counterintuitive, they are not particularly complicated. The trial and error process used by consumers and workers can, however, be a disastrous approach to making decisions about or within marriage. There is much less room for error in those areas. Too many decisions are irreversible. Just consider parenthood. What prepares us to be parents? Having become one, it is not the time to question whether it was a good idea. You need a clearer structure for making decisions. A business perspective can be a surprising source of guidance for making better decisions about marriage.

You seldom have adequate guidance about the decisions that will make marriage a success. Few of us have observed numerous families intimately and even the decision making of our parents may have been subtle or dysfunctional. Your contemporaries are of even less value as guides. They are as confused as you.

The value of a business perspective on marriage can be illustrated by observing the investment process. Businesses prosper due to key investments that are made possible by personal sacrifices. Investors sacrifice income that could be used for current consumption to buy shares in corporations that use the funds to increase their output and, hopefully, their profits. Both the investors and the businesses expect to be better off in the future due to this process.

In a similar fashion, families benefit when spouses invest in their marriage. They make sacrifices by doing things that they would not otherwise have done. Some can be casual and low cost, such as going to a concert that they do not anticipate enjoying—but they know they will be rewarded with the appreciation of their spouse. Some sacrifices can be substantial, however, such as when spouses limit their careers to provide childcare or to relocate due to a new employment opportunity for a spouse. The anticipated rewards for these investments are the reciprocal acts of the other family members—the increased income of their spouse and the love of their spouse and children. Both the people making the sacrifices as well as family members are potentially better off due to the investment.

This investment process is just one of the reasons married couples can be better off than people in other living arrangements, but its benefits may not be intuitively obvious. People do not like to make sacrifices. What about my career if I shift to part-time employment to adjust to childcare responsibilities? Why should I take the time and effort to complete my education when our current incomes are covering all our expenses?

THE FAMILY AS AN EFFICIENT BUSINESS

A business perspective can also provide insights about the roles that spouses might consider during marriage. While many people argue that the ideal marriage should consist of an equal sharing of responsibilities by the spouses both through employment and in the home, insights from successful businesses suggest that the process of increasing your overall welfare is more complicated. In many ways, a successful marriage can be viewed as an efficient business about which the business literature has numerous insights. Businesses convert inputs into outputs attempting to make a profit. In the pursuit of profits, most businesses rely on their employees assuming specialized roles that increase their productivity. Most families benefit from a similar process. The family members use their time, income, and skills to produce a variety of outputs such as well-adjusted children and a pleasant living environment. During this production process, most families benefit from the spouses assuming more specialized roles than they would have had if they had remained single.

Even in an era of two-income households, couples still benefit from differentiating their roles. In the 1980s, one of the most politically powerful couples in America was the Doles. Bob Dole was the Senate majority leader—and eventual presidential candidate—and Elizabeth Dole was the Secretary of Transportation in the Reagan Administration. However, in their domestic capacities, Elizabeth assumed the primary responsibility for cooking, for example. In their joint autobiography, *Unlimited Partners*, she notes the challenges that she faced as the family's cook, often having to rely on Lean Cuisine and a small library of thirty-minute-meals cookbooks.[7]

Like many couples who have created a successful marriage, Amy and I have become more specialized since we married. I enjoy eating, so even in my bachelor days I was a fairly good cook. Well, it might partly have been due to poverty during graduate school. However, Amy is a much better— and certainly more enthusiastic—cook than I, so she has assumed the primary responsibility for cooking during our marriage. Specialization is never complete, as I make the best fresh pasta on the planet. On the other hand, plumbing and electrical problems are outside her experience and, therefore, have become my responsibilities. In support of her cooking, I have also assumed responsibility for such pedestrian tasks as washing the dishes.

The gains from increased specialization are going to be particularly important for you when you become a parent. Both my wife and I had full-time jobs until we became parents. However, we then realized that we were probably going to have to temporarily alter our careers so that we could have the happy, well-adjusted children that we wanted. With a master's degree in early childhood education, my wife was much better prepared to work with the children, so she cut back from teaching full time to part time. Meanwhile, this freed me up to continue to focus on my career.

After the children reached an age at which they could be left alone after school, she returned to full-time teaching.

TAKING RESPONSIBILITY FOR YOUR DECISIONS

Both business and marital decisions can be difficult. The reason that you have to make decisions is because you cannot have everything. All decisions essentially require you to sacrifice something else. You will marry when you expect to be better off married to a particular person rather than remaining single. And you will stay married so long as you and your spouse continue to believe that to be true. Therefore, the solution to having a Smart Marriage requires you to choose the right person and then make good decisions during marriage. All of these decisions require you to reject alternatives.

In particular, having a Smart Marriage requires you to reject the victimization perspective that is too common in contemporary society. From that perspective, you are not responsible for your actions, since societal forces overwhelm you. One of the most pathetic examples of this process is when people who voluntarily married someone proclaim—when their marriage ends in divorce—the despicable characteristics of that person. They assume no responsibility for having made a poor decision in having married. Unless they are capable of that recognition, it is not likely that the quality of their decisions about a spouse will improve in the future. People, just like businesses, are less likely to be successful if they do not recognize and learn from their mistakes.

Mia Farrow has been married to Frank Sinatra and Andre Previn and had a long-term relationship with Woody Allen. Her lack of success in these relationships may be reflected in her unwillingness to assume responsibility for her poor choices. For example, in her autobiography, *What Falls Away*, she describes Woody Allen as hypercritical, short-tempered, emotionally frigid, and oblivious to anyone else's needs.[8] He was cold to her children—including his son—and mean to his parents. Moreover, he is a hypochondriac who has been in therapy for forty years. These are not the attributes that most of us would look for in a life-long partner, so one has to wonder why she devoted so much of her life to him. Eventually, the couple separated in 1996 due to the well-publicized relationship between Allen and Farrow's adopted daughter, Soon-Yi Previn. She justifies having stayed with him so long because she was emotionally dependent on him and afraid to lose her job working in his films.

Here, we assume—and emphasize—that you are responsible for the decisions that you make. Sure, life is uncertain, so choices can turn out different from your expectations. Marriage, like so many decisions about the future, entails risk. An analysis of business decisions usually shows that the more informed they are, the more likely that they will produce the desired outcomes. You have the opportunity to acquire more information and hopefully reduce your risks as your relationship gradually progresses from dating to intimacy, marriage, and parenthood. You can reduce your risk of making poor choices by evaluating the information acquired at each stage: dating, marriage, and parenthood. This evaluation is especially important because the cost of making a poor decision also increases with each stage. Ending an intimate relationship is emotionally draining, but it pales in comparison to the anguish for all parties associated with a divorce especially if there are children.

WHY DO PEOPLE MAKE BAD DECISIONS?

People are already making decisions in all the areas that we have discussed. They are dating, marrying, and becoming parents. While these people are unlikely to have used a business perspective in making these decisions, throughout this process they think that they are making good decisions that will result in a successful marriage. So what is wrong with the processes that they are going through?

Businesses and people make what appear to be poor decisions for a couple of reasons. First, conditions change in an unexpected way and their results differ from their expectations. Second, they do not have the correct framework or information at the time the decision was being made. You can do little about correcting for conditions that change unexpectedly other than being willing to adapt. Imagine the person that you love has an accident that changes the nature of your relationship. You would need to adapt or end the relationship. However, you can deal with the second cause by improving your decisions by utilizing a better framework and improved information. Each alternative has benefits (what you expect to gain), and costs (what you have to give up). You can make better decisions by more clearly identifying the benefits and costs of your alternatives and choosing those with the largest net gain. An improved framework would recognize the roles that you would expect as spouses that differ from those that you have assumed as a dating couple. If you think you are interested in being a parent, then it is better to think of potential spouses as the mother or father of your children rather than as just your lover.

WHY THE ALTERNATIVE SOLUTIONS OFTEN DO NOT WORK

By focusing more clearly on the costs and benefits of choices, a business-like approach to marriage differs from most of the popular marriage advice. The popular literature and numerous talk shows on radio and television dispense advice on how to improve marital quality. Yet most of the advice offered by family therapists and psychologists ignores why people do what they do. They give you advice on how you can improve your behavior without clearly understanding the reasons why you are making poor decisions. This advice does not get to the core of the poor decisions that many people make regarding marriage.

A common thread of this advice is better communication between the spouses, which is obviously an important component of marital success. However, frequently lacking is this question: Communication about what? If you think you are making the right decisions, when in fact you are making the wrong ones, improved communication is not likely to improve your judgment. Poor judgment occurs because people do not understand the decisions that will result in a successful marriage. It is no surprise that few marriages are saved by entering therapy.

In summary, to have a Smart Marriage, you need to make better decisions. This book uses a business perspective to help you in making those decisions. You are responsible for your decisions and your goal is to make yourself better off. As evidenced by the high divorce rate, making the best decisions about marriage is not easy.

WHAT FOLLOWS?

The first step toward having a Smart Marriage consists of identifying why it is particularly difficult to make the best decisions about marriage. To make better decisions about marriage requires us to look at some unique problems. Four traps cause people to make poor decisions. They consist of the Experience Trap because other experiences do not necessarily prepare you for making good decisions about marriage; the Emotional Trap because your emotions have such a strong influence on romantic decisions; the Self-Interest Trap because a misinterpretation of your self-interest can cause you to ignore the importance of considering others when you are making decisions; and the No-Fault Divorce Trap, which can limit your commitment to marriage with unfortunate results.

Subsequent chapters will lead you through the various stages in which you need to make critical decisions to establish a successful marriage. Initially, you are interested in a spouse. So we will explore the characteristics of people that you should be considering—and I am not talking about blond and blue eyed versus tall, dark, and handsome. That person should have many of the attributes of a person that you would consider as a potential business partner. Think in terms of someone with whom you are compatible in more ways than just physical attraction and yet someone whose skills and preferences present opportunities for both of you to benefit from more specialized roles during marriage. We will explore why commitment is so essential in both business and marriage. Finding the right person is the result of a search and marketing process in which you have to consider the characteristics of the person that you are seeking, how you will find that person and how you are going to convince her to marry you.

The next challenge is determining your roles during marriage and the balance between your careers and those roles. You should never lose sight of your goal of increasing your welfare. Often, that is not the same as increasing your income. A successful marriage is a central component of that welfare for most people—and probably you, which is why you are reading this book. In addition to intimate contact with someone you love, you will be better off married if you have access to more goods and services than you would have in any other situation. A successful family is very much like a thriving business as it converts inputs into outputs. Its inputs are time, money and skills with the resulting outputs being commodities. These commodities come in various forms from meals, intimate moments with those you love, to well-adjusted children.

Careers are an important source of the income necessary for the production of commodities, but they also detract from the time available for domestic activities. There are benefits from employment based on the commodities that it permits, but there are costs associated with it due to work-related factors and sacrificed alternatives. The goal from employment should be to maximize the net gain—benefits minus costs.

Central to most families are children, so they are discussed next. You should have children only because of the enjoyment that they will bring to your life. This enjoyment will be enhanced if you produce happy, well-adjusted children. From an economic perspective, you invest in your children by making sacrifices on their behalf in the anticipation of the enjoyment that they will bring to you. This is a critical area in which you have more choices today. Most couples had many children in the past. Now you have to decide whether you will have children, how many you will have, and when you will have them. These choices will be determined by weighing costs and benefits. Considering parenthood in a pragmatic way, you'll see, can be very important for marital success.

Not all marriages are a success, so we have to discuss divorce. In effect, a divorce is similar to a company going bankrupt—the future benefits (revenues) are not expected to exceed the costs. It is important for you to recognize that the costs of divorce usually increase with the duration of the marriage, so you are advised to evaluate your marriage critically in the early stages. This chapter also alerts you to the costs of divorce, thereby encouraging you to work harder to make your marriage—which you anticipated would be a success—a success.

With a divorce, the process of attempting to create a Smart Marriage starts all over again as most divorced people want to remarry. Although you may be wiser for your experience, you now have to face a broader range of decisions to create a successful marriage. You are in the position of a business that is considering a merger. You have to address whether your activities and those of your prospective spouse can be successfully consolidated. You, and many potential mates, may have ex-spouses and children who will complicate the process of making the best decisions. A review of past decisions is important to improve on your future ones.

So, let's start to create a Smart Marriage. It is important to realize that pragmatic thinking within a business framework is not in conflict with the emotional response that you want to make to someone you love and to whom you are physically attracted. You want that love and physical attraction to lead to happiness rather than frustration and pain. The framework developed here is most likely to complement your emotional preferences, resulting in a successful marriage. The first challenge is to avoid some critical traps into which too many people fall resulting in poor decisions about marriage. Those traps are the subject of the next chapter.

CONCLUSION

To create the successful marriage (a Smart Marriage) that most adults recognize as their most important goal, people have many more choices than in the past. Regrettably, many people lack an adequate framework for making good decisions, with the result that their marriages do not fulfill their expectations. Too often the result is divorce. Guidance for making better decisions can come from a surprising source. Business—and more specifically economics—studies the choices that people make and how they can be improved. This book uses a business framework for making better decisions before, during, and potentially after a marriage.

THINGS TO REMEMBER

- Having a Smart Marriage is based on establishing the successful marriage that is important for most people.
- Most people marry optimistically in pursuit of that goal, and yet so many are incapable of establishing the marriage that they anticipated.
- Don't kid yourself. You base your decisions on your self-interest.
- Other experiences may not prepare you for making the best decisions about your marriage.
- A business perspective on making decisions considering benefits and costs can be important for increasing the likelihood of marital success.

The Four Traps

2

No one starts out intending to make poor decisions about marriage. Still, the high divorce rate suggests that many people are making poor decisions about the person that they marry and choices that they make during their marriage. Therefore, your first task is to understand why it is so difficult to make good decisions about marriage.

In this chapter, four traps are identified that cause people to make poor decisions about marriage. The key to improving your decisions follows from a better understanding of why these traps can lead you to make poor decisions and how you can overcome them. Only then can you improve your decision making when looking for a spouse and weighing alternatives during marriage.

THE EXPERIENCE TRAP: YOU MAY HAVE LITTLE EXPERIENCE WITH THE CHOICES THAT RESULT IN A SUCCESSFUL MARRIAGE

The first trap exists because other experiences often do not prepare you for the best decisions before and during marriage.[1] A concern about the choices that you make about marriage is a fairly recent development; adults in the past had few alternatives other than to marry someone from a limited pool of potential mates and then to assume a predictable role within marriage. Historically, couples were essentially forced to make choices without thinking much about them.

Married couples were better off than single people, so people married as soon as men were capable of supporting a family. They usually chose someone (or had someone chosen for them) from a similar socioeconomic background. Couples assumed roles similar to those of their parents. When agriculture was the primary occupation, men tended to work in the fields, while women focused on domestic activities. Even with this specialization, they often worked together during, for example, a harvest. With the industrial revolution, the roles of husbands and wives became more distinct as the husbands emphasized income earning and wives continued to focus on domestic activities, especially raising children. Without thinking much about it, couples continued to specialize.

Because divorce was difficult and uncommon, there was little doubt in most couples' minds that their marriage was going to be for their joint lives. By conforming to social norms, married couples were better off than single people. They had access to more material goods and services and had little reason to question the roles that they had assumed. Most couples that were capable of having children had them. Because of the gains from marriage, arranged marriages have continued to be common in less-developed countries. In poor, traditional countries such as Pakistan, for example, 90 percent of marriages are still arranged.

MORE CHOICES

Having a Smart Marriage has been complicated by more choices. Adults now have many more options and, while that has improved the lives of many people, it has made it more difficult to make the decisions that will result in a successful marriage. The gains from marriage have become less obvious as there has been a convergence in the opportunities available to men and women. The employment prospects have improved for women and, responding to higher wages and improved opportunities, women have made a stronger commitment to careers. Most women no longer need a husband for financial support. Meanwhile, new products and services have reduced the importance of the services provided by some women in the home. Processed foods such as frozen entrees and cleaning services have reduced the gains to men from having a wife. There appears to be fewer benefits to men and women from assuming specialized roles in marriage.

Complicating decisions about how to act during marriage has been the increase in the importance of less-tangible gains from marriage. When there were substantial material gains from marriage, it could be a success even if the couple barely tolerated each other. At least there was food on the table and a roof over their heads. Many adults now, especially women, are looking for intangible qualities in a spouse such as communication, companionship, and empathy. There has been a shift toward "companionate marriages" in which the partners are more equal in the roles that they assume in marriage. Many adults have higher expectations about the quality of their interaction with their spouse. They want more than to just get along.

With fewer obvious gains from specialization during marriage, couples now have less guidance regarding the decisions that will increase their welfare. There are a number of schools of thought on the preferred roles that couples should assume. On the one hand, businesses understand that specialization of labor increases efficiency in most situations. This is true in most commercial situations such as factories and stores, but it is also evident in domestic situations. For instance, those who plan trips more frequently usually become better trip planners. On the other hand, some, such as feminist Gloria Steinem, argue that the preferred roles within marriage should consist of an equal sharing of all responsibilities. In this new environment, adults have much less guidance as to the best decisions about spouses, careers, domestic roles and parenthood. Moreover, it is common for married couples to modify their goals over the duration of their marriage.

When Susan Molinari married Bill Paxon in 1994, she hoped to become president of the United States and he was committed to being her campaign manager. They both had plenty of political experience as she represented Staten Island in Congress and he represented Buffalo. In the pursuit of the marriage that they wanted, those ambitions had to be altered. In 1995, they had a child and they soon became the model modern couple as they shared childcare responsibilities equally in their adjoining Congressional offices. At that point, they had avoided any major concessions to marriage and a family. But then Ms. Molinari recognized the tradeoffs that she was making and in 1997 she quit Congress stating that, "It was totally about family." She wanted to have more time to spend with her child. Mr. Paxon's leaving Congress in 1998 had less to do with family than with a power struggle with Newt Gingrich. As of 2003, the marriage was flourishing with Mr. Paxon serving as a senior adviser to a Washington law firm and Ms. Molinari being the president of a lobby firm. She is no longer interested in being president, because it would be too time consuming.[2]

The number and timing of children have also become new areas of conflict. When women primarily worked in the home, essentially all couples who could have children had them and often lots of them. With more options for adults, and attractive careers for women, parenthood requires much more planning and thought. Couples have substantial control over the number of children that they will have and when they will have them. They may have conflicting aspirations concerning parenthood resulting in disagreements about the number of children and when to have them.

PREFERRED ROLES

One of the first challenges facing a couple is to determine their best roles. Let's make it clear from the start: It is going to be very difficult, if not impossible, for you to "have it all." You cannot have a highly successful career, be there for your spouse when she needs you, and attend all of your children's soccer games. You must first clarify your priorities. Then you must ask, "How can I accommodate my other activities?"

Many women have had a particularly difficult time determining their preferred roles, because their range of options has expanded more than it has for men—so far. In many households, the husband has continued to be the primary income earner, so he assumes that role while providing—if he's smart—some support at home with domestic chores and childcare. For women, especially if they are a secondary income earner, the choices have become more difficult because of the conflicts between careers and domestic activities, especially motherhood. The earlier attempts to have it all—a successful career, a happy marriage, and usually motherhood—have gradually given way to the realization that few women are capable of being successful in all of these areas. Then the issue becomes the area or areas that will be emphasized.

Younger women often are more aware of these tradeoffs than were their mothers, many of whom were at the forefront of the women's movement in the 1970s. Consider the discussion between author Carole Hyatt and her daughter Ariel on the Oprah Winfrey Show.[3] Carole has written important books providing guidance for women in the workplace. These include *When Smart People Fail: Rebuilding Yourself for Success*[4] and *Women and Work*.[5]

Still Ariel felt, "My mom is a fantastic trailblazing woman, but a lot of times she was not there."

On reflection, Carole concurred noting, "I tried hard to be the supermom, but, frankly, I wasn't good at it. Looking back, it was costly. I had a very angry little girl, who wanted her mommy, and I didn't have the time, and I didn't know how to balance it, and it took me a long time to get to understand that you can't have it all." In other words, she was snared by the Experience Trap.

Ariel hopes to find a better balance, "When I have my own kids, I think that I'll probably end up staying home for the early part of their lives and then go back to my career." Since the labor force attachment of married women with young children has not shown a significant tendency to decrease, it will be interesting to see if Ariel is able to fulfill that commitment.

This transformation of the United States can be vividly illustrated by the evolution in the roles assumed by presidential couples. All presidents have been men and, with the exception of James Buchanan, they have been married. Traditionally, the wives of presidents had only domestic careers. In many cases, they had a substantial effect on their husband's decisions, but their influence was usually subtle. In some cases, it was more than subtle, such as when Edith Wilson assumed decision-making powers when her husband, Woodrow Wilson, had a stroke in 1919. More recently, the wives have been more visible such as Eleanor Roosevelt and Jacqueline Kennedy, but they continued to live in the shadow of their husbands.

This pattern changed with Hillary and Bill Clinton. They had a similar level of education and she had been the primary income earner during most of their marriage prior to his election as president. After his election, she assumed a visible policymaking role far beyond that of her predecessors. She was the first presidential wife to have an office in the West Wing of the White House and was chosen by her husband to lead the efforts to reform America's healthcare system. The negative reaction to her role within the administration caused her to have a much less visible, but not necessarily a less important, role during her husband's second term.

With the increase in dual career couples, we can expect for presidential spouses to have more accomplished careers than in the past. This will influence their roles during a presidency. However, like other couples, they will have to address the roles that they are going to assume in much more detail than did presidential couples in the past.

EXPERIENCE AS CONSUMERS AND WORKERS

Learning how to make better decisions as consumers and workers may not necessarily help you to make better decisions about marriage. While you have more alternatives than did your grandparents, you have had only a limited opportunity to develop the skills for making the best decisions before and during marriage. The trial-and-error process that helps you make better purchasing and career choices may not provide clear guidance to the best marital decisions. Seldom are your initial purchasing and career decisions life-long choices. Not only may you recognize later that there were better choices, you observe that your tastes and preferences can change over time. However, for a successful marriage, it is important that your first choice of a spouse be a successful one. Other living arrangements may not have prepared you for many critical decisions during marriage, especially those associated with parenthood.

When actors Uma Thurman and Ethan Hawke married in 1998, they found that conflicting careers can create difficulties for a successful marriage. When their six-year marriage collapsed, Hawke recognized that the difficulty of making the best decisions had contributed to their separation. He noted that a marriage works best on a farm, where you are together and everyone has real clear-cut roles. Because of their acting careers, they alternated jobs to be with their children, but as a result they were seldom with each other.

When Amy and I got married, we—like most of you—had very limited experience with the decisions that would make our marriage a success. It was the first time for both of us. However, we did have some things going for us. First, we obviously loved each other and were committed to marriage and parenthood. Regrettably, some people enter marriage with a "let's give it a try" attitude. Moreover, we recognized that we had complementary skills. Key among those skills was our degrees. I had a Ph.D. that limited my employment opportunities, but also permitted me to earn more. Amy had a master's degree in early childhood education that gave her employment flexibility as well as key parenting skills. We already had a sense of the roles that we would be assuming within our marriage. This gave us a foundation for learning how to make better decisions later.

In summary, experience can improve your decision-making capacities in many areas such as consumption and employment, but often it does not prepare you for making the best decisions about marriage. You have much more freedom than in the past to make choices that affect your marriage. When men and women assumed fairly predictable roles in marriage, this lack of preparation was less likely to lead to marital conflict and dissatisfaction. Now men and women have more choices about the person that they are going to marry and the roles that they are going to assume during marriage. This independence has increased the difficulty of making the decisions that will result in a successful marriage.

As you'll see in later chapters in this book, a business perspective can assist people in making better decisions. Practical guidance will be provided for making better decisions prior to and during marriage. Do not be offended by pragmatism. Your grandparents were not more romantic than you; they just had fewer choices. With more choices, you need to be more systematic in your evaluation of alternatives—especially if you want to avoid the Experience Trap.

THE EMOTION TRAP: DECISIONS ABOUT ROMANCE AND MARRIAGE RELY MORE ON YOUR EMOTIONS THAN MOST OTHER DECISIONS

Many decisions involve your emotions. You do not calculate the enjoyment anticipated from a choice such as buying a house, but instead you rely on your judgment about the enjoyment that you expect to receive from it. Just as people fall in love with each other, they also can "fall in love" with a house. Still, the nature of most choices forces us to scrutinize our emotions closely. The reaction can be very different between the love of another person and our attraction to a material good. In the latter case, you are quickly confronted with the cost of that choice. A house has a price and paying it will require you to make some very clear sacrifices of other things that you want to buy. The cost of the house can be time as well as money, as the house of your dreams may be far from where you work. Then you are confronted with whether this ideal house is worth the longer commute. Very quickly, your emotional reaction is affected by practical considerations.

An emotional reaction to someone else is not subjected to the same practical considerations. As many have said, "Love is blind." From a business perspective, the more appropriate conclusion is that the tradeoffs are much less obvious. What you are giving up—the cost—will seem insignificant relative to what you are getting—the benefit. It is easy to consider the benefits of the relationship and ignore the costs because you are not confronted with those costs. The costs are other experiences that you could be having, but those experiences may not be obvious.

Some of the worst cases in which emotions have destroyed marriages that otherwise would be successful occur due to infidelity. Researchers have shown that happily married people often have affairs. Shirley Glass, a psychologist, has noted that affairs often occur among people who work together.[6] These people permit their emotions to drive their decisions without adequate consideration for the costs of their actions. If discovered, an affair breeds distrust that can reduce the quality of the marriage and often result in divorce.

Infidelity and not assuming a fair share of parental responsibilities are some of the common causes of marital failure as people let their emotions control their behavior. These were two of the reasons given by Diandra Douglas when she divorced Michael Douglas in 2000 after twenty-three years of marriage. It would appear that Michael's emotions led him to believe that womanizing and absenteeism were more important than being a responsible spouse and parent. By the time of his divorce, his affair with actor Catherine Zeta-Jones was well known with them also marrying in 2000. In this new relationship, would he be able to control the activities that had led to the dissolution of his prior marriage? The answer so far is "yes" as he has become a loving father of their two children and an outspoken critic of other celebrities for their divorces.

In at least one area, overcoming this trap has probably been easier for Amy and me than for most couples. Businesses worry about their financial situation and economists talk about money all the time, so addressing the financial aspects of marriage has been second nature to us—or maybe it was just me. Money worries—along with infidelity—tend to be some of the major problems leading to divorce. Sure, just like everyone else, there have always been things we wanted to buy and places that we wanted to visit. However, we knew that we had to live within our income. For example, we have had to pay credit card interest debt just one time during our marriage—and that was the month when we relocated for my first teaching job. We never permitted our emotions to lead us into buying things that we could not afford. No sleepless nights have been spent wondering how we were going to make a mortgage payment or handle credit card debt. Neither of us had reason to blame the other for putting us in a precarious financial position.

In summary, emotions can lead you to overestimate the benefits and underestimate the costs of choices. This is particularly true in romantic situations affecting marriage. For some people, controlling their emotions and placing a strong emphasis on weighing benefits and costs may appear to be too manipulative and calculating, but emphasizing pragmatism is important for arriving at the psychological goal of a Smart Marriage. One way to attempt to deal with your emotions is to recognize the high failure rate in marriage and the importance of looking at decisions objectively. Relying too heavily on your emotions can be very costly.

If you are having great sex with someone with whom you find it difficult to develop other common interests, a Smart Marriage is less likely to occur. In subsequent chapters, we will discuss how you can make better decisions about getting married and your roles during marriage to limit the influence of misguided emotion. The goal is to force you to have broader consideration of your choices.

THE SELF-INTEREST TRAP: PEOPLE OFTEN MAKE THE WRONG DECISIONS BECAUSE THEY MISINTERPRET THEIR SELF-INTEREST BY FOCUSING TOO NARROWLY ON THEMSELVES

Self-interest has a central role in economic analysis. Economists believe that it is the primary force motivating individuals' decisions so that it has strong predictive powers about the choices that people make. However, unless you are careful, your sense of what is in your self-interest can lead you to make the wrong decisions. The misguided response to your self-interest can be illustrated by considering "egocentric people" and "introspective people." When making decisions, there is a critical difference between egocentric people, who make destructive decisions potentially resulting in marital failure, and introspective people, who improve the quality of their lives by increasing the likelihood of having a Smart Marriage.

EGOCENTRIC PEOPLE

Egocentric people only focus on the effects of choices on themselves. These people frequently make destructive decisions. In relationships, they are the individuals who, when an opportunity comes along to cheat on their partner, take advantage of the situation. There is no commitment. There is no concern for others. Sure they may get away with this violation of the trust of their partner, but eventually this type of behavior may be discovered and the relationship destroyed. In addition, egocentric people can pursue destructive behavior much less dramatic than adultery. An example would be spouses who spend their weekends fishing or playing golf, which they enjoy immensely, even though they know how it irritates their spouse.

INTROSPECTIVE PEOPLE

Introspective people, on the other hand, still make decisions based on self-interest. But they recognize that their welfare is improved by considering the response of others to their decisions as well as the longer-term repercussions of their actions. We are all social animals. We need others. If we want others to care about us, we have to sincerely care about them. Introspective people recognize the importance of compromise and reciprocity. They do things to make their partners happy and most of them assume that others will reciprocate by accommodating their preferences later.

CHANNELING SELF-INTEREST

Introspective people know how to channel self-interest. One of the keys to creating a Smart Marriage is recognizing the importance of becoming an introspective person—and finding someone with a similar inclination. You have to fight the inclination to be an egocentric person. Making decisions based on being an introspective person is ultimately in most people's best interest. Reciprocal acts are still essential for most of us to obtain the happiness that we seek. A common practice among businesspeople is to join organizations such as Rotary because of the opportunities to network. However, this networking will only be successful if other people feel that you are sincerely interested in them. Being sincerely concerned about each other has become more important for marital success.

SELF-INTEREST AND THE FAMILY

The role of self-interest has been misunderstood with regard to families. The recent decline in successful marriages and the accompanying increase in the divorce rate are often attributed to a shift toward more egocentric, self-indulgent behavior. Typical are William Bennett's comments in his book *The Broken Hearth: Reversing the Moral Collapse of the American Family*. It ascribes the divorce culture to the glorification of personal choices, autonomy, and individualism.[7] Sociologists Frank Furstenberg and Andrew Cherlin attribute the increase in the desire for personal fulfillment to two developments: the weakening of religious and other moral constraints and the demise of the breadwinner-homemaker family.[8] The behavior of many individuals is viewed as having shifted from a concern for their family based on altruism toward the goal of increasing their individual welfare.

These conclusions reflect a fundamental misunderstanding of self-interest, since there is strong evidence that all decisions are influenced by it. People have not become more self-centered so much as changes in society have caused some people to conclude that their welfare is improved by focusing more narrowly on themselves and less on the other members of their family. People can view a commitment to marriage as having less tangible and predictable benefits. This causes them to focus more on themselves and less on their families.

The benefits of marriage have become less tangible as the material gains from marriage have declined and the importance of psychological benefits have increased. Being less tangible, the benefits of marriage may be harder to recognize and appreciate. While people may want a successful relationship, if they perceive fewer benefits from marriage, then they are going to be less willing to incur costs to sustain it.

The commitment Amy and I have to marriage has been important in our avoiding this trap. We have always treated our marriage as a life-long commitment. Keeping each other happy within the relationship has been essential. One of our keys to avoiding the kind of arguments that are long remembered and often become the sources of marital aggravation is to step back when a conflict is developing. Because of concern for each other, we can usually come back to the topic later with a compromise that is acceptable to both of us.

In summary, many people misinterpret their self-interest as encouraging them to focus too narrowly on themselves. When making decisions that affect their marriage, some people do not appreciate that their self-interest is best served by considering the welfare and reciprocal acts of the other family members, especially their spouse. This can occur because the benefits of marriage have become less tangible and predictable.

You can improve your ability to create a Smart Marriage by recognizing the situations in which you will benefit from considering the welfare of others. Family meals, for example, are an important opportunity to become aware of other family members' concerns.

THE UNILATERAL DIVORCE TRAP: UNILATERAL DIVORCE HAS CREATED INCENTIVES FOR PEOPLE TO MAKE THE WRONG DECISIONS

Unilateral/no-fault divorce, which has been available in most states for the last few decades, has created incentives for people to make choices that reduce the likelihood that their marriages will be a success.[9] Marriages frequently benefit from spouses making sacrifices—doing things that they would not do if they were not married. Many of the rewards for making these sacrifices often do not occur until much later. A husband gives up an attractive job to relocate with his family because his wife has gotten a more attractive position elsewhere. The rewards for his action are the income and love from his spouse as well as the love of his children. However, the cost of the move for him is now and the rewards will occur much later. Therefore, a significant incentive for those sacrifices is the likelihood that there will be rewards. If those rewards become less likely because the marriage can be dissolved easily with only limited compensation, then people have a weaker incentive to make them. Rather than being an opportunity for increasing the family's welfare, the move—if made—can become the source of friction in the relationship now and later.

By making divorce easier, unilateral divorce has reduced the probability that sacrifices will be rewarded, thereby reducing the incentives for couples to make them. Between 1969 and 1985, all the states either replaced the fault divorce grounds of adultery, desertion, and cruelty with the no-fault grounds of incompatibility or irreconcilable differences, or they added the no-fault grounds to the fault grounds. More importantly, most divorces used to require mutual consent. Now, it only takes one spouse to dissolve a marriage. In the past, it was difficult to prove the fault grounds and marriages were frequently viewed as a failure by the spouses for other reasons. Thus, it was common for the spouses to mutually agree to a divorce and then fabricate the testimony necessary to establish the fault grounds. That is not to say that these divorces were the preference of both spouses. More often than not, one wanted it more than the other or one did not initially want it at all. However, confronted with the state of the marriage, especially when one spouse made it clear that divorce was desired, couples were able to negotiate a settlement.

A spouse who made sacrifices during the marriage had some leverage in those settlements to ensure compensation for those sacrifices. The couple could make their own arrangements, ignoring statutory requirements. In a community property state in which the laws provided for an equal division of property, the spouse that did not want the divorce could ask for a substantially larger amount of property.

That leverage effectively disappeared with unilateral divorce. The courts have been willing to accept the assertion of the no-fault grounds by either spouse as being sufficient to dissolve a marriage. You can imagine how ineffective it is to dispute your spouse's assertion of "incompatibility," since that conflict alone would justify the conclusion of incompatibility. The financial arrangements at divorce now tend to conform to statutes. These statutes provide spousal and child support as well as a property settlement after a divorce, but these funds can be difficult to collect and they seldom adequately compensate a spouse who has incurred sacrifices for the benefit of their marriage. The potential for inadequate compensation at divorce for sacrifices during marriage reduces the incentives for spouses to make them.

DENYING THE INFLUENCE OF UNILATERAL DIVORCE

The effect of unilateral divorce is subtle, so couples either do not recognize it or they want to deny its influence on their behavior. They attempt to pretend that a concern about their situation if they are divorced has not influenced their career decisions. Fulfilling jobs or financial necessity are the reasons usually offered if a couple is asked why they both work full time. They are not likely to admit that a concern for the perverse effects of divorce has in part been the basis for a continuing emphasis on their careers. Because limiting a career to provide childcare, for example, may not be adequately compensated at divorce, spouses have an incentive to attempt to avoid it. Circumstances may encourage them to emphasize their careers to a greater extent than is in their family's best interest.

While people may not acknowledge concerns about unilateral divorce, few women that I know are not familiar with the dire conditions of women who are divorced in middle age, especially if they have increased their specialization in housework and childcare during their marriages. The experience of their elders is not lost on the younger generation of women. Lia Macko and Kerry Rubin note in their book, *Midlife Crisis at 30: How the Stakes Have Changed for a New Generation—And What to Do About It*, that women who grew up while their parents were divorcing internalized the message that having a career was an important "divorce insurance policy."[10] To use an economic concept, Macko and Rubin have however discovered that careers have not turned out to be a "free lunch"; they can interfere with the ability of women to establish permanent relationships. Their lives are either too complicated or they are just too tired to find the right guy. While the career/family conflicts of married women—and men— are commonly recognized, the authors suggest that this conflict is also a concern of unmarried women—and men—as they attempt to balance a career with their attempt to find a spouse.

If the costs associated with limiting a career are not protected by the financial arrangements at divorce, then people have to take steps to protect themselves. My research has shown that unilateral divorce has been a major influence on the increase in the labor-force participation rate of married women.[11] By encouraging people to limit their commitment to their marriage, concerns about the costs of a unilateral divorce can encourage people to make decisions that increase the likelihood that their marriages will not be a success, potentially ending in divorce. It causes people to focus more narrowly on their own welfare and less on the welfare of the other family members.

Most marriages benefit from a long-term commitment that encourages sacrifices and reciprocity. Easily obtainable divorces discourage that commitment. Even though people are marrying later, it encourages them even then to approach it more casually than they would if divorce were more difficult. Then after the wedding, it discourages the choices based on a long-term commitment that are important for marital success. It encourages people to define their self-interest more narrowly and with less concern for other family members. This leads to couples placing too strong an emphasis on their careers than is often desirable for a successful family life. Finding the proper balance between careers and family life is one of the keys to creating a Smart Marriage.

Amy and I probably benefited from marrying in the 1970s rather than later. While most couples today may not be that familiar with the divorce laws, it is common knowledge that obtaining a divorce is not a difficult legal process. When we married, the common perspective was that dissolving a marriage was difficult, so it was best to choose a spouse carefully and work to make your marriage work. Our commitment to our marriage has not been altered by the knowledge that dissolution is much easier than when we married. Like many women, my wife has been the one making most of the sacrifices as we have moved and become parents. Because of our commitment to each other, these sacrifices have not been the basis of conflict between us. I am sure that others—who have since divorced—started out with the same commitment, so I guess that we have just been fortunate to have made better decisions along the way.

In summary, unilateral divorce makes it easier for either spouse to obtain a divorce. This, of course, is good news for someone who wants out of a marriage. However, most people get married with the expectation that it is a long-term commitment. Pre-emptive divorce laws that make acquiring a divorce easy frustrate that expectation. Easy divorce discourages sacrifices for the benefit of a marriage, since it makes reciprocal actions by the other family members less predictable. Without these sacrifices, the quality of the marriage is reduced.

Decisions during marriage can be improved if couples recognize the effect of unilateral divorce on their decisions and the decisions of others. Other people may not be finding their jobs as rewarding, necessary, and fulfilling as they profess. If you feel comfortable in the durability of your marriage, you have to consider whether your career choices are in your family's best interest or motivated by more egocentric motives. Guidance in making this determination will be provided by an investigation of the costs and benefits of your career choices.

Now we are ready to improve your decision making about marriage. Next, we will start with the process of finding the right person and then move on to better decisions during marriage and regrettably—if necessary—after your first marriage.

CONCLUSION

The first step toward creating a Smart Marriage is to understand why it is difficult to make good decisions about marriage. Four Traps frustrate the choices made by well intentioned people. These Traps were less relevant when people had fewer choices and family and friends were more involved in marital decisions. The Experience Trap occurs because other experiences often do not prepare people for making good decisions about marriage. People can fall into the Emotion Trap because people in romantic situations are less likely to accurately gauge the benefits and costs of decisions. Focusing decisions too narrowly on themselves can lead people into the Self-Interest Trap. Last, the introduction of unilateral divorce has caused some people to place too strong an emphasis on themselves and their careers to the detriment of the quality of their marriage. This can lead to the Unilateral Divorce Trap. The goal of this book is to help you avoid these Traps.

THINGS TO REMEMBER

- Most of your other experiences in life have not prepared you for making good decisions before and during marriage.
- You cannot let your emotions dominate your decisions about marriage, especially when considering a spouse.
- Your self-interest will be best served by considering those around you and the effect of your actions on them.
- Because it is easy to dissolve a marriage, you have to be sensitive to how that affects your marital decisions.

Why Do You Need a Business Partner?

So you are getting tired of casual relationships and the dating scene. You want to settle down. You want to get married. Maybe you are lucky enough that you have a particular person in mind—you are in love. Certainly, love has become synonymous with marriage. In the twentieth century it became commonly accepted that the only ingredient necessary for a successful marriage was love. The importance of love was everywhere. Most popular songs extolled it. Hollywood depended on it to sell movies. Romance novels and magazines became a cornerstone of the publishing industry.

Lost in all the attention given to love as a basis for marriage has been that marriage historically has been a pragmatic rather than a romantic institution. The primary motivation for marriage within what have often been called traditional societies was that married couples were better off than single adults. They had access to more goods and services than single adults.[1] Because marriage was a pragmatic arrangement, the characteristics of a preferred spouse went beyond love and physical attraction. In fact, love and physical attraction often had very little to do with the choice of a preferred spouse.

Because it is so fundamental to this book, let me emphasize again the historical importance of pragmatism—and the personal characteristics associated with it—in marriage. A romantic, in contrast to a pragmatic, approach to marriage is very new. It was not until the eighteenth century in Europe that individuals had much control over who they could marry. Prior to that time, marriage was viewed as far too important to be left to the inexperience and emotions of young people. The idea of arranged marriages continues to be common in most of the non-industrial countries of the world.

Even when people gradually acquired the ability to make their own decisions about a spouse, they did not have many choices. Usually they were restricted to a narrow range of potential candidates from a limited social and geographic pool. With the large flow of immigrants into the United States during the nineteenth and early twentieth centuries, many people still had stronger ties to their country of origin than to the United States. It was common for people to marry within their ethnic communities. This was especially true for the different religions, with the Catholic and Jewish communities making a strong emphasis of marriage to other members of their communities. When these social restrictions were coupled with the general lack of geographic mobility, the result was that when people considered marriage they were restricted in their choice of a spouse to a limited pool. Having married, couples again had few choices about the roles that they assumed.

The alternatives that adults have today were not serious options then. Cohabitation and living alone normally were not choices. In was not socially acceptable for a couple to live together without being married, while living alone often meant a boarding house or as a domestic servant. Adults wanted to marry and they wanted to do it as soon as possible. The limiting factor was usually the ability of a man to support a family either through his earnings or his ability to buy a farm or business.

Adults have many more choices today. Geographic mobility and marrying at a later age expose people to a broader range of potential spouses. The opportunities to marry someone from a different background have increased dramatically. After marriage, there are many fewer constraints on the roles that men and women can assume with the most dramatic changes occurring in the attachment of women to the labor force. While most adults still marry eventually, not marrying has become a more viable alternative. Cohabitation is common and living alone has become more widespread.

Marriage is still the goal for most adults. The potential for life-long love and affection within marriage has added an important new element to marriage that can undoubtedly increase the quality of life for many people. However, lost along the way has been recognition that most marriages benefit from a pragmatic foundation. By pragmatic, I mean that married people are better off in a broad variety of areas including such pedestrian accomplishments as well-adjusted children and peace of mind. This lack of recognition of the pragmatic aspects of marriage has probably contributed to the increase in people's dissatisfaction with marriage and the resulting increase in the divorce rate.

If you want your marriage to be a success, you have to recognize that a successful marriage consists of more than love and physical attraction. Just like past generations, you want to feel better off married than in any other situation. The characteristics of a partner who will assist you in accomplishing that goal go beyond those that make the person physically attractive to you. Think of it this way: You may have friends whose company you enjoy immensely, but with whom you would never want to go into business. Similarly, there are probably people with whom you might want to be intimate but who would not make a good spouse. The likelihood of marital success will be increased if you consider potential mates as a business partner—rejecting the ones with whom you would never want to go into business.

What is the difference between friends, lovers and a business partner? That is the subject of this chapter. A successful marriage is similar to a prosperous business. They both efficiently convert inputs into outputs. This process is obvious for a business; but it may appear to be a strange way to describe a marriage. Still, families convert inputs such as time, income and skills into outputs such as well-adjusted children, a clean house and peace of mind. It has become too easy to conclude when two people marry that their most important accomplishment is validation of their mutual attraction to each other without seriously considering the other things that they hope to accomplish in their marriage. If there are reasons to question whether you will be able to accomplish the goals that I just described (well-adjusted children, a clean house and peace of mind, for example) with this person, you have to wonder about the future durability of your marriage.

So, let's consider some of the attributes that you should consider when entering into a business partnership.[2] In most cases, these are exactly the characteristics of a spouse who will help you create a successful marriage. In most partnerships, the participants share the profits equally, while all partners are individually liable for all of its debts. This is true in both a business and marriage.

You have to seriously consider these attributes because it is too easy to fall into the Four Traps. The Experience Trap is a concern as dating has not given you the experience to judge the attributes that are important in a spouse in contrast to a date or roommate. Because you have been led to believe that marriage is based almost solely on romance, the Emotion Trap can let your emotions dictate the type of person that you find attractive. Interacting with someone in an environment in which neither of you have to make many sacrifices does not permit you to determine whether the two of you can avoid the Self-Interest Trap by understanding the importance of channeling your self-interest in ways that will make both of you happy. Last, there is still the potential for the Unilateral Divorce Trap because easy divorce due to unilateral divorce statutes may cause you to approach marriage too casually without realizing that even with easy divorce there can be very high costs for both of you and potentially your children if you make a poor match.

In the following section, we will explore the specific characteristics that are important for success in a business partner—and in a spouse. While investigating these attributes, it is important to be aware of tradeoffs. This is an important concept to economists as most choices require people to give up other alternatives. So the issue often is whether a given choice is worth the alternatives that have to be given up. Attributes of spouses have to be approached in a similar manner. Some attributes should be so important that they are essential, such as commitment, while others, such as a good sense of humor, become less important if the person has other, more significant, attributes. Certainly, as the number of essential attributes increases, the likelihood of finding someone with those attributes decreases.[3] So, you have to figure out what is important to you.

It would probably be helpful to consider a particular business. So, how about considering the characteristics of someone that you would consider as a partner in a combination microbrewery and pizzeria in your hometown? We will start out with some characteristics that are so important that they are almost essential for your success. These characteristics are commitment, compatibility, and complementarity.[4] Those characteristics will be followed by ones that are important, but not necessarily essential.

ESSENTIAL CHARACTERISTICS

COMMITMENT

In Business

The first attribute that comes to mind for me is commitment. This is essential. It is going to take time for the business to succeed. This is not a good time to align yourself with someone who suggests that the two of you give this business a try. For your business to be a success you are going to need a much greater commitment to it. Often you and your partner are going to have to make personal sacrifices. Money will have to be used in the business that could be used for something else. Time that could be devoted to more enjoyable activities will have to be committed to the business. Unless there is a commitment to the enterprise, your partner will lose interest in the face of these sacrifices.

Moreover, there will probably be a predictable pattern in your enthusiasm for the project. The planning and anticipation can be frustrating but very exhilarating. Then, you are exposed to the daily problems associated with implementing your plan. The exhilaration gives way to frustration. You have to work your way through this period to get to the time when you expect the business to prosper. Even when you get to the point when the business is living up to your expectations, commitment can continue to be important. We live in a very competitive world. Being successful now is no guarantee of continued success. In a business setting, your success is exactly the motivation for others to copy your ideas. A commitment to the business will keep you on your toes. How do you protect your success and how do you address new opportunities? These are your concerns and a commitment to the business is fundamental for asking the right questions and taking the best steps for success.

In Marriage

Commitment is also essential for a successful marriage.[5] Few would disagree with that statement, but the high divorce rate has to be viewed as evidence that too many people have made only a weak commitment to their marriage. When it was difficult to dissolve a marriage—which was the case for most of the history of the United States—few people were concerned about spouses' commitment to their marriage. Exit was seldom an option, so people had incentives to make their marriage work.

Easy, unilateral divorce (the Unilateral Divorce Trap) that was introduced in most states in the 1970s encourages people to reduce their commitment to marriage. However, commitment is probably the most important ingredient in marital success because most marriages benefit from a combination of sacrifices, reciprocity and commitment. By sacrifices, I mean that during marriage you do things that are potentially detrimental to you that you would not have done if you had not married, such as to relocate with your spouse. Why would a self-interested person (you) make these sacrifices? The answer is reciprocity as you anticipate that your spouse and potentially your children will reward you with love, earnings and their sacrifices. However, the timing of sacrifices and rewards will probably not be concurrent. You may have to make sacrifices in the anticipation of other family members' actions later. That is why commitment is so important. You want to be comfortable that both you and your spouse see your relationship as long term.

Commitment is also important because the satisfaction for most marriages follows a pattern similar to that of a business.[6] It often starts high, drops down and then recovers. Who is not euphoric prior to their wedding? You found that special person. You can envision all those happy years together. The planning for the wedding takes on a life of its own. Then you are married. Even without children, the perceived quality of the relationship can deteriorate with the problems and frustrations of everyday life, but it will frequently face a major challenge when you have children. Even though children are a primary goal of marriage for most of us, they often place a strain on a marriage as the parents adjust their careers and lives. The perceived quality of the marriage deteriorates and the likelihood of divorce increases. Without a strong commitment, some parents lose track of the potential for their marriage. When a couple has young children, the financial and emotional costs of divorce are very high for the spouses and their children and yet many divorces occur at this time.[7]

There is strong evidence that after an initial decline in satisfaction in most marriages, people find that their satisfaction increases. People tend to rate their satisfaction over the duration of a marriage as U shaped. It is particularly noteworthy that many people who consider divorce and reject it find five years later that they are happy with their marriage.[8] While a strong commitment to each other and the institution of marriage may not solve all problems, it will certainly increase the likelihood that a marriage will succeed.

Not only is commitment important for the success of a marriage, researchers have shown that it can be a significant factor contributing to whether you marry.[9] It can be hard work to find an acceptable spouse. The more you are convinced that marriage is important for your happiness, the more likely you are to be successful in your search. If you think that marriage is important for your happiness, do not hesitate to communicate that to the people you date. If your commitment turns them off, then you might be better off spending your time with someone else. Women who felt that marriage was essential to their happiness were almost twice as likely to be engaged or married four years later than those who said that they thought that marriage was not essential to their happiness.[10]

COMPATIBILITY

In Business

The next essential ingredient for a successful business relationship is compatibility. To put it in a different context, incompatibility can be very destructive for a business relationship. You do not necessarily have to like each other so much as your fundamental values have to be similar. Personal conflicts can interfere with the smooth operation of a business. It is important that you both have similar attitudes toward work—and leisure. A workaholic is not a good match for someone willing to trade off profits for more leisure. Since you expect to share the profits equally, you probably expect your partner to work as hard as you. If that is not the case, then conflicts are certain to arise.

Compatibility also extends to a range of decisions such as those dealing with ethical values and how the partners treat others. Conflict is reduced when the partners respect each other's decisions. An important area of compatibility is their time horizons. What is the rate at which they want to withdraw any profits from the business?

Often compatibility is something that partners develop over time. Jeff Bernstein and Brian Hinman met when they were five years old.[11] After college they started a business together, but eventually went their separate ways. However, in 1998 they reunited to start 2Wire, Inc., a broadband technology company, which had 500 employees and sales of over $220 million in 2005. Hinman acknowledges that the key to their success is that they just fit well together. Basically, they are not competing to be the chief executive officer.

While compatibility can be important, it has its limits. There will be times when the partners have to tell each other things that they know their partner does not want to hear. Being honest with each other can conflict with their harmonious relationship. These conflicts over decisions will have a smaller impact on the business if the partners are compatible in other areas such as values and work ethic.

In Marriage

To state that compatibility between the spouses is essential for marital success seems like stating the obvious. However, it is relevant to note that compatibility has become increasingly important for marital success. When marriage was a more obviously pragmatic institution, most married couples were better off than single adults, so compatibility was desirable—but not necessary—for a successful marriage. Married couples were wealthier than single people with more comfortable homes, better clothes and higher quality food. That is not always true today. There are fewer tangible gains from marriage, so it has become increasingly important for a happy, successful marriage that a couple is essentially each other's best friend. Being each other's "soul mate" is often viewed as the goal of spouses.[12] It is important that the two of you have similar values and interests and the ability to communicate with each other.[13] In the glow of love and physical attraction it may be too easy to ignore fundamental differences such as the religion in which your children will be raised. There are numerous compatibility questionnaires available for people considering marriage. You certainly would not like to rely just on some "score" from those tests, but they can reveal potential areas of conflict.

Education would appear to have an important effect on the importance of compatibility between spouses. With the increase in the average level of education, men and women are more likely to have similar interests and experiences. I am reminded of an experience I had in rural Australia in the late 1960s. Farmers in rural Australia were fairly prosperous, but their primary labor force was their children so they usually took them out of school as soon as it was legally possible. This was at an age that in the United States would have been middle school. At social gatherings, there was a sexual segregation of adults that would have been unusual in the United States at that time as both sexes separated to discuss topics appropriate for middle school educated people. The men discussed sports and business, while the women discussed children and domestic activities. I can only assume from my casual observation that these couples had fairly happy marriages. With more education, both men and women tend to expand their interests into politics, travel and cultural activities in a way that their interests converge. While this creates new areas for interaction, it can also create areas of conflict when political and cultural values diverge.

Being compatible does not mean that the couple should agree on all decisions. It just means that the areas of disagreement will be limited. It is easier to resolve a conflict between a trip to Paris or Florence than when a couple consists of one person who loves to travel and the other does not like to leave home at all.

COMPLEMENTARITY

In Business

Complementary skills and interests can also be important for business partners. An important element in essentially all successful businesses is specialization of labor.[14] Few people have broad skills and even when they do, they only have a limited amount of time. The relative strengths of different people can be described as their comparative advantage. Let's say that one partner is good at accounting, but very good at marketing, while the other partner has contrasting skills (good at marketing, but very good at accounting), then we would conclude that the first partner has a comparative advantage at marketing and the second at accounting. Because of their relative skills, it is not in their business's best interest for them to share each of those responsibilities. One should concentrate on marketing and the other on accounting.

Seldom will the specialization be complete as marketing campaigns may require both of their efforts and tax deadlines may require them to cooperate on data collection. Their success as a team might be more limited if both were particularly good at the same skills such as marketing. Who would do the accounting? Even if partners start out with similar skills, specialization can increase their skills and, therefore, their overall productivity. People who emphasize marketing or accounting become more proficient at those tasks the longer they work in those areas.

Regrettably, complementarity may not be enough as it can conflict with the need for compatibility. In the mid-1990s, Scott Testa started an Internet service company with an old college friend.[15] They seemed like a good match since Testa had experience in sales and marketing and his friend had a technical background. Their problems developed when they had to address the growth rate of the company. Testa wanted the company to grow rapidly, which would have required relinquishing some control to outside investors. Meanwhile, his partner was unwilling to give up that much control over the business, wanting to rely for growth on funds generated internally by the business. Unable to resolve this conflict, they were forced to sell the company prematurely. Testa learned from the experience, eventually founding Mindbridge Software, which has been a successful intranet and collaboration software development company.

In Marriage

Being complementary was a characteristic that was essential for marital success in the past.[16] Societies established clear guidelines for what men and women were expected to do and they usually were very different. Women were often taught domestic skills from an early age. Boys were expected to observe and work with their fathers. In many cases, couples' standard of living was very low. An inefficient allocation of responsibilities would have been very costly. Their different roles complemented each other.

The apparent need for spouses to be complementary has lost its importance among modern marriages. The reduced importance of complementary roles has probably accompanied the increased importance of compatibility. As people looked for mates with whom they were compatible, the likelihood increased that they would find someone with similar skills and interests. During most of the twentieth century, men had more education than women, resulting in a division of labor consisting of men as the primary income earners and women working in the home. The dramatic increase in the average education level of women has increased the likelihood that husbands and wives will now have similar levels of education and income-earning capacities.

With an increased emphasis on careers by both men and women, it became less clear who would assume responsibility for domestic chores. While subtle, the gains to a marriage from the spouses having complementary skills and interests continue to be a major source of the benefits of marriage. People tend to become better at an activity as they devote more time to it. An obvious example is cooking meals. But it is also true with plumbing and childcare. Being complementary is particularly important with income earning. While income is an important input into the welfare of a family, so is time. If both spouses are strongly committed to their careers, how are other welfare-enhancing activities such as a comfortable home, well-adjusted children and enjoyable meals going to be accomplished?

Most marriages—especially ones in which the spouses want children—probably benefit from a couple in which one places a stronger emphasis on a career than does the other. It is too easy to see income as the core ingredient in the family's welfare without an adequate appreciation for the other attributes of a successful marriage, such as a walk on a Sunday afternoon or drinking a glass of wine, which can require substantial inputs of time. If a couple wants a comfortable income and happy children, then there are going to probably be complementary roles for the parents. If the parents do not find these complementary roles attractive, then their marriage may be less successful.

IMPORTANT CHARACTERISTICS

CONCERN FOR OTHERS

In Business

Another important attribute necessary for success in business is a concern for others (the Self-Interest Trap). A frequent observation about business is that greed is its own reward. However, that is far from true. A concern for others is one of the most important ingredients in business success. In the business world, you are always selling yourself. You are selling yourself to employers, customers and fellow workers. A concern for others is often viewed as based on altruism. Economists are suspicious of that term and question how broadly it is relevant. The most successful people act on self-interest, but they know that a concern for others is important to success. Therefore, they act in a sincere manner. So when a customer comes into your pizzeria, you know that they will be greeted enthusiastically by your partner.

In Marriage

Before marriage observe how a potential spouse treats others. A concern for others, especially family members, is one of the cornerstones of a successful marriage. Again, I have just made a statement with which few would disagree, and yet too many people violate it in their own marriages. You have to avoid the Self-Interest Trap. Your concern for others has to be sincere. Do not kid yourself: The most important person in your life is you. Still, if you want to have a successful marriage you have to recognize that keeping your spouse happy within your marriage is fundamental to its success. If you want to be happy, you have to make others happy.

In the current environment of fragile marriages and unilateral divorce, there are incentives for people to focus their concerns more narrowly on themselves and less on the concerns of those around them.[17] Part of the problem goes back to why someone loves you. Do they want to possess you or do they understand that the key to their happiness is making you happy in this relationship? Too often people know what they want out of a relationship without considering what they are willing to put into it. A concern for others is often the key to our own welfare.

FINANCIAL RESPONSIBILITY

In Business

Businesses only survive if they are profitable (the revenues exceed the costs). Initially, any profits are important for reducing debt and expanding the business. Probably the number one reason that new businesses fail is a lack of working capital.[18] By this I mean that they lack the funds to meet the immediate needs of the business. Who cares if you have a great idea if you are not paying your bills? When suppliers are not paid in a timely fashion, they stop providing supplies and potentially sue. They may not care that you have a great long-term plan if they are not being paid on time.

Being financially responsible takes many forms. Does the business need the best equipment or is something less expensive best for the business now? One partner might want a new delivery truck with an attractive sign on the side to replace the plain truck that is being used for deliveries. Another important aspect of being financially responsible is the rate at which the partners take out the profits. Given the choice, most of us would rather spend now rather than later. However, for the business to grow and to provide for unexpected events, it may be important to maintain a comfortable cash reserve in the business. You have to resist the temptation to live the good life too soon.

In Marriage

In a book authored by an economist, it should not be a surprise that being financially responsible is viewed as an important characteristic of a spouse. While infidelity is a more dramatic cause of divorce, probably far more divorces are caused by a couple being financially irresponsible.[19] As homes get bigger, cars fancier, and consumer debt increases, we keep reading about the difficulty that couples have making ends meet. If spouses have unrealistic expectations about the amount that they can spend, that is going to place more pressure on their marriage.

Most people do not start their marriage with a comfortable financial situation and yet they often make some of the most ill-advised decisions at that time. If either party thinks that an expensive engagement ring is an important signal to others about the affection of the couple, they are starting off with the wrong attitude toward marriage. I might add that a similar comment about an expensive wedding is equally appropriate. Just like new businesses often fail because of a lack of working capital, a new marriage is vulnerable if it immediately faces a financial crisis.

Living within your means is important for marital success. There are things for which it is worthwhile incurring debt even early in a marriage. These things will usually have one important characteristic: They will be providing services as you pay for them. These include a house and potentially a car. On the other hand, to get in debt for past purchases will put pressure on the marriage in the future. The expensive vacation that attempted to salvage a fragile marriage may in fact destroy the marriage when the couple is confronted with the change in other expenditures necessary to pay the bills later.

HARD WORK

In Business

In a business partnership, you will share the profits equally. As I noted above, you have friends with whom you would not want to go into business. Often the reason is that they do not have the proper work ethic. As a friend, that is usually not costly to you. The same is not true if they become your business partner. Then their work habits can impose a cost on you. Their habits can not only impose a cost on you, but they can also alter your incentives. Even if you are willing to work hard, you will be tempted to reduce your effort if you know that half your effort benefits this other person who is unwilling to carry an equal share. You want to work hard and that commitment is reinforced by a partner who is also willing to work hard.

Matt Lauzon and Dan Marques, two high school friends, found out about the importance of being willing to work equally hard when they started a business based on their idea of a Rib Wrangler that would allow people to eat ribs without getting their hands dirty.[20] Although they had agreed to be 50–50 partners in the business, Matt eventually concluded that he was doing 90 percent of the work. He was almost happy when the venture failed, because their friendship—which was in jeopardy—survived. When Lauzon started another business selling diamond rings over the Internet, he and his partner drafted a written agreement that provided for more specific roles for the partners.

In Marriage

It is important for spouses to have similar work ethics. However, within marriage it is important to get a clear idea of what is work. Too often, there appears to be a sense that the only activities that are work are those for which people are paid. Nothing could be further from the truth. Work is best thought of as the alternative to leisure. Therefore, cleaning house and tending to children is just as much work as is earning income. Moreover, they both contribute to the welfare of the family. People want to believe that their partner is carrying their fair share. When that does not occur, the result can be bickering.

SENSE OF HUMOR

In Business

While maybe less important than some of the attributes discussed above, the importance of a sense of humor in a business partner should not be underestimated. It is interesting how people handle adversity. In a business setting, things will go wrong. A rainstorm on a Saturday night limits the customers on the patio of your pizzeria. You can let this situation depress you or you can laugh at your adversity and use it to plan for the future. What has happened has happened and there is nothing you can do about it. Of course, you can always blame your partner for poor planning. A sense of humor clears the air, so that you can consider actions that you can take to avoid these problems in the future.

In Marriage

A sense of humor is equally important in marriage as there are a broader range of decisions and situations in marriage than in a business. Most of those decisions will yield expected results and the outcomes will be anticipated. However, that is not always the case. If you respect your spouse, you laugh off the unanticipated outcomes and learn from them. Without a sense of humor, it is too easy to look for someone to blame. While it can be difficult to develop a sense of humor, you and your spouse can at least learn how to relax in the face of adversity.

ORGANIZATION

In Business

Poor organization is an attribute that you might tolerate in a friend, but would be less acceptable in a partner. Too often people think that money is the only true constraint facing a business. However, in a business setting, time is also an important restriction. How much time are you willing to put into making your business a success? Just being there will not guarantee success. What you do during the time that you allocate to your business is very important. Some people take pride in the long hours that they devote to their businesses. However, since you have families and other obligations, the critical question is, How efficiently do you use your time? Equally important is how efficiently your partner uses time and indirectly your time. Is he on time for meetings? When discussing issues concerning the business, does she get to the point quickly? People that are not well organized frustrate those around them.

In Marriage

While it may seem petty, being well organized (or just being organized at all) can have a significant effect on marriage. Modern life has become very hectic and often frustrating. Couples need to minimize unnecessary conflicts. Often these conflicts can be due to your spouse not arriving on time or not being able to accomplish necessary tasks such as paying the family's bills when they are due. While you may have tolerated your future husband being late for dates because of the anticipation associated with those dates, his tardiness after marriage may become less tolerable.

HONESTY

In Business

Businesses do not like uncertainty. A business benefits from honesty and directness between the partners. While uncertainty cannot be eliminated, it can be reduced by clear communication within the organization. Reality is always in the eyes of the beholder, but differing views of reality can be detrimental to the success of a business. If a partner has made a decision that is not producing the desired results, then it is important to address whether it needs to be modified. Your partner has convinced you—against your better judgment—to start a second location for your business—away from the hard-drinking college students at the initial location. That has not turned out to be a profitable decision. Still, since it was advocated by your partner and until he is willing to address the situation with candor, it could threaten the overall success of the business.

Jeff Bernstein and Brian Hinman, who have successfully managed 2Wire Inc. for almost a decade, have noted the crucial importance of honesty. When they disagree on something, they attempt to address the issue immediately rather than allow it to smolder, causing problems later.

In Marriage

Candor is just as important for a marriage. If you cannot trust your spouse, who can you trust? The issue of candor goes beyond what your spouse intends. Candor requires him not only to be honest with you, but also with himself. Often the most destructive lies are the ones that we make to ourselves. If people lie to themselves, that could create major problems for their marriage. This can be particularly important with the Self-Interest Trap. If people think that they are considering others' interests when making decisions, when they are only considering the effects on themselves, that is not a good sign for future success.

PRIOR EXPERIENCE

In Business

Last, let's consider prior experience. In many ways, there is no substitute for it. Often in a start-up business there is very little capital, so you can only make a few, minor mistakes and survive. If someone has been involved in a similar business in the past, she may help you avoid making the types of mistakes that have caused other businesses to fail. Even experience in some other kind of business can be helpful. The key ingredient for experience to be helpful is whether those businesses faced problems similar to the ones that you can expect to face with your pizzeria.

In evaluating their experience, there are a couple of factors that you should consider. One consideration might be whether their prior business was reasonably successful, but for some reason they decided to dissolve or leave it. It might have been too time consuming or they observed changing market conditions that would eventually challenge their ability to keep the business profitable. Clearly, this type of person can have valuable insights.

You also might meet people who are in other situations that might be less valuable. One would be a person who was in a business that failed. Either the owners lost their investment or potentially the business went bankrupt. Then, the value of the lessons learned is less clear. You will have to investigate more closely to see if this person benefited from the experience in a way that will benefit your new enterprise. If he identifies things that he could have done differently, you should give him serious consideration as a partner. On the other hand, if she blames other people and circumstances for the failure of her business, then she has obviously not learned much from the prior experience. This type of person probably will not bring additional value to your business.

A third type of potential partner is one who is actively involved in another business. Your pizzeria is initially going to need the full time effort of you and the person with whom you decide to associate. If the person has substantial obligations elsewhere, he is not going to be an attractive candidate to work with you on this project.

In Marriage

Some of the people that you will be considering as a partner already have experience with long-term relationships and possibly marriage. Subtly, you should determine if they learned things during those relationships that will assist them in making a relationship with you a success.

Less often you may even encounter widows or widowers, who have had experience with a fairly successful marriage. One issue could be whether that person is truly open to a new relationship. Most widows or widowers want to remarry. However, a concern can be the standard that they will apply to you. Will you be loved for yourself or will you be compared to the actual or idealized memory of the spouse who died? These are questions that have to be addressed before marriage.

Less attractive as a partner are people who are divorced as they are similar to individuals whose businesses failed. Just as with a failed business, it is important to determine what this person has learned. If he acknowledges and learned from his mistakes, then he can be an excellent candidate. These mistakes can be in behavior or in failing to recognize attributes in a spouse that caused the marriage to fail. Certainly, people who place all the blame on the failure of their marriage on their ex-spouse learned very little from the experience and they probably should be avoided.

Last, we have the people who have a substantial commitment somewhere else. Often these people will be married already. They will make a very poor partner. If they will cheat on their current spouse, they will certainly cheat on you. Plus, because of their prior commitment, they may never marry you anyway.

PRODUCING WELFARE-ENHANCING COMMODITIES

By this point I assume that you have an understanding of the characteristics that are important in a business partner and a spouse. Still, another set of considerations about this partner still exists. What exactly are you going to produce? Even if you have agreed to start a combination microbrewery and pizzeria, what specific products are you going to produce in your pursuit of profits? After the obvious choice of an India Pale Ale, what other types of beer are you going to produce? In addition to pizza, are you going to produce calzones? Are salads going to be important and if so what types? Your business will function more smoothly if you reach agreement on what your business is going to produce.

You want your family to be a welfare-producing enterprise, so it is also important to agree on what you want to produce. In addition to your love and physical attraction, your marriage will be a success if you are able to produce a life together that you continue to believe is superior to any alternative. Now you still need to turn to whether the two of you are going to be able to produce the welfare-enhancing commodities necessary for making your marriage a success. Essentially, the two of you—and hopefully your children—will use your time, money and skills to produce the things that increase your welfare. We will call these things "commodities."

So an additional concern when considering a spouse is the commodities that the two of you want and how you will produce them. It is important now to discover what the two of you feel are important goals and how you are going to accomplish them. If you want expensive commodities such as luxurious cars and gourmet restaurants, how are you going to fund them? If your hobbies are time consuming, how will you find that time? Dating and potential living together may not have provided you with answers to these questions, so you may have to dig deeper. So here are some additional questions that you need to address to your future partner.

Where do you want to (or are willing to) live? This will have a strong influence on the commodities available to you. This is more than a question about climate as living expenses differ dramatically across the country. The big cities are generally much more expensive than smaller cities such as Albuquerque, New Mexico, for example. If your partner wants to live close to parents in the San Francisco Bay area, that will influence many of your other decisions. A need to spend a large amount on housing will influence other decisions about careers and other commodities available to the family.

What are the careers that you prefer? You obviously know how your partner feels about her current career—don't you? But, it would be best to dig a little deeper. If she is frustrated with her current job, it is better to find out about that now rather than later. The commodities that you will be able to produce will be different if she prefers a high income, but time intensive, career rather than one with more free time, but less income.

What if one of you gets an attractive offer somewhere else? This has increasingly become a challenge for couples. At one time, a family moved when it was in the best interest of the husband to move. That is obviously no longer the case. It is common for both spouses to work and frequently the wife can be the primary wage earner. Then you have to address whose career has priority. Income should not be the only consideration as it may be wise to consider the net gain from employment. The net gain is the difference between what someone is paid and the amount necessary to attract them to the job. What are you going to do if one of you is offered a more challenging and interesting job elsewhere that pays less?

Do you want children? How many? When? These are essential questions that affect many of the commodities that your family will produce. What changes are you willing to make to accommodate children? If you cannot have your own children, would you be willing to adopt? Again, you are being forced to address questions that were not major issues in the past. The number and timing of children will strongly affect both your careers and your domestic commodities. You only have a certain amount of time, how will you spend it?

If you have children, in what faith will they be raised? While dating, different religions may not have been a concern. However that may change with children. Religious preferences may also have an effect on the commodities that you produce. Amy is Jewish and religion has not been important to me, so it was easy for us to decide to raise our children within the Jewish faith. Other couples with conflicting religious preferences have been less fortunate.

How do you want to handle your money? Who is going to pay the bills and who is going to do the taxes? You are managing an enterprise, so these are essential questions. Money worries are a major cause of marital discord. As much as people do not want to be in debt, they also do not want to be surprised to discover that they are in that state. These concerns are particularly important early in marriage as you adjust to combining your incomes and expenditures.

The issue of handling money ties into the question, What do you consider necessities and luxuries? If you view some high-priced commodities as necessities, then the two of you are going to have to sacrifice other things in the pursuit of earning income. Be aware that there are tradeoffs.

How much are you going to save? Even though the average couple in the United States has a very low personal savings rate, do not let the acts of others guide yours. It is important to establish a nest egg early in your marriage. You do not ever want to be unable to pay your bills. You want to also avoid less extreme circumstances such as continuing in an unpleasant job out of financial necessity. There are lots of reasons for establishing a solid nest egg early. If your prospective spouse does not agree, be cautious.

How do you see the two of you dividing up household chores? This can be a major battleground and hiring a cleaning service is not always an easy answer, especially early in a marriage. The question may not only be what has to be done, but also how often these things have to be done. How often do you feel that the living room has to be vacuumed?

What are your views about home cooked meals? If neither of you enjoys—nor even tolerates—cooking, that will create problems later. We feel that meals at home have been very important. They are the time when you get to catch up on the other family members' activities. Again, early in marriage eating out should not be a common practice and just getting by with snacks is also a poor choice. So, who's going to shop and cook? There are lots of options. Who does the main course and who does the salad? It helps to find out what your partner does and does not enjoy doing. Now for the tough one: Do you have any problems cleaning up especially after messy meals? Well, someone has to do it!

What is your idea of a good vacation? It is great to have a challenging and rewarding career, but leisure offers more alternatives and hopefully more enjoyment. Enjoying your leisure is fundamental to what most people want to accomplish in life, but it will only be enjoyable if both of you are on the same page. That does not mean that both of you have to enjoy exactly the same things. We recently walked the Inca Trail in Peru. That was not Amy's first choice of a destination, during or since, but she tolerated my enthusiasm. Next is Italy that she prefers (and I do too). Where would you like to go, what would you like to do when you get there, and where would you prefer to stay?

You might even inquire about things such as whether they want pets and what types?

These questions are meant to alert you to the importance of your family as a producing unit. With some people you will be able to produce the types of commodities that both of you agree will make your marriage a success, while with others that may not be possible. This production process is the subject of a later chapter, which will give you a better idea of why these are important questions that you should be asking now—before you marry.

CONCLUSION

Marriage is not just candlelight dinners and great sex. It is also a productive relationship in which two people attempt to improve their welfare. Some couples will be more successful than others in production and it is suggested here that they are more likely to have a successful marriage. What are the keys to more efficient production in marriage? This chapter suggests that in addition to the love and physical characteristics that attract you to someone, you should also be attracted by the attributes that would make for a good business partner. Some of these attributes, such as commitment, compatibility and complementarity, are essential in a business partner and a spouse. Others, such as being financially responsible, hard working and concerned about others, may appear to be less essential, but seldom will a marriage be a success without them. A sense of humor, as well as being well organized and candid are important attributes in any relationship—business or marital. Among people with prior experience, single people, widows and widowers are much more desirable than either divorced or married individuals. Just as businesses produce products, families produce commodities. Before marriage, it can be important to determine the commodities that the two of you feel are most important. Your challenge now is to find that person with whom you can accomplish these tasks—if you have not already. That is the task of the next chapter.

THINGS TO REMEMBER

- For your marriage to be a success, you and your spouse must feel that you are better off in it than you would be in any other arrangement.
- That feeling is generated by the two of you producing desirable commodities just like successful businesses produce desirable products.
- In addition to being attracted to your spouse, that person should have the type of attributes that you would want in a business partner.
- Some of those attributes will be essential such as commitment, compatibility and complementarity, while others will be less important.
- Among people with prior experience, single people, widows and widowers are much preferable to divorced or currently married individuals.
- Because your family is going to be a productive unit, you will benefit if you prefer similar commodities.

Acquiring Your Partner

Now it is time for you to get to work. You have some ideas about the characteristics of the person that you should consider marrying, so you have to determine how to find your future spouse and then convince that person to marry you. If you are waiting to fall in love, have a reality check. That's a little bit like a company waiting for consumers to find out that it has a great product. It will probably go broke before that happens. Initially, a business has to figure out how to acquire inputs to produce an appealing product. Then it has to determine the customers who might be interested in buying its product and how to convince them to actually buy it.

That is exactly what you have to do. If you are single and want to get married, you have to ask yourself: Why have I not found that particular person? Alternatively, if you have found that person, but have been unable to get a long-term commitment, you have to ask yourself why? Finding the right person who wants to marry you is similar to experiences that businesses have buying and selling.

In a business setting these two activities are described as purchasing and marketing, and these tasks are usually handled by different divisions within a company. In your search to find and attract a desirable spouse, you will have to integrate both activities. This process is particularly important because of the Experience Trap. The process of finding a spouse has become much more difficult and your prior experiences may not have adequately prepared you for finding the person for whom you are searching.

The Emotion Trap also continues to be a concern. In a business environment, you are usually exposed to the cost of your choices because they normally involve money. This is less likely to occur while dating. Love can make you focus on the benefits of a relationship, while the costs are often vague—and potentially ignorable. Moreover, you also are less likely to be questioned about your romantic decisions by parents or other members of society than would have been the case in the past.

At least some of the increase in the divorce rate has to be traced to these two Traps, as too often people marry and then eventually decide that it was a poor decision. So, you want to make sure that you make good decisions.

PURCHASING: WHY A SPOUSE IS LIKE MOZZARELLA

While these activities often have to be pursued simultaneously, let's start with a consideration of purchasing. Remember that I am suggesting in this book that many of the key decisions necessary for you to have a happy, fulfilling marriage are similar to those necessary for a successful business. Purchasing is particularly important for avoiding the primary reasons that businesses—and marriages—fail. Both usually start optimistically with the idea that they are going to be a success. Regrettably, some fail. In both cases, most of those failures can be traced to inadequate preparation or unexpected outcomes. These problems are more likely to occur during purchasing if the company has not adequately investigated its alternatives. The business that we have been considering is a combination microbrewery and pizzeria. Good quality mozzarella at a reasonable price is essential for the success of your pizzeria.

PURCHASING MOZZARELLA

Let's first consider the steps that successful businesses go through when they are purchasing. Purchasing decisions have to be based on a search that involves benefits and costs with people expected to search so long as the benefits of additional search exceed the costs. The benefits are finding a better product while the costs are the time and money involved in the search. To make better decisions, a business wants to increase the benefits and reduce the costs of additional searching.

When a business decides to acquire something, its analysis has to develop through some specific steps.[1] What does it want? Where will it find it? What are the tradeoffs between different attributes? How long is the relationship among the different businesses going to be maintained? Supply chain management addresses these concerns and it has become increasingly important for successful businesses. The supply chain consists of the flow of inputs into outputs and then their distribution to customers. Traditionally, this process was fairly straightforward as a steel firm, for example, acquired iron ore and coke, converted them into steel, and then formed the steel into beams that were delivered to customers to be used in the construction of a building.

The purchasing activities of businesses have changed dramatically recently as business practices have altered the traditional roles of purchasing professionals. They now have become more involved in the earlier stages of product development. These professionals also have had to adapt to new technology such as the Internet and computers as they have attempted to limit their inventories and control the quality of their inputs.

Supply chain management has also observed a shift from tactical to strategic decision making.[2] Tactical decisions have a narrower focus than strategic ones. With the tactical approach, for example, a business's purchasing decisions are isolated from other aspects of the business. Purchasing agents are told the parts that are needed by the manufacturing function of the business and it is their job to locate those parts at the lowest cost and make sure that they are available when needed. More recently, the purchasing decisions have become more strategic as there has been a shift toward purchasing being more integrated into the other aspects of the business. People in purchasing work more closely with those in manufacturing to determine the parts that are needed and how to acquire them.

Your business has to go through a similar process when it purchases its mozzarella. Evaluating potential suppliers is one of the most critical functions of your pizzeria as you use your resources to investigate them.[3] You will usually interview prospective suppliers and visit their plants and distribution centers to assess their capacities. It is important to make certain that the supplier is capable of delivering the desired goods or services on time and in the correct quantities without sacrificing quality. You may enter into long-term contracts, because you may have to rely on one or a few suppliers.

FINDING A SPOUSE

The process that a company goes through to find cheese is similar to the process that you have to go through to find a good spouse. Just like a business, you are involved in a search process that involves benefits and costs. You should be attempting to avoid those two reasons why businesses and marriage fail: inadequate preparation and unexpected outcomes. In both cases, the acquisition of information is important for minimizing the likelihood of failure.

While it is popular to view the prelude to marriage as a search to fall in love, an economist would describe a successful search process as one that continued so long as the benefits of additional search exceeded the costs. To put it another way, people marry when they decide that the benefits of additional searching no longer exceed the costs of that search. The benefits of searching are finding someone more desirable than current alternatives, while the costs can be much broader. Certainly, one cost might be the loss of someone with whom you already have a relationship. Other costs are time, money and frustration. Many people today recognize that these costs can be substantial and as a result they are looking for ways to reduce them. I noted recently in one airline in-flight magazine that there were two ads for match makers and one from the dating service It's Just Lunch. Clearly, those services see people who travel regularly on airplanes as a frustrated audience waiting to purchase their services.

When considering the best strategy to find a spouse, it is easy to fall into the Experience Trap by continuing to do what you have done in the past—which has not generated productive results so far. To be successful, you need to expand your horizons. In your case, let's look at this process starting with the end result. You want to live the good life with a successful marriage being an essential ingredient. To create that marriage, you need a partner with an attractive combination of the attributes that we discussed in the last chapter.

Just like purchasing for a business has confronted important changes, so has the process by which potential spouses meet each other. As recently as 1970, the median age at first marriage was 23.2 for males and 20.8 for females—in contrast to 27.1 and 25.3, respectively, recently. When people married at a young age, neighborhoods and schools were by far the most common places in which they met their future spouse. The uncertainty of the world after graduation from high school or college often caused couples to marry just after they graduated.

Now that many people have left school before they start to seriously think about marriage, the process by which people "acquire" a spouse has become much more complicated. Just as with businesses, computers and electronic devices have become much more important. However, because of the subjective nature of the process, other methods continue to be very important. It was sort of easy to "fall in love" in the past when the most likely candidates for your spouse were right in front of you in your neighborhood or at school. With that being less likely today, the acquisition process has become more complicated and you have to become more systematic in your planning.

Like purchasing by businesses, the acquisition of a spouse has also seen a shift from being tactical to strategic. As recently as fifty years ago, the process by which people acquired a spouse could be viewed as tactical. The decisions necessary to acquire a spouse were much narrower than today. People met the person that they eventually married in normal activities in their neighborhood or at school. Very little planning was required or necessary. It was highly likely that they could have a successful marriage with someone to whom they were physically attracted with only a limited consideration of their other attributes. Most young adults already understood the roles and responsibilities that married men and women were expected to accept, so those roles were assumed and less likely to be a basis of conflict after a couple married.

Now, the process has become much more complicated as it has become more difficult to identify and contact potential spouses and it has become much more important to consider attributes that are not obvious when you first meet someone. You have to think strategically. Now you have to work much harder to identify potential spouses. Certainly, the computer and other electronic devices have changed the process. Still the evidence suggests that the process of locating a spouse has not improved in efficiency as much as has been the case for the manufacturing process. Introductions by friends, family and acquaintances continue to be the primary way by which couples meet.[4]

LOCATING ALTERNATIVES

Just as a purchasing professional has to start out with the need to acquire production inputs with certain requirements, you have to start out with certain characteristics of a spouse in mind. While the specific goal is a spouse, what you really want is someone who has an attractive combination of the attributes noted in the last chapter. At the top of your list probably should be commitment, compatibility and complementarity. In contrast to physical attributes, these characteristics may not be obvious to a casual observer. Your initial challenge, therefore, is to acquire a general understanding of how you can identify the people with the attributes you desire.

COMPATIBILITY

A good place to start searching is with compatibility because it is easier to identify that attribute than some of the others you should be considering. Compatibility is a broad attribute that includes both similar interests as well as the ability to effectively communicate with each other and solve problems as they develop. A good place to start looking is among people who enjoy the things that you enjoy. Religious and recreational interests are obvious choices.

While you may appreciate that compatibility is an important attribute of a spouse, it may not be easy to determine when you and someone else are truly compatible. Compatibility on a date or in a relationship can be very different from the compatibility necessary for a successful marriage. Differences in religion that create few problems during dating can cause major problems during marriage especially if you become parents. Your social activities may give you some idea about your compatibility, but your initial dates may not offer evidence of the types of places to which others like to travel, for example. It is amazing how often conflicts in travel preferences will cause conflict between spouses. An active social life may mask you from really "knowing" the person that you are dating.

So, rather than just subjectively determining that someone else is compatible, you have to address compatibility in a more systematic manner. A good place to start is with a key set of questions to ask people that you date. If you are only interested in having a good time, there is no need to know more about the person you are dating. However, if your goal is marriage, it is important to get to know them—and quickly wouldn't be a bad idea. There is a high opportunity cost associated with spending time with someone who you eventually conclude is not good marital material. Without playing twenty questions, you should direct the conversation in a way that you get answers to these questions. There are books that give guidance as to the type of questions that you should be asking.[5] It would probably be a good idea to get some idea of your partner's views on the six most controversial issues in marriages: money, sex, time spent outside the marriage, in-laws, children, and religion.[6]

COMMITMENT

The next attribute to investigate is commitment. Considering commitment in the past was not a major issue for couples, because the gains from marriage were obvious—married people just lived better than single people—plus it was difficult to obtain a divorce. The importance of commitment has increased because the gains from marriage have been less obvious and divorce has become much easier. Men and women would appear to gain less from being married than in the past. Women now can have successful careers and men can have a comfortable bachelor existence without marriage. However, although the gains from marriage are subtler, most people still recognize it as their ultimate goal. Some people are going to be more committed to a successful marriage than others and your job is to find the more committed ones.

While young adults enjoy being single, eventually most of them want to marry. Economists have an important concept called diminishing returns. The incremental enjoyment of an activity tends to fall as you do more of it. Being single can be very enjoyable. For the first time in U.S. history, adults have a long period between when they leave the relative poverty of education and when they marry. What a great time! They finally have an adequate income and there are few responsibilities other than work to interfere with their enjoyment. Still, diminishing returns often starts to set in as people look for more of a focus in their lives. While they may have been willing to consider marriage with the right person, eventually the importance of finding that right person may increase. They become more willing to make a long-term commitment to a relationship.

Because commitment is such an important attribute of a spouse, it should be addressed early in a relationship. Never forget that wasting your time with the wrong person has a high opportunity cost—the lost opportunity to be investigating other relationships. I am not suggesting that you demand a commitment on the second date. However, if you are willing to assess a person objectively there should be some evidence of a willingness to commit in the foreseeable future. Two obvious concerns when considering commitment are polar situations: people who are middle aged and have never married or those who have been married numerous times. Finding a spouse is difficult enough without any additional challenges. These people are clearly a challenge when it comes to commitment and so their position has to be addressed directly and carefully.

Researchers have identified some important characteristics of people who are ready to make a long-term commitment to marriage.[7] These are the people that you need to identify. The most important factor influencing commitment is separation from school with the result that people with a high school degree tend to commit to marriage before those with a college or graduate school education. It is a common pattern for people to want to start their careers and enjoy their higher incomes before they seriously consider marriage. Still the single scene eventually starts to lose its attraction for many adults and they start looking for a more permanent relationship. These are the people for whom you are looking. Not everyone in those age brackets is looking for a spouse and that becomes more obvious when they remain single into their thirties.

Another aspect of commitment is the difference between the desire and the ability. Most people in a serious relationship eventually decide that they want to make a commitment. An added concern for you is whether they have the ability to make a successful commitment. Let's face it—the characteristics of some people make them more likely to be able effectively to commit to marriage than others. Others may think that they are committing when their actions eventually suggest that their commitment was feeble. Often these will be people with inadequate role models.

The most important characteristics of people who are most likely to have the ability to make a credible commitment resulting in a successful marriage are those who grew up in intact families, have strong religious beliefs, more education and a higher income.[8] These are the people who tend to have the most successful marriages based on their low divorce rates. Because a religious commitment is associated with a lower divorce rate, religious groups are also a good place to start looking. To suggest that you are better off associating with people with more education and a higher income seems elitist. Regrettably, a higher income not only provides a more comfortable lifestyle, it increases the likelihood that your marriage will be a success. This suggests certain strategies. Becoming more involved with the local symphony is preferred to attending an event touting bikini contests or free wings. Golf and tennis are better pursuits than bowling.

While getting a commitment from someone when you are ready to make one yourself can be frustrating for both sexes, it can be a particular problem for women.[9] Men and women would appear to have different "clocks." There is a limited age range during which women can become mothers. Most women in addition recognize that it is more likely that their children will be happy and well adjusted if they grow up in a household with their biological parents. So it is important to be married—or at least in a stable relationship—when they have those children. Most women would like to end their child bearing years by age forty, if not earlier. So it is important for them to marry early enough to accomplish that goal. Men, meanwhile, do not face the same constraints; their primary concern is to be an active father, which they may expect to continue at least into their fifties.[10] Therefore, women may be the ones who need to be most concerned about whether a partner is willing to make a commitment. This research suggests that if a woman in her early twenties wants to marry she should avoid men of a similar age. The more likely candidates for a successful marriage are men who are somewhat older.

Women have to be especially concerned about "stringers," the men who have had one or more long-term relationships with other women and didn't marry them.[11] This is not a time to seek a challenge. Find out why those relationships failed and find it out quickly. Research indicates that there is a time at which men are ready to marry.[12] You have to find whether this man is just not the marrying type or whether he was just not at that time in his life at which he was going to be willing to commit. Researchers have noted that men often leave a long relationship and then quickly marry someone else.[13] You do not want to be the person who "wasted" time in a long relationship.

COMPLEMENTARITY

Determining whether a potential spouse and you are complementary can be more of a challenge than determining whether you are compatible and willing to make a commitment. When people are dating, they are less likely to be in a situation in which they would benefit from assuming more specialized roles. Often they are living alone or with roommates. Therefore, it may be difficult to visualize the roles that the two of you would assume if you married.

So a concern is how do you find people with whom you are complementary? While work is a common place in which people find a spouse, this approach should be used with caution since co-workers will often have similar career goals. Lawyers in a large firm may both consider their careers to be essential to their future goals with much less interest in domestic work. If they marry, they will have fewer gains from being complementary—although they may have a successful marriage by buying domestic services.

The activities that are most likely to help you find someone who is compatible may also be helpful in finding someone with whom you are complementary. Recreational and religious groups consist of a broad variety of people. While seeking someone who is compatible within those groups, you should also consider those with whom you are complementary. Women with strong career goals should be considering men who enjoy working around the house.

Seeking someone with whom you are complementary requires you to avoid common stereotypes. We are far removed from marriages in which the roles of the spouses were clearly defined. However, while the earnings of the typical woman are still less than that of the typical man,[14] that could change as the educational attainment of women increases.[15] Not only are women earning a majority of bachelor degrees, the percentage of advanced degrees going to women has increased dramatically over the last few decades. Between 1970 and 2002, the percentage of medical and law degrees going to women increased from eight and five percent to 44 and 48 percent, respectively.[16] The probability is increasing rapidly that the spouse with the higher income-earning capacity within a marriage will be the wife. For these women, men willing to increase their work in the home should become increasingly attractive.

Most marriages still benefit from couples assuming differentiated roles. This differentiation will vary from slight to extreme based on their preferences and skills. A challenge for many women is to find men who are capable of adapting to this new environment. My research has shown that men often do not see adequate benefits from their wives' employment to justify—in their minds—increasing their own efforts around the house.[17] To be blunt, many women have to find men who understand that comparative advantage does not mean that women do most of the housework no matter how much the women earn. It is appropriate during dating to address the roles that the two of you see for each other during marriage. Whose career is most important? How are you going to allocate (or buy) domestic tasks? What changes do you expect with parenthood?

In conclusion, compatibility, commitment, and complementarity are important for your marital success. Initially, you have to consider how to identify people with those attributes. Having developed a process for determining the people who are most likely to have the attributes for which you are looking, you have to develop a plan for finding a particular person.

A Specific Acquisition Plan

After a purchasing agent has decided on the characteristics of what the business needs to buy and how to identify the right products, the next step is a plan for locating an actual supplier. For a business this may be as simple as looking in the yellow pages or a trade association directory. Finding a spouse is a lot more complicated. There is a difference between where people think others met the person that they married and where they actually did.[18] This is especially relevant given the perceived importance of the Internet. It turns out the best place to start is with your family and friends (and their friends). That is how most people have found their spouses. These people are followed by about equal chances of meeting someone by chance or at a party, bar, club or work. Surprisingly, online dating came in last among the choices in a recent survey at only three percent.

To find the right person, you need a plan. Just like a business has to closely scrutinize potential suppliers, you want to identify and evaluate potential spouses. Now we want to consider the different methods that you might want to use to find a spouse. Most of these methods also permit you to market yourself to them. Still, if we think about this process sequentially, you need to find the person that you are seeking before you can sell yourself to that person. So, our first interest is in finding someone that you want to marry.

Our purpose here is not to give all the information that you need to use these services. Instead, we are going to analyze some of the popular methods available today. Although people are familiar with dating, few have a lot of experience in finding a spouse. This is a new challenge for them and they do not want to fall into the Experience Trap. Consequently, they are not in a position to evaluate the methods that will work for them. While the ideal person could appear at any time, no business would rely on luck in finding customers and you certainly should not rely on luck in finding a spouse.

An important concept in business, especially in financial analysis, is diversification. Most activities—both investing and dating—are risky in that outcomes are uncertain. One way to reduce risk is to diversify so that not all of your investments—or dates—perform poorly at the same time. In a similar manner, your search for a spouse should consist of a variety of activities—you need to diversify your portfolio.

An important consideration is the benefits of each approach relative to its costs. You should recognize by now that we are not talking about money. The primary benefit of the search is a spouse with the cost being a combination of time, money, frustration and other alternatives. The preferred methods have the highest potential benefits relative to their costs. Here are some of the more obvious choices.

LUCK

Let's get rid of this quickly. Sure, the costs are low since you are expending so little effort, but unfortunately the benefits are also low because of the limited likelihood of success. Rely on luck until you become serious about finding a spouse. If you were lucky, then you probably do not have to read this chapter and you have probably already moved on to the next chapter. For the rest of you, relying on luck is an unacceptable strategy. Few successful businesses have been based on it and fewer have survived on it. Of course, it can occur, but it is much more likely to occur if you have planned for it. The probability of success is increased if you have made plans that increase your likelihood of success. So, let's move on to more realistic alternatives.

FRIENDS, FAMILY AND ACQUAINTANCES

This is the place to begin as the benefits can be high while the costs are low. Do not hide your frustration from others about not finding the type of person you desire. Let others know that you are looking for the ultimate permanent relationship. There are lots of people like you out there. The fundamental problem is the flow of information between you and those people. That is why friends, family members and acquaintances are so important. They are in the best position to provide reliable information. Let's face it. There is a range of quality of information that you have about others and that they have about you. Family and friends are the people in the best position to provide others with reasonably accurate information about you and about them to you. Few other methods are as capable of identifying whether others have the characteristics that are important for marital success. Similar information about you can be channeled to others.

Of course, you need to question the suggestions of these people because it can be awkward if their suggestions lead to conflicts between people that they have viewed as friends. Why are they interested in the two of you connecting? Are they just suggesting that you meet someone because they sincerely think that you are compatible or because they feel sorry for the other person's inability to establish a relationship?

WORK

Work continues to be an important source for potential spouses,[19] although it is a source that has to be used with extreme caution for both legal as well as emotional reasons. When your organization tolerates office romances and a couple is realistic about the appropriate bounds, the initial benefits can be high relative to the costs. The benefits consist of the ability to become familiar with a person's attributes before you date, while the initial costs can be low because you are not using time or money to find someone else. Eventually, the benefits are the same as they would be in any process that results in marriage, but the costs can be particularly high because of the continuing working relationship if the romantic one fails.

While relationships with subordinates and bosses open up the possibilities for sexual harassment cases, most other types of relationships are tolerated in most companies.[20] Companies are most concerned if the romance is within a couple's work group. Overall, discretion is probably more important than secrecy.

While finding a job that you enjoy is too important to be compromised, among alternative positions you may want to consider their possibilities for marital prospects. It is just good old supply and demand. Employment in an engineering firm is probably a good idea for a woman looking for men, while teaching may be a good place for a man to find single women.

RELIGIOUS, CULTURAL AND SOCIAL GROUPS

Groups of people with interests similar to yours are also a good place to look. The foundation of any marriage has to be physical attraction and compatibility. These are the groups in which you are most likely to find people with whom you are compatible. The best groups are the ones in which there are opportunities for personal interaction. You want activities such as hiking groups in which you interact with people on an informal basis. Classes and lectures may be less appealing because of the lack of interaction with others. Another opportunity to interact with numerous people is political campaigns. Basically, the idea is to get out of the house—or your apartment.

INTERNET DATING

Internet dating is an attractive alternative because the costs, especially in terms of time, can be fairly low.[21] Rather than hanging around a bar and meeting no one, you can investigate and contact people fairly easily through these services. However, the benefits can be low because the initial information is often distorted and unreliable. These services generally allow people to provide personal information and then search for other individuals using criteria such as age range, gender and location. An important component of these services is the ability of members to upload photos and browse the photos of others. Sites may offer additional services such as online chats and message boards. They sometimes allow people to register for free but most offer services that require a monthly fee. Many sites are broad-based with members from a variety of backgrounds looking for different types of relationships. Other sites are more specific based on the type of members, interests, location, or relationship desired. Of course, you would want to focus on the ones that emphasize an interest in marriage rather than more casual relationships.

There have to be at least two concerns with these sites. First, as noted above the information that they contain may not be particularly accurate. Talk about perverse incentives. People want to attract responses so they have an incentive to describe themselves in the most favorable way. In fact, they have an incentive to overstate their positive attributes and understate their negative ones. Others, knowing that this is going on, even if they would prefer to be honest, feel compelled to act in a similar manner. However, knowing that this is going on creates incentives for readers to discount what they read.

The problems associated with questionable information are not fatal, but they have to be addressed. In initial exchanges, it is important to attempt to confirm the accuracy of the information contained on the various web sites. A good place to start is with questions that indirectly establish the other parties' age. If they say that they are a certain age, ask about experiences that they had in school and try and connect them to particular dates. What were they doing on 9/11?

A second concern with these sites is whether matches that they have created have resulted in weddings and whether those marriages have been successful. Some of the commercial Internet sites such as Match.com have been very aggressive in publicizing the number of marriages that have resulted from contacts made via their web sites. An unresolved question is, How successful have those marriages been?[22] People often rely on connections made through these services when other methods have not been successful. In some cases, they may see few benefits in additional searches and, therefore, they are more willing to marry someone that they meet in this venue. However, with reduced expectations they may be disappointed with the choice that they make.

While some characteristics of a potential spouse are essential such as commitment and complementarity—neither of which you can determine through a profile on a web site—when using these online services it can be important to show some flexibility with regard to other attributes. A person a little shorter or older than you prefer may not be all that bad. It has been suggested that you can always avoid going out with someone you contact online, but you can't meet them if you never contact them.[23]

ARRANGED MEALS OR DRINKS

There is often no substitute for personal interaction. Here we are dealing with a tradeoff between money and time as this method is more expensive, but less time consuming than some of the other methods. While we have discussed the important characteristics of a spouse that are most likely to result in a successful marriage, successful relationships most often begin with an attraction between two people based on physical appearance and body language. One problem with Internet dating is that people can devote substantial time establishing a relationship that quickly dissipates when the couple actually meets. Therefore, another way to diversify your portfolio is to consider opportunities involving personal contact.

Typical of these opportunities is It's Just Lunch![24] which specializes in sending people on casual dates over lunch, brunch, or drinks after work. While this alternative can be more expensive, it can have the benefit of prior screening and personal contact. These arrangements attempt to also limit the cost of unwanted contacts by limiting the parties' knowledge of each other's contact information until it is mutually agreeable. The personal screening is particularly important for the success of the companies that arrange the meetings as people will no longer buy the service if they experience or hear about poor matches. Opportunities such as this for informal face to face meetings for which there has been some preliminary screening can be a very valuable means for meeting people with whom you may be compatible. Meeting for drinks may be more productive than a meal. Not that I want to suggest that you should be cheap, but it always seems to me that a meal can be a distraction when you are attempting to have a productive conversation. I hate to have a business lunch at a place with particularly good food as I never seem to be able to remember what the food was like.

Even for a casual meeting, you need to do your homework. Read carefully any information that is provided to you and then think about the questions that you want answered. You do not want the conversation to be an interrogation, but still you are wasting time if you just want to confirm that the person is physically attractive. At the same time, it is probably a good idea to consider which topics you should avoid at this time. Leave politics and frustrating prior relationships for later.

SPEED DATING

A recent development is a concept known as speed dating in which people have brief interchanges at a specific location such as a bar or restaurant. One of the leaders in this field is 8minuteDating.[25] At 8minuteDating events, people have eight one-on-one dates each of which lasts eight minutes. If both parties are interested in meeting again, the organizers provide contact information so they can set up another date. Again, this is a method that can be more expensive while reducing other time and frustration costs.

Regrettably, this may be a poor way to screen potential spouses. Sure, it fits into the popular myth of love at first sight. However, I do not buy that myth and neither should you. It does provide you with the opportunity to meet lots of people in a short period of time. Of course, that leads to the quantity over quality approach. In the modern era, it is so important that spouses are compatible, committed and complementary. Therefore, a short exposure to someone during which you confirmed their physical attractiveness as well as certain mannerisms may not provide particularly valuable information. Moreover, you have to be concerned about people who find this approach attractive.[26] Because this book has emphasized the importance of certain attributes, you should be concerned that these activities attract people who think that they can make quick judgments about others.

Some of the advantages of speed dating are that it allows singles to meet a large number of new people in one easy event. Research shows that people at these sessions often make up their minds about whether they want to see their current partner again within three seconds.[27] It is especially efficient for busy professionals or those with limited social circles. It also levels the playing field for men and women. Men do not have to play their traditional role as the aggressor—both men and women are forced to meet and interact. The structured interaction helps shy people to overcome their inhibitions. The time limit ensures that no one is stuck talking to someone longer than they wish. The matching process occurs after the event, ensuring people do not have to face rejection in person. This helps avoid awkward situations and uneasy interactions between participants during the event. Participants are almost always guaranteed that the people they meet are single or at least looking. This is generally not the case when one goes to a bar or a club. It is something that women who like to go out in groups can do together. However, it has been criticized because it reinforces first impressions, which may not be reliable indicators of long-term compatibility. It also tends to put less extroverted subjects at a disadvantage.

MATCH MAKERS

Now we get to the big bucks approach to finding a spouse.[28] In some ways this may be the most expensive and yet the least costly method for some people. As we have already noted, time and frustration are also costs of the dating process. A good match maker has the ability to reduce those other costs. The acceptance of organized dating systems, however, has created a resurgence in the role of the traditional professional match maker. Those who find dating systems or services useful but prefer human intelligence and personal touches can choose from a wide range of such services now available. The common pattern here is for couples to consist of successful, wealthy men and attractive women. The men usually pay a fee with the women being able to participate for free. You certainly get personalized attention at a price.

These services are particularly important when potential spouses have a unique characteristic but they are dispersed within the population such as deeply religious Jewish singles. It may be difficult for them to find each other, so match makers provide a clearinghouse for them.

So you now have a plan on how you are going to locate your future spouse. You can increase your likelihood of success by considering a variety of approaches. Fundamental to this process is putting out the word to family and friends that you are seriously looking for someone. You are going to combine that strategy with joining some recreational groups and Internet dating services. If you have tried these approaches without success, then it is time to move on to the more expensive services such as arranged meals, speed dating and match makers. Your next task is to convince someone that you meet to marry you.

MARKETING: SELLING THE BEST PEPPERONI PIZZA AND YOU

Using insights from purchasing, you have decided on the type of person that you are seeking and the places and methods that are most likely to help you locate such people. If that process is successful, you still have at least one additional challenge—how do you convince that person to marry you? That critical additional step benefits from insights from marketing.

MARKETING PIZZA

Consider how you get the word out that you have the best pepperoni pizza in town. Again, you are confronted with the tradeoffs between benefits and costs. You have to consider the different marketing strategies with that concern in mind. Some approaches are potentially very beneficial in their ability to attract customers, such as a television ad campaign, but they are also very costly. An alternative is word of mouth, which is very inexpensive, but it may not be very beneficial in attracting customers. A company's marketing strategy consists of determining which customers the company will serve and how it will create value for these customers.[29]

The major marketing tools are classified into four broad groups, called the four Ps of marketing: product, price, place and promotion. As a first step the firm must create a need-satisfying product. It must then decide how much it will charge for the product (price) and how it will make the product available to target consumers (place). Last, it must communicate with target customers about the product and persuade them of its merits (promotion).

Let's consider these tools in more detail. Product means the combination of goods and services that the company offers to the target market. Some of the variables that influence the product are variety, quality, design, features, brand name, packaging and services.[30] The task of a business is to combine these attributes in an attractive package. Your pizza is a combination of flour, tomatoes, cheese and other ingredients, but an important part of your product is the environment in which the pizza is sold. People can be as concerned about the quality of the service and attractiveness of your restaurant as they are of the pizza itself. These are all components of your product.

When introducing a new product businesses have to consider strategies based on segmentation, targeting, and position.[31] Segmentation consists of dividing a market into distinct groups that might require separate approaches. Targeting is the process of evaluating each market segment's attractiveness and selecting one or more segments to enter. Last, you need to position your product by arranging for it to occupy a clear, distinctive and desirable place relative to competing products in the minds of targeted consumers.

A business's next concern is price, which, of course, is the amount of money that customers have to pay to obtain the product. For retail products, there are few variables other than the list price, although there may be sales and specials. Most consumers will not consider price in isolation but will compare it to the perceived quality of the product that they are receiving. They will buy the goods that have the highest ratio of value to price rather than just the lowest priced product. Because of the enjoyment that they receive from your product, you want customers to think that your pizza is a bargain relative to its price. You will have less discretion in your pricing as the number of alternative pizzerias increases. It is common among restaurants such as yours to alter your price based on market conditions with the result that they have a lower price at lunch than during dinner and an especially low price during "happy hour."

Place consists of a company's activities that make the product available to target consumers. There are good and bad locations for restaurants. For a retail business such as yours there can be a difficult tradeoff between rent and access to customers as rents tend to be high in the areas in which you are most likely to have customers. A remote location might have a low rent, but there are few customers there.

Promotion is the activities that communicate the merits of the product and persuade target customers to buy it. Some promotional activities that a business might consider are advertising, personal selling, sales promotion, and public relations. Of course, these will vary with the type of product being sold. For your pizzeria, advertising and street appeal may be particularly important because you want to reach a broad range of potential customers.

An important component of promotion is first impression, as you might not get a second chance to acquire customers' business. Business consultants have suggested that a good way to capture a consumer's attention is to think of your business as a theatrical production.[32] They suggest that companies need to have a systematic theme that makes their product come alive for potential consumers. More than just having great pizza, you should design your pizzeria so that it has a warm, friendly environment that suggests that your customers are in a small town in Italy.

Overall, researchers have shown that consumers go through five stages in the process of adopting a new product.[33] Initially, consumers become aware of the new product, but they lack information about it. Then they seek information about the new product. Next, they consider whether trying the new product makes sense. Then they try the new product on a small scale to improve their estimate of its value. Last, they decide to buy and regularly use the new product. These steps would appear to have applications elsewhere.

MARKETING YOU

I hope that the parallel of marketing concepts to your attempt to attract a spouse are not too subtle. Translated into the context of this book that means your marketing strategy should be to determine the type of individuals who would find you attractive and then to convince them that you are sufficiently valuable that they should marry you. Sorry to put it this way, but you are a product. What kind of product do you want to be?

While in the purchasing mode you were considering the type of persons that you would want to marry and where to find them, the marketing phase reminds you that only certain types of people are likely to find you attractive and to attempt to attract others may be costly in terms of lost alternatives. If you have strong religious beliefs, then it is probably a good idea to focus your marketing efforts on people with similar beliefs. Even with a strong physical attraction, different religious beliefs are likely to conflict with the compatibility that is essential for marital success. Other interests are less restrictive, but outdoors-oriented people are more likely to find happiness with other outdoors-oriented people, while people with a strong interest in the arts should search for similar people. If you have no interest in camping, for example, then you would be wise to avoid people who focus their lives on outdoor activities.

You as a Product

So, your goal is to create a "product" that someone else would find attractive with the ultimate goal being to make them want to marry you. It is important for businesses and you to consider strategies that encompass segmentation, targeting and position. You want to segment potential spouses, target the ones with the highest likelihood of producing a successful marriage and then position yourself to get them to marry you.

The primary way that you will segment your market is by choosing people with whom to associate. Then your targeting becomes particularly important. Of all the people that you might date, you want to target those who are marriage material. You want to focus your efforts on people interested in marrying, particularly on those most likely to result in a happy, fulfilling marriage. This is not an easy process and it may require some difficult choices on your part.

Having segmented the market and targeted the groups who are the best marriage material, you have to position yourself. This consists of the way that you are defined by the "buyers" in the market relative to others. Positioning involves implanting in the minds of others your unique attributes while differentiating yourself in their minds. In the process of positioning yourself, the extent to which you can alter or emphasize different characteristics can have a big effect on your success in attracting a mate.

Researchers have described certain attributes as necessities and luxuries when people are being considered by the opposite sex.[34] Physical attractiveness in women is viewed as a necessity by most men and status and resources of men similarly by women.[35] Kindness and intelligence are also necessities for both. In many cases, the result is essentially a threshold value. Being unemployed makes a man a particularly unattractive candidate in the eyes of most women. Meanwhile, having the type of job associated with being a college graduate makes him someone that many women would consider. However, having crossed over a particular threshold, that attribute becomes less important relative to other attributes, which researchers have described as luxuries. So being an attractive man may not be important to many women if that man is unemployed, but it becomes important if he has a decent job. Similarly, research has shown that being reasonably kind and intelligent is viewed as a necessity for many people, while being unusually kind or intelligent does not make them that much more attractive after they have reached a certain threshold. This suggests that it is important for men seeking a spouse to have a reasonable income and for women with the same goal to make sure that they are as physically attractive as possible. While this conclusion may appear to be unacceptably reactionary, economists are more interested in what people do than in what they say and it would appear that many women still prefer rich men and many men prefer attractive women.

Self-confidence is sexy.[36] Of course, this is more easily said than done. To the best of your ability, you want to act as if you have your life under control without being arrogant. While this attribute may be commonly accepted to be important for men, it can also be important for women. We are in a new era in which people are marrying after both men and women have had an opportunity to have a broad range of experiences and careers. Men want to be proud of the woman they marry. Both men and women want to brag about their spouse's accomplishments.

PRICING YOU

Then, we need to turn to pricing. This may seem a strange concept in courting. However, some relationships can appear to be more costly than others. We have all heard the term "high maintenance" applied to someone. It has been suggested that women with lots of makeup and expensive clothes may turn off some men as appearing to be too costly.[37] Costs can assume a variety of forms other than money. Some are time such as the other person not being punctual. Others can be psychological when a person has a tendency toward depression. Some people are just very demanding of others' attention and time.

Just as with pizza, people will compare your attributes to the cost of associating with you. It is probably a good strategy to not come across as being too costly. We all have insecurities and minor neuroses, but dating is not a good time to advertise them.[38] You want to emphasize your positive attributes. If a woman is sincerely looking for a marital partner but states to potential mates that her career has a central role in her life, she may project that considering a marriage with her could be very costly.[39] A man would have to make numerous changes to accommodate that career. The price might be too high. In a similar fashion, a man can radiate a lack of sincerity that would suggest infidelity and its costs later if the couple were to marry. If you want to convince someone to marry you, you may have to communicate that your flexibility and commitment makes your "price" low enough to attract the type of people that you want.

One clear example of those who can appear to be costly to others are single parents.[40] Most of the research deals with single mothers, but some of the same problems may face single fathers. While out-of-wedlock childbearing can increase the likelihood of the mother marrying the father, it greatly diminishes the likelihood of subsequent marriage to other men. Men just plain do not look forward to raising someone else's children. Compared to women without unmarried births, those with unmarried births are more likely to cohabit than to marry. Moreover, they are more likely to have less educated and older spouses or partners.

PUTTING YOU IN THE RIGHT PLACE

Being in the right place is important in both finding a spouse—and being found. Under purchasing, you investigated where you could find potential spouses. The goal here is to place you in those environments. Just like successful real estate investing depends on location, location, and location, successful courting depends on being in the right place. Here it is wise to follow the advice of people in finance and diversify your portfolio. In a similar fashion, you need to diversify the places where you can be "found." So while reminding your family and friends of your availability and preferences should be your first course of action, it would also be appropriate to use other methods such as Internet dating and special interests groups. Getting out can be difficult for people who have demanding jobs, but, if you eventually want to marry, it is important that you pursue activities that will place you in contact with others.

PROMOTING YOU

Your last concern is how to promote you. Essentially, you need to sell yourself. There are lots of valuable insights about this process in the sales literature. Jeffrey Gitomer in his *The Little Red Book of Selling*[41] emphasizes the central principle that you should not "sell" so much as you should make people want to buy. He suggests that by reducing risk you can convert selling into buying. People are anxious about the future—their future. It's risky. If you can convince them that they can have an attractive future with you, the risk level goes down and your selling efforts now become their buying activities.

The only person that can sell you is you. So complaining about all the losers that you are meeting is not constructive. Why are you meeting losers? What is wrong with your strategy? To sell yourself you have to be proactive. Gitomer emphasizes that to be successful you have to have self-inspiration, self-determination and hard work. Forget about luck. Hard work creates good luck. Keeping positive with a touch of humor is important for successfully selling yourself. He notes that such pedestrian things as your telephone voice message can be an important selling device. The one that he uses is, "Hi, this is Jeffrey Gitomer. I wish I could talk to you but I can't. Please leave your American Express number and expiration date, and I'll get right back to you." The bottom line for successful selling is being positive and sincere.

Rachel Greenwald has written a book giving advice for women trying to find a husband after age thirty-five.[42] She emphasizes the importance of promotion for success in finding a spouse. Especially important are two important lessons from advertising. First, it is essential that you have "brand consistency" by which she means that your image remains the same every time you meet a potential spouse. The easiest way to accomplish this is to have a clear understanding of your own values and goals. Second, the key to branding yourself is identifying you as someone different. You are a Jewish girl who enjoys outdoor activities such as backpacking. This brand can be important for people who can fix you up and for those with whom you have dates. Equally important is "brand recall," which means that people remember who you are. So when a Jewish guy says to a friend of yours that he cannot find a woman who is interested in backpacking, you immediately come to mind.

While online dating can serve an important role in finding potential spouses, it is also an important device for selling yourself. Because there are lots of potential candidates out there, this is a much more competitive environment than a dinner party or a picnic. You have to start out with a profile—and it has to be a good one. Just like your essay to get into college had to be well thought out, this profile has to be well written.[43] It has to present you as a unique, positive person with a sense of humor. A current picture is essential. Emphasize your uniqueness with three catchy attributes.

First impressions are important for products and they can also be important for you. When you are at casual events, one suggestion is to wear something from an interesting place that you have visited. A unique T-shirt is particularly visible, while just having a golf shirt with a logo on it may be best at other times. Not only does it differentiate you, but it can be the basis of a conversation. When approaching you, others do not want to have to start out with some dumb, potentially embarrassing question or comment.

Your first impression visually and verbally should be consistent. Do not dress provocatively and then talk about your conservative religious values. In fact, dressing provocatively is not a good strategy for attracting the type of men who are looking for wives rather than one night stands. Men are more likely to approach a woman who is dressed in an outfit with which he is comfortable.[44] An important aspect of first impressions is conveying a positive personality. Without looking artificial, it is important to smile when you are in situations in which you might meet someone new. While there has been a gradual change in men's and women's priorities,[45] men still emphasize looks over accomplishments and women are attracted to successful men, so these are the attributes that you should attempt to stress in any initial meetings.[46]

Your marketing effort has attracted the person that you now think that you want to marry. However, for your marketing effort to be a success you need for the two of you to get married.

CLOSING THE DEAL

In both business and matrimony, you cannot consider your efforts a success unless you can close the deal. You have a goal. It could be a sale or in your case it could be a wedding and the successful marriage that follows. Closing the deal consists of obtaining that goal.

CLOSING A BUSINESS DEAL

First consider a closing from the perspective of salespeople. After presenting their case for why the customer and the product are a perfect match and handling the prospect's objections, they try to close the sale. Some salespeople do not handle the closing well. They may lack confidence, feel guilty about asking for the order, or fail to recognize the right moment to close the sale. They need to know how to recognize closing signals from the buyer, including physical actions, comments, and questions. Salespeople can use one of several closing techniques. Most importantly, they have to believe in their product. They can ask for the order, review points of agreement, offer to help write up the order, ask whether the buyer wants this model or that one, or note that the buyer will lose out if the order is not placed now. The salesperson may even offer the buyer special reasons to close, such as a lower price or an extra quantity at no charge.

CLOSING YOUR DEAL

Alternatively, consider a closing from your perspective. You have decided that you want to marry a particular person and you are convinced that the two of you can create a successful marriage. The most important attribute of an effective closing is a conviction that what you are selling is the best product. In your case, you have to believe in the importance of this marriage for you and your partner. You have dated for a while and you may even have lived together. Traditionally, men were expected to propose, so the task for a woman was to either wait patiently or provide inducements and hints. Now both men and women can take the initiative.

Delay can have a high opportunity cost. Researchers have shown that it is important for people seriously interested in marriage to make their intentions well known early in the relationship and eventually insist that your partner make a clear commitment.[47] So, if your partner does not seem to be in a hurry to get married, you may have to give a tactful but clear ultimatum. It is best to choose a time when your partner is in a positive mood.[48] As important as the decision to marry is—what is more important?—pressing that topic at the wrong time can result in a reaction that threatens the relationship.[49] You can propose that the two of you get married or you can threaten to end the relationship if your partner is not willing to marry. Some authors–arguing that they understand men–discourage this approach, but they appear to lack a sense of the opportunity costs of procrastination.[50]

That may be particularly relevant for women as research has shown that men often propose to someone that they have dated only briefly after having ended a long relationship.[51] You do not want to be the person in the relationship that ended. Richard Kirshenbaum and Daniel Rosenberg suggest that no matter how much a guy may love his significant other, he feels that change is the enemy.[52] So, the women in their lives may have to convince their boyfriends that marriage is man's best friend. However, if you need an incentive to make that hard decision, remember opportunity cost. Time passes quickly for both men and women—especially for those with demanding careers, so you cannot afford to waste it.

COHABITATION

Before we leave this chapter, let's consider the benefits and costs of cohabitation. Within the context of this chapter, you should never cohabitate with someone unless it is part of your purchasing or marketing plan. When you are not looking for a spouse, it can be a way to have a more intimate relationship with someone that you find attractive. We also know that two people living together can do that more economically than if they were living separately.

However, it can become less attractive if you are looking for a spouse. By precluding other relationships, cohabitation can have a high opportunity cost. On the other hand, it does provide an opportunity to get a clearer understanding of whether your partner has the characteristics that will result in an attractive spouse. Moreover, it does present an opportunity for you to market yourself. As a minimum, it is important to establish that anyone that you might consider living with has the potential to be a spouse. It may also be important to establish deadlines for a commitment to marriage from your cohabitating partner.

However, be careful. People who only have one episode of cohabitation have normal rates of marital success based on their divorce rates.[53] However, people who have cohabitated with more than one person have an increased risk of marital disruption. While living together can be a valuable source of information about a future spouse, researchers have noted that many of the people who cohabitate with more than one person take a more casual approach to marriage with the result that their subsequent marriages are less successful. Cohabitation is not the same as "pre-marriage," as it does not usually involve the types of conflicts and sacrifices that are at the core of marriage. The partners do not have to face up to parental responsibilities and career choices. It is like two lawyers sharing a secretary and office space rather than two individuals starting a pizzeria.

MARRIAGE EDUCATION

To help you run your pizzeria, you might benefit from getting a master's degree in business administration—an MBA. That degree would provide you with important basic skills, so that you are less likely to make fundamental mistakes as you establish your business. Couples considering marriage can also benefit from a marriage education program. These programs focus especially on improving relationship skills such as clear and positive communication and problem solving. These programs are available from a variety of community and religious organizations. They can be particularly valuable if you find that someone else has attractive attributes, but for some reason you often argue and disagree. Then improved communication and problem-solving skills may be particularly important.

PREMARITAL AGREEMENTS

Businesses frequently establish contractual relationships with others. Starting your pizzeria you would need to contract with a construction company to remodel your store. Then you will have to enter into contracts with your suppliers. While these contracts could result in a lawsuit if either party does not fulfill its obligations, they are often just a means for recording the parties' agreement. What is to be done and when is it supposed to be completed?

Having decided to get married, an increasingly important consideration is whether the two of you should draw up a premarital agreement. There are two reasons why you should at least consider a premarital agreement. First, it is more likely than in the past that they will be enforced. Traditionally, the states felt that they were the only bodies that could define the rights and obligations during (and potentially after) marriage, so contracts by spouses affecting their marriage were frowned upon. Even for the limited range of issues that could be addressed such as the determination of the separate property of the spouses, it was not uncommon for an agreement to be voided at divorce as being unconscionable. As evidenced by the passage of no-fault divorce laws, the states have reduced their restrictions on how couples manage their marriage. Most states have passed statutes that make it more likely that a premarital agreement will be enforced if specific conditions are met.

You still have to be aware of what a contract can and cannot govern and the formalities necessary in its creation. Essentially all of the things that you can agree to will occur at the dissolution of your marriage—if that occurs. The courts will not usually enforce conditions that occur during marriage such as the spouse who will wash the dishes and how often you will have sex, so forget about those things.

One important thing that many couples contract about is the recognition of the property that they are bringing into the marriage that they want to remain their separate property if the marriage is dissolved. There are seldom problems with the enforcement of these provisions. Meanwhile, the courts will closely scrutinize provisions such as pre-arranged spousal support. There are other areas in which an agreement will not be enforced. For example, you will have no control over child custody and support as the state continues to have pre-emptive rights in those areas.

A second reason that you might want to consider a premarital agreement is because of the change in the nature of marriage. First marriages are occurring at later ages and some marriages are only for a short duration. With marriages occurring when people are older, it is more likely for the spouses to already have property that they want to protect if the marriage is dissolved. With unilateral/no-fault divorce, a marriage can be dissolved by either spouse and this can occur early in a marriage. Even with a short duration marriage, if assets are commingled, there is a chance that they will be treated as marital (in contrast to separate) assets if the marriage is dissolved. An agreement about the assets being brought into the marriage by both parties can make it easier to avoid the appearance of commingling. Premarital agreements become particularly important if this is a subsequent marriage, but that topic will be discussed in a later chapter. Here we are dealing with a first marriage with the hope that there are no subsequent marriages.

Just as with a business, a premarital agreement can be an important planning device even if some of the provisions are unenforceable or you have no intention of suing even if they are. During dating it is easy to ignore questions such as what career adjustments you are going to make when you become parents or one of you gets an attractive job offer elsewhere. This is a good time to address these types of issues with a written document.

THE BIG ROCK AND EXTRAVAGANT WEDDING

Ok. So you pulled it off. You found that special person and the two of you have decided to get married. The next step is to get engaged and plan the wedding. It is easy to become euphoric about the future. In this euphoria do not lose sight of the fact that the two of you are probably about as poor as you will ever be. This is not the time to throw financial caution to the wind. You will be starting your marriage out on the wrong foot if you purchase an expensive engagement ring or have an extravagant wedding. Neither is remotely necessary for the successful marriage that is your goal. Concerns about money can be one of the leading causes of marital disputes,[54] so initially it is best to limit expenditures that are discretionary such as engagement rings and weddings.

A wedding is the transition between dating and family life. Too often the wedding becomes an end in itself. Do not lose track of what it is. It is a ceremony to officially begin your marriage. Your marriage is the big deal, not the wedding. While others may be concerned with where, when, and how many bridesmaids, the concern here is how much? Couples can easily be trapped into making poor decisions about the scale of their weddings.

This is an important time to address the tradeoffs that frequently confront businesses and families. The money spent on a wedding could be spent on many other things. A couple will seldom be poorer than they are shortly after they marry. On the one hand, your incomes are lower than they will be in the future. At the same time, you may be in the process of acquiring expensive possessions such as a home. Eventually, you will probably become parents, which will cause your expenses to go up while your combined income may go down. A common problem with new businesses and marriages is a lack of capital. I strongly encourage you to evaluate your wedding plans critically. When I grew up in Pittsburgh and attended a few weddings of friends' relatives, I thought that the ideal wedding consisted of a ceremony followed by a polka band, lots of beer and a spread of cold cuts. That still sounds good to me.

It is important to think economically no matter who is paying for the wedding. If you are paying for the wedding, the financial tradeoffs are obvious. However, those tradeoffs are still important if your parents are paying for some or all of the expenses of your wedding. Many parents pay for a large wedding because they think that is what their child wants. Essentially all parents want their children to be happy, so tell them that you want to use some of the money that they would have spent on other things. Use your imagination. Invite your family and friends. Have a good time, but save the money for later.

Amy and I were married in her parents' backyard with about fifty family and friends. I thought at the time (and I still believe) that our wedding was the culmination of the most important decision that I (we) ever made. Given the magnitude of the decisions reflected in a wedding, it can be a little nerve-racking. You do not have to make it any more stressful than necessary. Therefore, I am a big fan of keeping it simple. That has at least two benefits. First, there are fewer complications that can cause the marriage to start out with unnecessary anxiety. Second, it can be cheaper.

Now that we have worked through this complicated process for finding a spouse, let me note the method that Amy and I used. Well, we used the method that I told you to ignore—luck. We met when I was the leader of a group of students to England and Amy was a student. No, it was not love at first sight, but we did one smart thing—we stayed in touch. Little did we realize that marriage was in the future. We were fortunate enough to see each other regularly over the next few years, eventually marrying six years later. As I said earlier, if you were lucky, you did not need this chapter.

Conclusion

In this chapter we have used principles from purchasing to identify how you can find someone with the characteristics that are important in a spouse. Having found that person, you have to use marketing techniques to convince her that she should marry you. An important aspect of marketing you is closing the deal. Because the successful implementation of a purchasing and marketing plan will lead to an engagement and wedding, you are cautioned about spending too much of your limited resources on the engagement ring and the wedding.

While luck is an acceptable approach to finding a spouse, it is even less likely to help you make the best decisions during marriage. So the next chapter provides guidance on the decisions that are most likely to result in the type of marriage that you will consider a success.

THINGS TO REMEMBER

- You are shopping for a spouse so it is important to identify the approaches that will help you find someone with desirable characteristics.

- A good place to start your search is by letting family, friends, and acquaintances know that you have reached a point in your life at which finding a spouse has become a priority.

- In the process of marketing yourself, you have to think of yourself as a unique product that is priced to sell, available in the right places and enthusiastically promoted.

- Having found and won the person that you were seeking, it is not a time to make extravagant purchases on an engagement ring and wedding.

The Family as a Business

Now that you are married, let's consider the future. Even though people are marrying when they are older, they are also living longer. If your marriage is a successful one, you will be married to your spouse for much longer than you were single. Your challenge now is to make those years together productive so that you never doubt the enthusiasm with which you approached your wedding. You can make your marriage more productive by thinking about it as if it were a business.

Ignore notions about love and physical attraction being the only important requirements for a successful marriage. Realistically, your marriage will be a success if both of you continue to feel that you are better off together than you would be in any other arrangement. People marry because they are in love, but they stay married because they feel that they are better off married to each other. The key to a successful marriage is making the decisions that accomplish that goal. In the past, clear role models and, frequently, necessity assisted people in making the best decisions. These decisions were usually reflected in the roles and tasks that spouses assumed during marriage.

Most marriages still benefit from people changing their behavior when they marry, but they have much less guidance now about the best decisions that will result in a successful marriage. With the high divorce rate, it has become more difficult to identify exemplary role models. Frequently, parents—especially if they have divorced—are poor role models. Even among apparently happy couples the decisions that result in their success are not obvious to others. Moreover, the convergence in the opportunities available to men and women has made the traditional roles for spouses inappropriate. Many women are doing what men used to do in the workplace and many men have either purchased or undertaken the tasks usually performed by women in the home. Still, a marriage will not be a success just because two people who love each other have taken marriage vows and are living in the same house. Now, people have to think about these decisions.

In looking for guidance to avoid the Four Traps, couples can benefit from considering the lessons that businesses have learned. Marriage presents many couples with a range of decisions for which they have little experience. With little experience, emotions may have too much of a role in decision making. Being single longer may lead spouses to place too much emphasis on their own interests. Also, easy divorce may discourage people from making the type of commitment that is important for marital success. All the Traps—Experience, Emotions, Self-Interest and Unilateral Divorce—are present in these decisions. Parenthood will be an obvious area with new challenges, but so will the allocation of household chores and career choices. So let's consider the parallels between what businesses are attempting to accomplish and their methods for obtaining their goals in contrast to the challenges facing families.

A Successful Business

The success of a business is usually judged by its ability to generate profits. While it should be obvious, let me just remind you that profits are the difference between a business's revenues and its costs—what comes in and what goes out. A business is profitable if it is able to buy inputs and convert them into outputs that buyers value more than the inputs. In effect, profit is the additional value created by the business.

Seldom, in fact, does a business have any other option than focusing primarily on profits. Other businesses are always looking for attractive opportunities, so they tend to gravitate toward situations that appear to be profitable. This dynamic process tends to reduce the revenues and potentially increase the costs of the businesses that are already there—reducing their profits. If a business does not make a concerted effort to be profitable, a possible outcome is no profits at all in which case the owners may have to dissolve the business. Therefore, most businesses have no other option than to attempt to find the combinations of revenues and costs that produce an acceptable level of profits.

In establishing your pizzeria, you have made all the right steps necessary for starting a profitable business. You chose a partner with the right attributes. Together you chose the best products and suppliers while formulating an effective marketing plan for your business. Now, you have to consider how you will operate your pizzeria profitably.

Advantages of a Partnership

While you could have started this business on your own, there are advantages to having a partner. These advantages consist of increased specialization, economies of scale and insurance. The first advantage is the ability to specialize. Assuming more specialized roles will probably be important for your success. The activities in which people specialize tend to be based on comparative advantage, which exists when two people have levels of productivity that vary among activities. Some people will have a comparative advantage in working with numbers, while others will be more productive in dealing with people. Comparative advantage is based on relative skills rather than absolute ones. Your partner may be better with numbers and also better when dealing with people than you, but her ability with numbers is much higher and her ability with people only slightly better than yours. Comparative advantage would suggest that she specialize in the numerical aspects of your business while you focus on interacting with people. One of you may focus on maintaining the books for the business, while the other implements your marketing plan. Often you may share the same task such as greeting customers.

Another important consideration for making your business a success is attaining economies of scale that occurs when the cost per unit decreases as production increases. Because most small businesses have fixed costs such as rent and the cost of equipment, you can create economies of scale by allocating those costs over numerous sales. It will be difficult to generate a profit if you have high fixed costs and only few sales. Therefore, working together it is more likely that your business will have enough sales to capture those economies of scale.

Another advantage of partnership is a form of insurance. Insurance is often used by businesses—and individuals—to reduce the risks they face. By paying a predictable premium, a business receives some protection from uncertain events such as a fire or accident. An initial risk of business is the financial one, which is reduced if the cost of starting the business is shared with someone else. Another risk facing a new business is what the employees are doing when the owners are not around. Initially, it will be difficult for you to afford the kind of employees that you can trust to run the business when you are not there. To make sure that the business is running smoothly, it is important for one of the owners to be there. With two owners, providing coverage becomes less of a task.

In conclusion, you can benefit from going into business with a partner. With a partner, there are opportunities for assuming more specialized roles that increase overall productivity. Together you will be in a better position to obtain the economies of scale that can be important for your business to be a success. Last, by spreading the workload and the risks between two people you are providing insurance for each other, thereby increasing the probability that the business can overcome any normal obstacles that it faces.

A Successful Family

Just as a business can be viewed as a success if it is profitable—it creates additional value—the same framework can be applied to a family. Families

will be successful if they are able to create additional value for their participants. Families convert inputs of time, money and skills into outputs.
A family is usually viewed as a success if the participants conclude that they
are better off in it than in any other arrangement. They feel better off in
the family because of what the family provides for them. Economists
observe that individuals attempt to maximize their "utility," with that term
reflecting broad concepts such as welfare, satisfaction, happiness, and all the
enjoyable things that life can provide. A successful family is an important
part of this process for most people. While families do not face competition
from other families, they do face competition from other alternatives. The
other alternatives for spouses are to be single again or in another relationship. The key to a successful family is to produce enough "utility" that
those other alternatives do not become more attractive.

Because of the Experience Trap, many people do not have adequate
preparation for making these decisions. Initially, we have to understand
why families should be viewed as producing units. Families increase their
welfare by using their resources to produce "commodities" with their
production consisting of combinations of time, money and skills. The analysis of consumer behavior traditionally focused on the acquisition of goods
and services, but it is more appropriate to recognize that individuals do not
necessarily receive enjoyment from just the acquisition of goods and
services.

Enjoyment comes from combining goods and services with time—and
skills—to produce commodities.[1] People do not receive enjoyment just
from buying a compact disc, but from buying it with money and then listening to it, which requires time.[2] Commodities often can be produced
using a variety of time-money combinations. A vacation can consist of an
expensive weekend in Cancun requiring lots of money and limited time or
a week camping in Yosemite that requires less money, but more time.

Of the commodities that a family can produce, what are the ones most
likely to increase its welfare? Of course, this will vary from family to family,
but researchers can provide some insights. Jonathan Clements of the *Wall
Street Journal* asked six academics who studied "happiness" about the
changes that they had made in their own lives in pursuit of that goal. Their
insights provide some initial guidance. One person noted that experiences
incur diminishing returns—the observation that the incremental enjoyment
of an activity tends to fall as you do more of it. You are excited about a
promotion, but then the excitement associated with the new job gradually
declines. Therefore, he recommends celebrating even less important events
such as a victory by your favorite college team.

Another pointed out that commuting is one of people's less enjoyable
experiences because you have so little control over the problems that you
may face. He made an obvious choice—he reduced his commuting time by
moving closer to his office. Noting that the income associated with a
choice such as a higher paying job initially can be exaggerated relative to its

effects on commuting and friends, a highly successful economist reduced the time he devoted to research and spent more time with his family and friends. Since time is our most precious—and scarce—resource, another economist suggested making sure that you use it to create memorable experiences. In his case, he cited going to the 2001 Super Bowl with his father as one of those experiences.

While all of the respondents undoubtedly have comfortable incomes, none of their reactions was to aspire to more income. While discussing the commodities that bring happiness to people, it is important to recognize that income is just one of the resources that people use to increase their welfare. Some of the most enjoyable things that people do require time but not very much money.[3] The commodities that ultimately make us better off also require time and skills.

INCOME IS JUST ONE OF THE PRODUCTIVE INPUTS

Because income is tangible, people can fall into the Emotion Trap by placing too much emphasis on it as a basis for increasing their welfare. Many young people state that getting rich is their primary goal in life.[4] Their emotions convince them that the key to happiness is the acquisition of things. The costs associated with generating the income are often under-estimated. The importance of time-intensive activities can often be unap-preciated because they are less obvious and certainly less tangible. Acquiring skills can also be time consuming as becoming a better cook or golfer is usually not instinctive. Buying a better car or going on a more expensive vacation can be viewed as obvious welfare-enhancing commod-ities. Meanwhile, going to a child's soccer game might be viewed as enjoy-able—if it is not too inconvenient—but its contribution to your welfare may be less clear.

This emphasis on becoming wealthy—rather than focusing on happi-ness—may be a reflection of the Unilateral Divorce Trap that you should attempt to avoid. In retrospect, most people conclude that their most enjoyable activities were intimate relations, socializing and relaxing. Many of these activities are associated with a successful family. Looking forward, many young people may conclude that investing in a family—in contrast to a career—is a very risky proposition. If you observe that others are empha-sizing their careers over establishing and maintaining relationships, you may be wise to avoid their choices. The way to avoid the Unilateral Divorce Trap is to make wise decisions about your partner and then consider the choices that are in your collective best interest.

The importance of income in the production of commodities would appear to experience diminishing returns. In other words, the empirical evi-dence is that people tend to be happier as their family income increases up to around \$50,000 to \$90,000 and then it tends to level off.[5] That could be due to two forces. First, people have to work harder or make more sacrifices to earn income above that level. Second, they probably have already bought most of the items that they view as important. Just like a business can make a mistake by attempting to increase its market share rather than its profits, a family can be misled into attempting to increase its income rather than its access to commodities. A problem with the Experience Trap is that you can only make decisions about the future, but you will judge those decisions after they have taken place.

In summary, a successful family is one that efficiently converts its resources into commodities that ultimately increase its members' welfare. Commodities come in a variety of forms. Some are tangible such as an enjoyable meal and a clean house, while others are intangible such as peace of mind and well-adjusted children. Some families will be better able to make this conversion than others. The families that do it reasonably well are the ones that are mostly likely to fulfill their members' expectations so that they continue to be happily married. So, let's investigate the means by which you can convert your family's resources into valuable outputs.

COHABITATION IS LIKE SHARING OFFICE SPACE

Marriage has been—and continues to be—a more welfare-enhancing living arrangement for most people than any other. First we will consider why people are better off living together and then we will explore why marriage and cohabitation have importance differences. Cohabitation is not the same as marriage. Because of the limited commitment by the partners, living together is more like sharing office space than running a business. The production that we are considering here essentially requires two people to be living together. However, living together is no longer synonymous with marriage as unmarried cohabitation has become more common.

A first concern with regard to increasing your productivity is why that process benefits from marriage. Because living together has become extremely common, it is important to understand why it is not the same as marriage and why marriage continues to be an important institution for increasing most people's welfare. The strong bonds created by love and sexual attraction are an important part of what makes couples feel that they are better off together, but we also have to consider pragmatic forces that encourage people to marry.

Traditionally, the decision for a couple to live together was synonymous with the decision to get married. That is no longer the case. Before the broad availability of contraceptives, it was uncommon for couples to live together without being married because regular sexual relations usually resulted in their becoming parents. Social mores tended to require marriage as a prerequisite for regular sexual relations, because children potentially could be a burden on society if the parents did not marry. Society responded by placing a significant social stigma on premarital sex.[6] With effective contraceptives, living together does not have to lead to children and, therefore, it has often been separated from the decision to get married.[7]

INCENTIVES TO LIVE TOGETHER

A first step toward creating a successful marriage is the recognition that couples are better off living together than on their own.[8] There are advantages for people living together besides love and physical attraction. These advantages are similar to those experienced by successful businesses: specialization, economies of scale, and insurance. While they can be important for couples living together, they do not necessarily make marriage attractive.

GAINS FROM SPECIALIZATION

Just as with a business, there are gains from specialization when people live together.[9] Specialization increases the welfare of individuals by expanding the commodities available to them. Commodities produced at home can be an important component of individual welfare; these commodities often can be time intensive, including home-cooked meals, a clean house and an attractive lawn.

The production of these commodities benefits from specialization. We often observe that businesses increase their output and profits by specialization. They gain from specialization that reduces the time lost as workers move between activities and permits employees to develop the unique skills necessary to perform specific tasks faster. The same principle is appropriate for the production of commodities by consumers. When people specialize, they can become more efficient in the production of commodities. People who cook frequently usually become better cooks. Even programming a VCR or TiVo can require specialized skills.

The activities in which people specialize tend to be based on comparative advantage.[10] Some people will have a comparative advantage in earning income, while others will be more productive in domestic activities. Remember that comparative advantage is based on relative skills rather than absolute ones. A woman may be a better cook and have a higher income-earning potential than her partner, but her income potential is much higher and her cooking ability only slightly better than his. Comparative advantage would suggest that she specialize in income earning while her partner focuses on cooking. As a practical matter, specialization by couples is seldom absolute as couples often share responsibility for earning income and doing domestic chores. Within a relationship, however, men and women tend to increase their specialization compared with when they live alone.

ECONOMIES OF SCALE

Households also provide opportunities for economies of scale that are not available to someone living alone. The size of a comfortable house does not normally increase as much as the increase in the number of occupants; thus the cost per occupant falls as the number of occupants increases up to some point. A two bedroom apartment is usually not twice as expensive as a one bedroom apartment. In addition, some commodities consumed in a household can be shared like a television set or a kitchen. Most households can reduce the number of these shared commodities relative to the number that they would have if the members were living on their own. Having to buy fewer shared commodities translates into a lower cost of living for each person in the household.

INSURANCE

The last reason that people benefit from living together is insurance. People generally do not like uncertainty, so they frequently buy insurance because they prefer certainty—a fire insurance premium—to uncertainty—having a house that has been destroyed by a fire. This characteristic of human behavior is called "risk aversion" with the common conclusion being that increased certainty can contribute to people's welfare.[11]

Because insurance cannot be purchased to cover all uncertain events, people frequently have to make other arrangements to reduce uncertainty. People may prefer a current known situation over an uncertain future. Many interpersonal relationships have that characteristic. A person might currently be having a satisfactory relationship with someone. If this relationship ended, will the next one be better or worse? How much effort will it take to adapt to a new relationship? If they have a good job now what will happen if they become unemployed or are forced to accept a lower paying job? They have excellent health now, but will someone be there to help them if their health deteriorates? Since these are questions that people often face, they can attempt to reduce future uncertainty by maintaining a current relationship.

In summary, people can increase their welfare by living together. These benefits follow from increased specialization, economies of scale, and insurance. So far we have been discussing the reasons why people are better off living together. But why do they benefit from taking a step further and marrying?

INCENTIVES TO MARRY

Taking a longer term perspective is what differentiates marriage from cohabitation. A credible commitment serves a central role in success both in business and in marriage. Although we have identified numerous reasons why adults are better off living together, we have not established a clear reason—other than one based on romance—that would explain why you would increase your welfare by marrying. From a pragmatic perspective, the reason that marriage continues to be so important for most adults' welfare is that some of the benefits from living together are enhanced by a more formal, long-term arrangement that traditionally has been provided by marriage. Because we live in a world with easy, unilateral divorce, it would not be wise to marry anyone whose commitment to marriage is anything less than unequivocal. Both specialization of labor and economies of scale involve investments that are encouraged by a long-term arrangement. In addition, marriage can be viewed as providing more substantial and predictable insurance than that available to couples who are living together.

A Credible Commitment

An interrelated combination of sacrifices, reciprocity, and commitment differentiates the production in marriages from that among people who are living together. In contrast to unmarried couples, married couples are more likely to invest in their relationship by incurring personal sacrifices. They do things that—if they were single or unmarried—they might prefer not to do. They relocate for the benefit of their spouse's career. They alter their career for childcare responsibilities. Why would rational people do that? I would caution against assuming that it is due to altruism. Rational people—even when they are in love—prefer that there are benefits associated with the costs that they are incurring. The benefits of their sacrifices are the reciprocal acts of the other family members: the love and potentially the income of their spouse and the love of their children. Since those reciprocal acts will often occur later, the durability of their relationship is important. That is when commitment becomes so important. Without a credible commitment, the whole process falls apart. Why incur sacrifices if there are limited expectations of reciprocal acts? So conveying a clear expression of commitment to your spouse is essential. Of course, the most obvious expression of commitment is getting married.

A clear and unambiguous commitment is what differentiates married from cohabiting couples. So a combination of sacrifices, reciprocity and commitment increases the welfare that a couple can derive from specialization, economies of scale and insurance. Let's investigate why that is the case.

Specialization

Most families benefit by more specialization than is common among couples living together.[12] While this increased specialization can benefit their family, it often requires people to do things that they might not have done if they had not married.[13] While this increased specialization is often associated with parenthood, it can occur for other reasons. Seldom does a long-term relationship permit both parties to pursue the careers and activities that they would have pursued without the relationship. Frequently, promotions entail a relocation that requires other parties to make a sacrifice either in their career or their lifestyle.

Sacrifices can result from increased specialization. A couple can often limit increased specialization until they have children. They can maintain their careers, while dividing the responsibilities within their household. Children change this situation by increasing the pressure for a couple to specialize. The arrival of children usually results in one parent increasing the emphasis that she—OK, let's assume that it's the mother—places on household activities.[14] Mothers traditionally tended to have a comparative advantage in caring for children because their earnings usually were less than that of fathers. However, this pattern is changing as the employment opportunities and incomes of mothers have increased relative to fathers. The likelihood is increasing—but not by much—that the primary provider of childcare is the father.[15]

The parents may be tempted to share the responsibility for child rearing equally. However, on closer inspection most couples conclude that it is less costly to them for just one parent to alter employment than for both to alter theirs. Higher paying jobs often require unexpected overtime and travel.[16] If both parents reject that type of employment, they may be worse off than if only one parent makes that choice and the other, if they are employed, accepts employment that accommodates childcare.

Even among couples who remain childless there may be pressures to increase their specialization as their relationship continues. While they may have viewed their careers as equally important when the relationship began, new opportunities may alter their view over time. An opportunity for one of them elsewhere may require the other to make a major career or lifestyle adjustment. Even without relocation, one may have a high-paying job that provides tremendous self-fulfillment for that party, while the other has a stressful job that no longer is rewarding. It may be in a couple's best inter- est for the party with the less rewarding job to find more flexible–and potentially lower paying—employment that accommodates the other party's career, thereby potentially increasing their collective welfare. Rather than both spending much of their weekends catching up on domestic activ- ities that could not be accomplished during the week, the party with the more flexible job could accomplish more of those activities during the week freeing up time for both of them to enjoy their weekends.

This increased specialization that occurs among married couples can have longer lasting effects than those commonly associated with people living together. Although this increased specialization is usually in the best inter- est of the couple and any children, it requires people to alter their behavior and it can be revealed as costly if the relationship ends. Skills developed in one household may have little value in another relationship and even less value in the marketplace, leaving a spouse who has emphasized domestic work vulnerable if the relationship is dissolved.

While this can be a problem in relationships of short duration, it is partic- ularly a concern in longer ones. If someone specializes in income earning, that skill will be intact if the relationship ends. Of course income-earning partners would lose their share of the household commodities provided by their mate, but these commodities may have decreased in value after any children have grown up and left the home. During relationships, people who increased their specialization in domestic activities may have developed skills producing household commodities that do not have substantial value outside the relationship and yet their income-earning capacity has deteriorated because of their working primarily at home.

Because this specialization can be revealed as costly, a credible commitment is important—no, it is essential. This is especially true because of the limited protection provided people who make these sacrifices during marriage. A couple can fall into the Unilateral Divorce Trap because the financial arrangements at divorce seldom compensate spouses for these sacrifices. People who emphasize housework can be worse off if their relationship is dissolved compared with the situation they would be in if they had never entered the relationship in the first place. Knowing—but maybe not acknowledging—this, spouses may resist increasing their specialization, thereby potentially reducing the gains from marriage.[17] Traditionally, women, who emphasized domestic work, were reluctant to specialize unless they had the expectation of the relationship being of a long duration and marriage was associated with that expectation. Now both parties may reduce their investment in their relationship due to the limited protection provided by marriage.

Because the gains from specialization have declined it is easy to become convinced that they are no longer important. Do not be deceived. They are still very important for increasing the welfare of most married couples. There has been a decline in the obvious gains from specialization due to the convergence in the opportunities available to men and women as well as the decision for many couples to have fewer–and in some cases no–children. Still, most couples continue to want children. Even with these changes, specialization—and the sacrifices associated with it—continues to be an important reason why couples are better off than single people. The specialization that occurs in married couples is usually more extensive than among unmarried couples. The sacrifices associated with this specialization are encouraged by the reciprocal acts of the other family members. These reciprocal acts become more likely when a couple feels comfortable with its commitment to each other. Therefore, that spouse directly and all family members indirectly benefit from a more formal arrangement provided by marriage.

ECONOMIES OF SCALE

Married couples benefit from many of the opportunities for economies of scale enjoyed by others who live together. They share a kitchen and a television set. However, the economies of scale associated with parenthood increase the importance of a long-term relationship. When a couple becomes parents, they share the enjoyment provided by their children. So long as the couple continues to live together, there are economies of scales from their both being able to enjoy their children.

These economies of scale no longer exist if they separate. Then they are more likely to have exclusive access to their children. Not only is there a loss of economies of scale, the quality of the interaction may decrease for the noncustodial parent. Again, we observe the importance of the sacrifices made by parents, the importance of the affection that they receive from their children and the commitment by the parents to each other and their children. A more formal arrangement such as marriage increases the likelihood that the couple will continue to live together, thereby being able to take advantage of these important economies of scale.

INSURANCE

Another important anticipated benefit from marriage is insurance against an uncertain future.[18] Insurance can be important for both couples with children as well as those who are childless.[19] By its most fundamental nature, insurance requires someone who has not incurred a cost to compensate someone else for the cost that they have incurred. With fire insurance, it is the insured party's house that burned down not the insurance company's office. Without a long-term agreement, the insurance company probably would prefer to return its premium and walk away from its obligation.

A similar situation can occur with relationships. While two people might informally agree that they will be there for each other in sickness and in health, when one of them gets severely ill the other might want to shift the responsibility for nursing to someone else if there are no strong emotional or legal ties. Marriage formalizes that emotional and legal obligation, increasing the likelihood that someone will be there if a spouse has unexpected medical, emotional or financial problems.[20] Marriage also provides some insurance against the potential costs of spouses altering their career plans for the benefit of their relationship. However, any limiting of a career can have costs later if the relationship is dissolved. Marriage can provide some insurance for the person limiting a career against those future costs.

Last, it is commonly recognized that people often gain from increased predictability. This predictability is relevant for psychological as well as financial outcomes. A strong commitment by spouses to each other has been shown to be an important source of satisfaction in marriage.[21] However, this commitment can be psychologically costly if it is ultimately discovered that one spouse's commitment was not reciprocated. Marriage provides insurance that encourages this commitment by both parties. The basic nature of insurance is that spouses may have to make a sacrifice to tend to the needs of each other. These potential sacrifices are encouraged by the understanding that there will be reciprocal acts during the duration of the marriage. Still, without a credible commitment, no form of insurance has much value.

Families benefit from key investments that often require sacrifices that are encouraged by the long-term prospects of the relationship. These investments will assist you in producing the commodities that will increase your welfare. So how do you go about producing those commodities?

THE COMMODITIES PRODUCED BY FAMILIES

So we have arrived at a very important conclusion that married couples can be more efficient in the production of welfare-enhancing commodities—the things that make life worthwhile—than single people or unmarried couples. So what should you produce? Seldom do businesses produce only one product. When they produce more than one product, they have to decide how to allocate their resources among their different products. So you are opening a pizzeria. Producing pizza is obvious. But, how about selling calzones and salads? Since you are also a microbrewery, what beers should you brew? Families face the same dilemmas. You need to consider the different types of commodities that you could produce and the roles that each category serves in enhancing your family's welfare.

You start out with two inescapable restrictions: your time and abilities. Some of the time is used to generate income, while the rest is used to produce commodities directly. Some people are more productive than others because of their skills. These skills result from using time to improve your inherent abilities. Since these resources are limited, people have to make choices about the commodities that they are going to produce.

A family can produce three types of commodities. The first use of resources is to produce commodities that directly benefit only one person. We will call them private commodities. They range from a round of golf to a day at a spa. Second are shared commodities that benefit more than one person. These commodities are particularly important for marital success. They are numerous, including a clean home, enjoyable meals and well-adjusted children. Last are gifts.[22] A gift is created when spouses do something that does not have direct value to them, but they feel that it will be valued by someone else. While you might think of traditional commodities such as flowers and jewelry as gifts, they usually come from communal funds, so their cost is shared by both spouses. While these items are usually appreciated, true gifts reflect the sacrifice by one spouse for the benefit of the other. An example of a gift would be spending time listening to your spouse's concerns and frustrations.

All of these commodities have an important role in making marriage attractive to the spouses. Therefore, let's consider them in more detail.

PRIVATE COMMODITIES

Private commodities can be an important component of most people's welfare. Most private commodities are available to someone living on their own. Even single people enjoy a round of golf or a day at the spa. Still, specialization of production during marriage can free up resources that otherwise would not be available. With one spouse shopping for food and the other doing the laundry, both may end up with more free time than they would have had if they had to do both of these activities for themselves. Even without more free time, each spouse has individual needs that private commodities can meet.

Still, spouses have to be careful as the resources that are used in the production of private commodities detract from the resources available to the family for the production of other commodities. Here you have to be careful to avoid the Self-Interest Trap by being aware of the impact of your consumption of private commodities on the welfare of the other family members. An extreme example of someone who has fallen into the Self-Interest Trap would be someone with an addiction to gambling that dramatically reduces the time and money available to the other family members.

SHARED COMMODITIES

Shared commodities are an important reason why historically married couples have been better off than single people. Here specialization of labor combines with economies of scale to improve the family's welfare. Because the benefits of these commodities are shared among other family members, the family's limited resources can go much further toward increasing its welfare. Many of these shared commodities are also available to unmarried couples. Still with a long-term commitment, a married couple can make more substantial investments in specialization. One can become more proficient at carpentry on domestic projects with the expectation that the couple has a long-term commitment to each other—and also to their house. Someone who is not married may be unwilling to make a similar investment. These investments can be important for increasing the family's welfare.

Married couples also have incentives to improve the quality of their shared commodities that may not exist for unmarried couples. Given unique tastes, a couple may want to make changes in their house that they know will not increase its market value. Still those changes are important to them, but incurring the costs will only be reasonable if they plan on living in the house for an extended period. Having concealed wiring for a surround sound system in the basement may be important to them, but they know that most potential buyers would not pay more for the house because of it.

The most important shared commodities in most families are children. Like any production process, there is no guarantee of desirable results. However, if a couple attempts to be good parents, it is more likely that they will be happy with the results. Being productive as parents benefits both the parents and their children. People can be productive as parents just as they can be on a job or in the kitchen. By increasing their productivity, they can accomplish better results. Most parents want children that increase their welfare and children want to grow up in families that have that goal.

Married parents are more willing to make an investment of time and money in their children than parents in other living arrangements. Unmarried couples tend to make a much weaker commitment to their children, with them spending less time with both parents.[23] When a child is born to a married couple, it is likely that it will spend a majority of its childhood in a two-parent family. Parents usually want well-adjusted children and they are more likely to have them if they are married and stay married.[24]

Because of their emotional bonds, married couples have incentives to shift resources from private commodities to the production of shared commodities. This may be important for improving their collective welfare.

GIFTS

The last use of families' resources is the production of gifts that use a limited, but important, amount of the family's resources. Because of companionate marriage, there has been an increase in the emphasis on spouses doing things together. Gifts have become increasingly important for accommodating this process. They could consist of going to a concert that you know that your spouse will enjoy much more than you. They can also be psychological by sincerely listening to your spouse's concerns and empathizing. Because the person producing the gift often does not receive any direct benefits, people can easily fall victim to the Self-Interest Trap. While you may enjoy your hobbies and your spouse's home-cooked meals, you may wonder why you should "waste" your time doing things that only your spouse wants to do or things from which only he will receive enjoyment. Why go to a new exhibition at the city museum that your spouse has suggested?

If you want a reason it is reciprocity. In a loving relationship, you attempt to meet your spouse's needs in the anticipation that she will reciprocate. The reciprocal acts can be gifts as well as shared commodities. Love can induce people to act altruistically, but their activities in other areas would suggest that eventually they look for some rewards for any sacrifices that they are making. Self-interest has strong explanatory power when people act as consumers and workers and it cannot be denied even in emotional interpersonal relationships. So, if you want others to do things that you want them to do, you better be prepared to do what they want you to do. Hopefully with those we love this sense of reciprocity comes automatically. Still, sometimes it requires conscientious effort.

DEVELOPING A PLAN

The key to a successful marriage is for a couple to find a desirable combination of these commodities. Because of the Experience Trap, you have less guidance from your parents and society, so you need to develop a plan. We have identified specialization of labor, economies of scale and insurance and the potential sacrifices associated with them as being the sources of the welfare gains that can make a marriage continue to be attractive to a couple. Because you are constrained by your limited resources, you are going to have to make choices. You obviously cannot do everything. If you produce more of some commodities, you will have to produce less of others. In making the best decisions you are constrained by your time, money, and skills; so you need to address how those limited resources will be allocated.

NOW AND LATER

There are two dimensions to planning: now and later. These time frames are based on the flexibility of your constraints. The situation is similar to the one that you face with your pizzeria. Over a short period of time, some of your constraints are fixed and unavoidable, while over a longer period of time you should be able to alter most of those constraints. You currently have a lease on the space for your pizzeria, but you do not have to renew it. Maybe later you will decide that you want a bigger place or one in a different location. While your current lease restricts your ability to do that now, you can do it later.

Within your family, you face similar constraints. In the short run, the allocation of your resources is relatively inflexible. There is only so much time in the day, week, etc. You can alter its allocation somewhat, but you are constrained by your current jobs, commuting and sleeping. Your money is determined by your earnings and the generosity of your parents and friends (lots of luck!). Your skills are the ones that you have developed so far. So in this initial period, your challenge is to allocate these resources in the most efficient manner.

In the long run most of these constraints can be altered, although changing your spouse should not be viewed as an alternative. While you will never have more time, you will have more flexibility as to how you use it. You can alter your careers. You will certainly be able to alter your financial resources by adjusting your careers and investments. Last, your skills will change over time. While you will have more flexibility over time, you will also be confronted with tradeoffs when considering the changes that you want to make. Often, increasing your income will require the sacrifice of free time. Alternatively, seeking more leisure time may require you to reduce your income. Attempting to increase your skills as a cook, wine connoisseur or golfer may require you to reduce both leisure time and income.

There will be different elements in your short-run and long-run plans. In the short run, you need to figure out how to allocate your relatively fixed income and time. In the long run, essentially all of your constraints of time, money and skills are variable. While the business may create a written strategic plan, a family could develop something that is more informal.

THE IMPORTANCE OF COMMUNICATION

To adequately address the tradeoffs that you will inevitably face, communication becomes very important.[25] In a business setting, the need for clear communication may be more apparent than in a marriage. Partially, this is due to the fact that costs of not communicating are more obvious to business partners. When things are going wrong, the situation needs to be recognized and remedial steps need to be taken. If they are not taken, the business—and especially a new one—may fail. The marketing plan was created by your best friend and you hesitate to hurt his feelings by pointing out why it is not working. However, if you do not communicate your concerns, changes may not occur and the business may fail.

A concern about the sensitivities of your spouse as well as a lack of clear costs of silence can lead couples into not communicating about their concerns. Yet, couples now have to make far more decisions than those in the past. Without clearly defined roles, a couple has to determine the commodities that it wants to produce and how they are going to produce them. A lack of clear communication can lead to frustration.[26]

Communication is particularly important when you are addressing the allocation of your resources as you need to develop problem-solving skills to deal with the conflicts between your preferences. When you were living alone, almost all the commodities that you produced were private commodities. Now that you are married, the production of shared commodities and gifts has become an important component of your collective welfare. A particular problem here is the Self-Interest Trap. What is the proper balance between private and shared commodities (and gifts for that matter)? Rather than agreeing to remodel the house (a shared good), one spouse might buy an expensive set of golf clubs (a private good). This can cause the other spouse to respond by buying other private commodities such as clothing. Often as purchases are shifted from shared commodities to private ones, overall household welfare is reduced. Clear communication is important for avoiding this deterioration in your relationship. It helps to informally discuss these issues, so we have always placed a strong emphasis on having dinner together.[27] There are numerous books and programs to assist couples contemplating marriage as well as those who are already married to assist them in solving these conflicts.[28]

YOUR PLANNING GOAL

In making your plans, let's consider your goal and then address how to implement a plan to accomplish it. Your goal is to maximize the value of the commodities that you can produce subject to your limited resources. You want an enjoyable and fulfilling life. The idea of maximizing something seems like a daunting task. However, it becomes more manageable when approached incrementally weighing the benefits and costs of alternatives. Because of diminishing returns, the incremental benefits of commodities tend to decline as the resources devoted to them increase. For many the enjoyment from visiting Disneyland, for example, would be expected to decline as it is visited more frequently. By choosing the choices with the highest benefit/cost ratio, you will be as well off as you can be. At any given time, I might view being in Paris as more beneficial than being in Albuquerque. However, the cost of a visit to Paris is greater than staying in Albuquerque, so I spend most—but not all—of my time here.

YOUR SHORT-RUN PLAN

The key elements in your short-run plan are money and time as they are the limited resources that you have to allocate. Your skills are an important ingredient in your production process, but since they are fixed in the short run, they will be ignored during this time period. Although the production of most commodities requires both inputs of time and money, we will discuss these inputs separately here. Initially, it is assumed that you are not yet parents. Since money can be a major source of conflict between spouses—especially early in marriage—let's consider it first.

MONEY

For our purposes, your income and your money at any given time are fixed. We have to be careful with terms here. Income is flow per time period. It can be so much per hour, week, or year. Meanwhile, money is an asset that has a given value at a particular time. So if you have an income of $2,000 per month that is directly deposited into your bank account, your account—which is money—is increased by that amount when the deposit is made. A higher income means that you will have access to more money and that is important because money is one of the major inputs into your production of commodities.

So, how are you going to allocate that limited money? You have to weigh the psychological enjoyment of alternative commodities (the benefits) against the other commodities that could be produced with the same money (the costs). I have felt—and continue to feel—that the benefits to me of owning a Ferrari would be very high. Certainly, they would be higher than the Honda that I own. However, when subjected to a benefit/cost analysis, the Honda was a clear winner.

Many people, including spouses, do not like to talk about money, and yet it can be a major cause of problems within businesses and families. Some have argued that 70 percent of divorces are caused by money.[29] Would it be reasonable for business partners to not talk about the financial condition of the business? Certainly, for new businesses a lack of working capital (money) is a common cause of their failure. A good idea can fail because the business did not have the resources to develop an adequate consumer base. In a similar fashion, money—or the lack of it—can be a major problem of families. While it is a particular concern early in marriage, it can continue to be a problem throughout marriage for many couples.

For most of us, there never appears to be enough money to buy all the things that we want. As constrained as you may feel, I have to start by pointing out how much better off you are than your ancestors. Between 1901 and 2002, the average family income increased three times even after adjustment for inflation.[30] The impact per person was even greater as the typical family declined in size from 4.9 to 2.5 people. In 1901, people had very little discretion in their spending as 80 percent of their expenditures were on food, clothing, and housing. Even with the increase in the quality of those items, by 2002 families were spending approximately 50 percent of their expenditures on them. The changes in expenditures on food are particularly relevant as they fell from 42 to 13 percent over this period. The change in the expenditures on food at home was even more dramatic as people started to spend more on food outside the home. The message here is that most people actually have substantial discretionary income, and if you feel that you don't, it may be time to more closely scrutinize where your expenditures are going.

Part of the reason that many people feel very financially constrained is due to what we have all come to expect—the things that have become necessities. In 1971, 45 percent of American households had clothes dryers, 19 percent had dishwashers, 83 percent had refrigerators, 32 percent had air conditioning, and 43 percent had color televisions. Now, most people expect to have—and actually do have—most of these things. So what are the new necessities? One of the easiest ways to become comfortable with your current financial situation is to re-evaluate your necessities considering which ones are luxuries. Save the luxuries for later.

New businesses usually develop pro forma budgets reflecting the revenues and the expenses that they expect. Then they can track their actual revenues and expenses in comparison to those that they expected, making adjustments when necessary. Your budget does not need to be as detailed as that of a business, but it does require some planning. Given the age at which most people are marrying today, most of them have had more experience spending their income than in the past. Without a formal plan, they have probably figured out the expenses that they can reasonably incur within their current or anticipated income. The challenge now is to integrate the incomes and expenses of two people. This is going to require more planning.

Incomes and Expenses

Any financial planning has to start with a consideration of your incomes and expenses. The relevant income is obviously not gross as you will only have access to your after-tax income. Do not just rely on the sum of your take-home pays. Marriage may alter your taxes and, therefore, your take-home pay. This is particularly true if the two of you have similar incomes. While the marriage penalty—if it applies to you—is usually not large, it is worthwhile to compare your tax return after marriage to the ones you filed before marriage and adjust your disposable income if it is appropriate.

Like any business, you will have fixed and variable expenses. In many ways, the fixed expenses will be unavoidable, especially in the short run, while the variable expenses will be more flexible. In the short run, these fixed expenses are given and benefit/cost considerations may be irrelevant. However, this analysis is still important for allocating your discretionary income. Many of the fixed expenses and some of the variable ones can be viewed as necessities. It is important to identify the expenses that you just cannot avoid. Rent or a mortgage payment needs to be at the top of your list. Next comes anticipated utility and insurance bills. Work-related expenses such as commuting costs and meals have to be recognized.

After addressing your fixed—regrettably unavoidable—expenses, you have to consider how to allocate the rest of your funds. Your focus should be on the benefits and costs of alternatives to all family members. Some of your other expenses will be incurred in the production of shared commodities such as meals at home and joint entertainment. Other funds can be allocated for private commodities. You might figure out an amount that each of you can spend on private commodities with no questions asked. This amount should be equal with no reference to your relative incomes.

A Joint Checking Account

An important first step is to set up a joint checking account to keep track of your incomes and expenditures. A business—even with two partners—usually only has one checking account. That helps the partners easily observe the cash situation of the business. One checking account is also important for families for a slightly different reason: Marriage is a partnership. Marriage can be viewed as the ultimate arm's length transaction. Neither person had an incentive to say, "I do," unless they thought that they were getting more than they were giving up. Ah, benefits and costs again! What they are getting can take a variety of forms. Certainly, physical attraction is at the top of the list, but it also includes income-earning capacities, personalities, social connections, domestic skills, and a variety of other attributes. By marrying, both spouses are acknowledging that the other is bringing commensurate value to the relationship.

So what does this have to do with your money? Separate checking accounts emphasize your individuality and they can overemphasize your separate incomes.[31] A joint checking account recognizes that you have entered into a joint venture. The higher-income spouse thought the marriage was a great deal on the day of the wedding. So it is no longer relevant to discuss how much income each spouse will contribute to the marriage. The answer is simple: All of it. Currently, it is too easy to fall into the

Unilateral Divorce Trap in which the spouses treat their marriage as an experiment rather than a commitment. A joint checking account is a symbol of their commitment to their joint venture. Even with a joint checking account, it may be appropriate to have two credit cards.

Financial Responsibilities

The next question is, How are you going to divide financial responsibilities? There are economies of scale in the two major activities that you need to address: bill paying and tax preparation. Some people actually enjoy these activities and, if you married one of them, you are lucky and the allocation of responsibilities is easy. Give it to her. Regrettably, most people find these activities to be work and, therefore, something that they would prefer to avoid. The decision as to who should assume responsibility for these activities should be part of your decisions about the overall allocation of household activities. If one of you assumes more domestic responsibilities with parenthood, that may also influence who assumes responsibility for balancing the checkbook and making sure that taxes are filed. At least in our household, Amy does the bills and I do the taxes.

Financial Planning

As part of your financial planning, the first objective should be to avoid or alternatively pay off high-cost, non-deductible debt. Then, part of your discretionary funds should be devoted to savings that will be used to produce commodities in the future. Savings are not just for your retirement years, as they can provide an important buffer for the uncertain events that are likely to occur. You never want to be locked into an unpleasant job just because you do not have the reserve funds to permit a transition to a better one. An obvious place to start a savings program is with the match to the maximum amount that your employer is willing to contribute to a tax-deferred plan such as a 401(k) or 403(b) account.

We do not have space here to provide details about the wide variety of savings opportunities, but one insight from finance may provide a helpful incentive to encourage you to save. The Rule of 72 shows that an amount invested now will double in value over a period of time that is equal to 72 divided by the rate of return on the investment. So, for example, an investment that is expected to generate a six percent rate of return will double in value in 12 years (and quadruple in value in 24 years). Therefore, it is important to start the saving process early.

The next consideration is where to place your savings. The funds that you have set aside to cover unexpected events should be easily accessible. For those funds, a money market fund or bank savings account would be reasonable. However, you want a higher return on the funds that you are saving for retirement. Financial analysts have shown that there tends to be a tradeoff between risk and return with riskier assets having a higher return.

Most of the risk associated with the investments that you might consider is in the variability of their value and return rather than their going bankrupt. The higher return to risky assets is just a reflection of the forces of supply and demand. People generally do not like risk, so fewer are willing to invest in risky assets with the result that those assets have a higher return.

A first concern is the amount of risk that you are willing to assume. With a longer time horizon, you can probably afford to take slightly more risk now than would be appropriate later when you are closer to retirement. After a house, over the long run the stock market has probably been the best place for the typical investor to place funds. While their returns—dividends—are more variable than the interest from bonds, on average stocks offer a higher return.[32] One way to reduce your risks investing in stocks is to diversify your portfolio.

You probably do not want to actively manage your investments. Do not be misled by your friends bragging about their successes in the stock market unless they are willing to give you all their financial records. The stock market tends to be highly efficient and by that I mean that it rapidly incorporates all available information. Unless you have information that few other people have—and even then it may be illegal to use it—you are unlikely to get a higher than average return. Moreover, you may waste a lot of money on commissions learning a lesson.

Since it is difficult to beat the average return being experienced in the stock market, your goal should be to make sure that most of the funds that you invest are working for you. Your funds are not working for you if they are incurring sales, transaction and management fees. That leads to a strategy focusing on buying indexed, no-load mutual funds. A mutual fund buys a portfolio of stocks (or other assets). No-load means that the fund has no sales commission, so you have to identify and contact the mutual funds company to make an investment. Since these funds are sold by large, visible companies such as Fidelity and Vanguard that should not be difficult. When a fund is indexed, its managers are buying an array of stocks that conform to those included in a standard stock index such as the Standard & Poor's 500. Indexed funds are not actively managed by a professional staff and trades are only made to reflect investments and redemptions, so they have low management and transaction fees.

Meals

While meals require the use of money, time and skills, we focus on the money input here. Meals at home are an important shared commodity for a number of reasons. Preparing meals does not rate high among people's enjoyable experiences and cleaning up afterwards rates even lower,[33] but it can be important for couples to eat meals together. The cooking, eating and cleaning up can be a shared experience. It is a good time to catch up on the day's events and personal frustrations. Since I am an economist, I also have to point out that meals at home are cheaper than eating out. Do not fall into the eating out trap.[34] At the end of a hard day, you may feel that you deserve to eat out rather than at home. You cannot escape that this decision reflects tradeoffs. Unless you have a lot more money at this point than we had, one of the easy ways to reduce expenses is to leave eating out for special occasions. Even pizza and beer at a restaurant is more expensive than the same items in your home. The good life should be part of your long-term plan, but now you need to economize. Your financial resources are more limited than they potentially will be in the future. Saving during this period can be difficult—with obvious tradeoffs in sacrificed activities—but establishing a financial reserve is very important. Meals at home are an obvious area in which to spend less.

Appreciating and Depreciating Assets

Another important consideration early in marriage is the nature of the assets that you are purchasing, because they are frequently bought using credit. There is a big difference between assets that have the potential to appreciate and those that will depreciate over time. The primary asset with the potential to appreciate is a house, which also has attractive tax benefits. Mortgage interest and property taxes are deductible and there may be no taxes on some sales. Some people have criticized investing in houses because of the small return over the last thirty years as the price of houses has only increased two percent more than inflation.[35] However, given the small amount that you will probably have to pay as a down payment, that is still a very attractive return on your investment. Therefore, the purchase of a house should probably be a top priority in most markets.[36]

Less attractive—especially early in marriage—are the purchases of assets that depreciate. Numerous appealing purchases have the unattractive characteristic that they depreciate in value over time—and often at a rapid rate. The most obvious of these purchases are automobiles, but it can extend to essentially all household items such as electronics and furniture. While you need to have some of these things, this is not the time to have the best. It would probably be a good idea to postpone purchasing the better quality items until your finances have improved. You certainly want to avoid incurring too much debt purchasing these assets. Take advantage of high depreciation rates by buying some used goods.

Vacations

While vacations are important commodities for most of us, early in marriage is probably not the time for spending large amounts of money on them. It is easy to conclude that you are working hard and, therefore, deserve to treat yourself to an extravagance. Nothing depreciates more rapidly than the memories of a good vacation, so a basic rule of thumb should be to never go into debt for a vacation. Diminishing returns should help you justify less expensive vacations initially. The enjoyment that I receive from camping in Yosemite—which is still substantial—has declined over time. Fortunately, with a higher income, we have been able to afford other enjoyable vacation experiences.

In conclusion, in the short run your financial resources are relatively inflexible. Some expenses are fixed and generally unavoidable. Among your discretionary expenditures, saving funds for uncertain events and retirement should be an early priority.

TIME

The other constraint that you have to address in making your short-run plan is your time. The process of allocating your time does not have to be particularly formal, but it is important to realize that time needs to be devoted to work-related activities and sleep as well as the production of private and shared commodities and gifts. Since your collective time is limited, there will be tradeoffs that have to be resolved to increase the value that you receive. Essentially, you can use your time for three activities: earning income, working in the home, and leisure. For many people, it would appear that the enjoyment associated with the use of time increases from employment through housework to leisure.

Initially, you need to recognize the time over which you have very little control. Work, commuting, and sleep are obvious here. For the remainder of your time, the benefits and costs are relevant. One consideration has to be the time allocated to housework much of which results in the production of shared commodities. Here the benefits may be more pragmatic than pleasure. Time has to be devoted to the purchase of inputs and production of those commodities. If you were living alone, you would have to do all of these things yourself. Within a household, there are economies of scale as one person can do things for both of you.

The allocation of these responsibilities should be based on comparative advantage—the lowest cost provider. When it comes to buying food, that person might be the one with the job with the shorter hours, more flexible schedule, or convenient commute. The allocation of other household tasks should proceed in a similar manner that takes into consideration each spouse's other time commitments and skills. If a spouse enjoys cooking and has a less stressful, demanding job, he could specialize in planning and cooking meals. You have to collectively decide the tasks that you feel are important and who is going to do them. It is important that both of you feel that the other is producing comparable value.

Leisure Activities

While the time devoted to income earning and housework can be productive, the activity that is most likely to be enjoyable is leisure. Now it is time to turn to more enjoyable endeavors. A good place to start is with the shared experiences that you view as important. Do your jobs permit you to eat together nightly? Are there social activities that you enjoy doing together such as dancing or going to the symphony? Will Saturday be date night?

The production of gifts may come up in your decisions about shared commodities as both of you may not have similar tastes and then compromises may be necessary that can be viewed as gifts. Do things that you would prefer not to do with a positive attitude. You need to avoid the Self-Interest Trap that would encourage you to resist doing things that you do not enjoy. Remember, keeping your spouse content with your marriage is the most self-centered thing that you can do. Other gifts such as empathy and understanding are not particularly time intensive, but they will require some time when they are appropriate.

After considering the shared commodities that you feel are important, you should consider the private commodities that each of you views as important. Have you been devoting your Saturdays to golf? Does your spouse have something that he wants to do during that time? If not, when does he have activities that can be done alone or with other people? A successful marriage requires a balancing of the time used to produce shared and private commodities and gifts.

Time-Intensive Leisure: Vacations

While we have essentially discussed a typical week so far, another important use of your time even over the short run is vacations. How much vacation time does your job permit? When is that time available? Will your vacations coincide? If you use your vacation to visit relatives, are you interested in doing that alone or do you feel that it is important to makes those trips together? How will you use your vacations?

Although the rewards from your job can be tangible both in terms of accomplishments and income, do not lose sight of the importance of vacations. While the next chapter discusses the process of finding an interesting and rewarding job, seldom have I had a day at the office that was more enjoyable than my best vacation experiences. If for no other reason than the recurring concept of diminishing returns, it is important to get way from the office. All good things benefit from some change.

In conclusion, in the short run the flexibility of your resources is limited by prior decisions. However, it is important to weigh benefits and costs when considering how to use your discretionary income and time.

YOUR LONG-RUN PLAN

Now that we have considered your current situation, it is time to look at the future. In planning the future, you face fewer constraints. There is still a limit on your time, but you have more flexibility with how you use it.

While your income and skills are often linked to your use of time, you will also have more flexibility about them. Over the long run, many more choices have to be scrutinized within a benefit/cost framework.

One problem with the Experience Trap is that you can only make decisions about the future, but you will eventually judge them in retrospect. You will only know how good your decisions are after you have made them. A good frame of reference—if it is possible—is not looking forward, but picking a point in the future and looking back. What do you want to have accomplished by the time you are sixty-five? Surveys suggest that people in retrospect place a much greater importance on relationships and less on wealth than people do looking forward.[37] Now, and periodically during the remainder of your life, make sure that you step back and consider the uses of your time that are most important to you.

THE ROLE OF CHILDREN

Before we consider the plan for your time, money, and skills, we need to consider the one factor that may dominate those decisions at least for the near future: children. A central consideration in your long-run plan will probably be children. These decisions involve whether you will have them, how many you will have and when you will have them. Do not kid yourself that you can continue using your resources as in the past with little change. Children—if you elect to have them—will dramatically alter your life. That is why you have to consider them in making your long-run plans.

The progression contemplated here consists of courtship, marriage and then parenthood. That is not based on a moral judgment, but rather on the process that is most likely to increase your welfare. Children will dramatically affect your careers and leisure time, thereby strongly influencing the commodities that you can and will produce. Because children are so important, they are the subject of a complete chapter later in this book. At this point, we deal with their general influence on your decisions.

Becoming parents is an irreversible decision, so approach it with caution. You want to produce children that will be a source of enjoyment to you. One of the keys to that result is having them grow up with both of you. A first step toward that goal is to wait long enough after your wedding that both of you are comfortable that you have the type of marriage that is going to last. The high divorce rate is well known. Fifteen percent of married women and 10 percent of married men get divorced before their fifth wedding anniversary.[38]

Having children will not salvage a failing relationship. As important as children are for most of us, the quality of most relationships tends temporarily to deteriorate when couples become parents.[39] Parenthood can be very frustrating. There is the Experience Trap as little in our prior experience prepares us for it. While eventually parenthood can be very rewarding, changing diapers and feeding a cantankerous child is usually at the bottom of many people's list of what they prefer to do. You should be sure that your marriage has a solid foundation before becoming parents.

When considering children, let me remind you of diminishing returns and its effect on how many children you will probably have. It is reasonable to have children as long as the incremental benefits exceed the incremental costs. The benefits associated with parenthood have changed over time as children have shifted from being a source of domestic labor and retirement support to a form of consumption. Diminishing returns would suggest that the potential enjoyment from children tends to decrease as you have more. It is not that you love the last one less, so much as the one you don't have would not have been expected to bring enough additional enjoyment to warrant the cost. Meanwhile, the incremental cost of children is fairly constant, although there can be some economies of scale in clothing and living arrangements. This analysis may seem harsh—and certainly not the way you want to consider parenthood—but research has shown that the combination of declining benefits and increasing costs explains why people are having fewer and frequently no children.[40]

The importance of children is just one of the changes that will occur during your marriage. Your opportunities, constraints and preferences can also change. We will now address how those forces will influence your allocation of time, money and skills. Remember, most commodities will require some or all of these resources. Here, we analyze them separately.

TIME

While we addressed money first when considering your short-run plan, the primary consideration over the long run is time as its allocation also determines your income and skills. In poll after poll, most adults report discontent with their work-life balance.[41] How much time will you have and how are you going to use it? You have some control over the amount of time that you will have—and its quality—based on your lifestyle choices.[42] People who do not smoke and control their weight tend to live longer while being active for more of those years. You can essentially use your time for three purposes: income earning, working in your home and leisure. Because your time is fixed, each choice is going to incur tradeoffs.

Income Earning

The time devoted to income earning has a central role in the production of many important commodities, so let's consider it first.[43] While in the short run we accepted your job as a given, that is no longer the case over the long run. There are two considerations here: acquiring the skills to earn income and then earning the income.

Your first concern has to be the acquisition of marketable skills with education being the obvious source. Additional education is important for obtaining a higher income because of the skills that you acquired in school as well as it opening the door for valuable on-the-job training later. College graduates earn substantially more than high school graduates,[44] so continuing your education may be very important for your future welfare.

It is attractive to devote time to education when you are relatively young because the opportunity cost is smaller and the benefits are higher. By opportunity cost, I mean the alternatives sacrificed in its pursuit. Wages are lower for younger workers and before parenthood there are fewer conflicting obligations both for single and married people. The benefits are higher because the period over which there will be a return is longer. Like other activities, your time should be devoted to education so long as the benefits exceed the costs.

The time devoted to income earning should be based on a combination of the career opportunities that you consider and the commodities that bring value to your family. In other words, how hard is it for you to earn income and what does your family want to do with the income that you earn? The incremental productivity from income earning is the net gain from employment—the difference between the value the family members place on the commodities that it can produce and the effort needed to generate it. So, if someone has a high-paying and enjoyable job and her family has a relative preference for income-intensive commodities—luxuries—that person should make a major time commitment to income earning. Maybe at the other extreme would be people who view most of their job opportunities as unpleasant and have a family that prefers time-intensive commodities—like camping; then this person might want to limit his commitment to income earning. Since income serves an important role in the production of commodities for most families, an advantage of marriage is an increase in the possibility that at least one spouse will find a career that has the ability to generate substantial net benefits for a family.

The relevant income is the amount that is available after taxes and job-related expenses. Each spouse has to address the financial gain from employment incrementally. In most households, there is a primary income earner usually based on a higher income, but it could be based on that person having the largest gain from employment: He enjoys his job. While the primary income earners may vary their career over time, it probably is not realistic in most cases to consider limiting their career or leaving the workforce before retirement.

If one spouse is primary, then the other is secondary. Remember, both spouses brought equal value to the marriage, so being a secondary income earner is not meant to denigrate their importance, but just to place their contributions to the marriage in proper perspective. Since the primary income earner is assumed to already be committed to employment, the financial gains from employment by the secondary income earner is after deducting any expenses incurred due to their employment. These can consist of cleaning services, childcare, and additional meals away from home.

An important influence on the allocation of your time to income earning is where you choose to live. This will affect your commuting and the importance of time devoted to income earning. Commuting is one of the least enjoyable activities for people,[45] so it is desirable to reduce it. This can be accomplished by living in a smaller town or closer to work in a large city. The second alternative confronts the complication that more desirable neighborhoods are usually more expensive. The combination of dual income households and a limited supply of desirable housing has driven up housing costs in many metropolitan areas much more than inflation.[46] When considering employment opportunities, you should consider the cost of living in different locations.[47] If a couple decides to live in an area with high housing costs that places pressure on them to devote more time to income earning. Living in an area with lower housing costs can reduce the pressure to devote time to income earnings and, hopefully, reduce the frustrations of married life.[48]

One concern when allocating your time to income earning can be the tangible rewards from devoting time to it in contrast to its value in other uses. The most obvious example of this process is the importance given to becoming rich by many young people today. Sociologists have noted that work has become home and home has become work for some people.[49] Making choices can be hard work. Some people find that they are more comfortable in the structured environment of work for which there is a predictable structure and tangible financial rewards than they are in their homes where they are confronted with an array of choices and the returns to their efforts are often vague. You want a high net gain from the time that you devote to employment, but its primary role is to provide the financial inputs into your production of commodities, most of which are produced away from your job.

Work in the Home

The second use of your time is producing commodities in your home. Some of these activities you would prefer to avoid, so we will describe them as work. How do you allocate responsibility for those activities? Comparative advantage should be a good guide. However, this will often suggest new roles for husbands and wives. As the incomes and education of women have increased relative to men, comparative advantage would suggest that couples' welfare would be increased by men increasing their emphasis on domestic activities.[50] So far, many men have been reluctant to increase their share of domestic chores.[51] You need to avoid traditional stereotypes and arrive at an equitable distribution of these tasks. Some of the increase in the dissatisfaction of wives leading to divorce can be traced to the imbalance in the effort in marriage as some men expect their wives to provide most of the domestic work while being employed.[52] This is an area in which adequate communication about frustrations can be very important.

One of the most important commodities produced in the home will be well-adjusted children. While interacting with your children is often an enjoyable experience, let's consider that some of the time they require you would prefer to use doing something else. If the benefits are similar from either parent, the choice of which parent should be primarily responsible for child rearing will come down to the lower cost provider. Because of comparative advantage these responsibilities will often fall to the secondary income earner.

An initial decision is whether childcare will be provided by a parent or someone else. Childcare can be provided by a variety of people other than parents such as daycare centers or relatives. A relative is certainly an attractive alternative, if one is available and compensation is reasonable. Otherwise, you are going to have to pay for it. While others may be—but not necessarily are—better trained for raising children, you have to be concerned with the quality—and therefore the benefits—of what they produce.[53] The quality of commercial childcare can be a concern because the interaction between children and adults early in life has been shown to be important for their future success.[54] The quality among childcare facilities is difficult to judge.[55] Therefore, the benefits to a child—especially as an infant—from parental-provided childcare can be high.

In making the decision about how to provide childcare, you have to consider the cost of alternative providers such as a childcare center or a parent. The cost for an infant at daycare will tend to be higher than that for older children. Frequently, people complain that childcare facilities will not provide the quality of service that they want. As a business school economist, I can assure you that markets will provide any legal—and some illegal—commodities for which a sufficient number of people are willing to pay. The profit motive is a very powerful force. If you find that businesses will not provide the quality of childcare that you prefer, the problem is that not enough people are willing to pay for that quality of service. Part of the problem is that a commodity that many felt was provided at home for free is actually expensive to provide either in the home or in a market.

When considering the cost of the time devoted by a parent, it is important to recognize that childcare expenses are only incurred when the secondary income earner considers employment. Therefore, the couple has to consider their financial loss from that parent providing the service. The couple needs to carefully consider the income available to the family after deduction of taxes and job-related expenses that include childcare costs.

The benefit/cost ratio of parental-provided childcare will change over time. Initially, the benefits both to the child and a parent may be high relative to the costs. Under those circumstances, it may be reasonable for a parent to forego or limit employment. Eventually, the relative benefits of professional daycare may increase, while its relative cost declines. It then may be more attractive for the parents to buy more childcare services. The result could be more hours at a job for the parent who had assumed primary responsibility for childcare.

A problem with parents allocating time to childcare is the Unilateral Divorce Trap. Limiting a career to provide childcare can potentially be costly to those parents if their marriage is eventually dissolved. It is likely that the parent providing it will earn less in the future because of this decision. Seldom are spouses adequately compensated for that sacrifice at divorce. While few are willing to acknowledge this concern, my research confirms that it exists.[56] One reaction is for both parents to continue to place a primary emphasis on their careers after becoming parents even if that is not the best decision for the family.

If you are comfortable with your spouse and your commitments to your marriage, then parenthood is a critical time to consider your allocation of time. You want to allocate your time in a way that increases the probability that you will have the type of children that you want. I have suggested elsewhere that a couple might want to write a contract providing compensation for a spouse who limits a career to provide childcare if the marriage is dissolved.[57] Hopefully, the marriage is a success and continues, but this type of agreement can reduce the potential anxiety of a parent who provides childcare.

As we conclude our discussion of the allocation of time to childcare, let me reflect back on our situation. When we married, I had a Ph.D. in economics and Amy had a master's degree in early childhood education. Without much discussion, we concluded that I had a comparative advantage in income earning and Amy had one in child rearing. When we had our first child—four years after we married—we were fortunate that Amy worked in a church-related pre-school with an infants' program. Therefore, she was able to continue as a part-time pre-school teacher—that was important to her—after the birth.

Having had our first child, we had to discuss two important economic principles: diversification and diminishing returns. As to diversification, it is a dangerous investment strategy to place all your funds in one stock and it is equally dangerous to place all your hopes and aspiration in one child. So we decided to have a second child. How about a third child? That is where diminishing returns came in and we decided that two children were enough. Eventually, when the boys were able to take care of themselves in the afternoon, Amy shifted to a full-time teaching position.

Retirement

Although you do not have to make definite plans, one consideration about the allocation of your time is when the two of you are going to retire. You will retire when you decide that the benefit/cost ratio is higher in that activity than in income earning. Because of affluence, some people are retiring earlier.[58] While many people deny that you can expect a higher income than your ancestors, in most cases you will. People tend to want more of most commodities as their incomes increase and some of those commodities are time intensive. They want to buy more time with their affluence. Consequently, people tend to enter the labor force later and leave it earlier than in prior generations.

Your decision about retiring will be based on weighing the value of your time in income earning in contrast to other uses. What are the types of commodities that you value and how well do your careers accommodate your ability to produce them? People who have substantial net gains from employment will tend to work longer than others. These are people who either enjoy their jobs or who have a strong preference for money-intensive commodities. One consideration is that the time devoted to income earning may experience diminishing returns as it become less enjoyable or your job may require more effort. When you retire, you will still have twenty-four hours in day, so an important consideration is the commodities that you will be producing at that time. Many can use that time profitably, but others may find that much time a challenge. I started writing this book after I retired as there is only so much golf that one can play.

The Timing of Activities

Another consideration is the allocation of time to activities that are often limited to a particular time period. One of these is observing your children's activities as they grow up. Often their first accomplishments such as walking, talking and scoring a soccer goal will not be repeated. You probably want to be there for these events. Another activity is your leisure. You can only play adult soccer so long and the ability to backpack may deteriorate with age. The point is that you do not want to look back with regret for not having had certain experiences knowing that they are no longer available. In my sixties, I climbed Mt. Kilimanjaro—with our sons—and walked the Inca Trail—with Amy—with a concern about how much longer I would be able to accomplish those tasks.

Buying Time

An important tradeoff is using the time devoted to income earning to pay others to produce commodities for you. In effect you are buying time. We have already considered childcare, but there are other situations in which people now pay others to do things traditionally done by families. You want a clean house and an attractive yard, but you can buy some of these commodities from others. These purchases are a reflection of comparative advantage. If your education and experience would only justify a low-paying job, then it probably does not pay for you to hire someone to maintain your lawn. However, if you have the potential for a high-paying job and no one in the family enjoys lawn work, then a more productive use of your time is to earn income and pay someone to do the things that you would prefer not to do.

Leisure

Leisure continues to have a central place in the allocation of time. This allocation is important in all phases of your life, but it will be most abundant when you retire. Some of this time will be used to produce private commodities, while other time will be used for shared commodities. I'm not a psychologist, but I have heard enough people say—and experienced it myself—that many experiences are less valuable when they are not shared with someone else. What is the value of a great sunset unless you can nudge someone and say, "Wow"? However, leisure activities are still subject to diminishing returns. So, most people have to use their time to pursue a variety of activities.

Reflecting on Our Use of Time

As you consider the overall allocation of your time, it is also worth dwelling again on diminishing returns. I look back on when I was single and then our lives together as phases. I enjoyed being single, but eventually the enjoyment of that state declined as diminishing returns would suggest. Our marriage has benefited from phases that neutralized the effects of diminishing returns. Initially, we got to know each other better while doing the things that young couples do—driving to Alaska in our old van. Then, parenthood presented new and evolving challenges. When the boys left for college, we were ready for new adventures. With more money and time, new opportunities opened up. Our careers continued to have a central place in our lives. Now we are semi-retired and that opens up even more opportunities, especially those that require more time. The lesson from our experiences is that you can defeat the effects of diminishing returns by creating new opportunities.

In conclusion, your allocation of time is the one factor determining the commodities that your family produces. Consider the benefits and costs of its use in different activities with the understanding that its benefits often diminish with the intensity of each use. The rewards from using it to generate income are obvious, but you should be sensitive to the more subtle value of working at home and participating in leisure activities.

MONEY

The money available to a family is less constrained than its time. Many of the decisions about money have already been reflected in the time devoted to earning it. There may be other sources of income, but for most people they will be limited.

In your long-run plan, the timing of income flows can be important. Early on you may spend more than your income—this is called debt. Going into debt is normally only reasonable for buying things that you will use in the future, so that you are paying for them as you use them. So finance your house—and maybe a car, but not a vacation. Education is important for increasing your income, so you may have to borrow to finance it. Because people are often young when they borrow these funds, they may be naïve about the sacrifices that may be necessary later to pay them off. Unless you are financing a degree—such as one in medicine—that has the potential for a high salary, this is not a good time to finance the good life with student loans.

Be a Smart Consumer

It is also important to be a smart consumer. These people carefully weigh the benefits and costs of their purchases and avoid attempting to impress others by what they buy. They are more likely to shop at Costco and Trader Joe's than at Whole Foods. They drive Hondas rather than Acuras—and certainly not Mercedes Benzes. When was the last time you considered the unit price at a supermarket? If you buy wisely, it reduces the pressure to earn income—even when you would prefer to do something else.

Certainly, one thing to avoid is spending money that you do not have. Eventually, you are going to pay for all your expenditures. The issue is only when. If you pay later, you will have to pay additional finance charges and finance charges can be over 25 percent. The average household has credit-card debt of $7,753 and only 30 percent of cardholders pay off their balances in full each month.[59] You want to be one of those 30 percent. In our household, the credit card has always only been a transaction card—with a percentage reward—as it has been used to facilitate transactions rather than to provide us with credit.

For most people, their incomes tend to increase over time.[60] This is true even after adjustments for inflation because of increases in productivity. If your income increases relative to your fixed expenses, you will have more discretionary income. Many of those fixed expenses are associated with necessities, so it is important to control them. You can get into financial trouble when the money-intensive commodities that you consider necessities grow more rapidly than your income.

Children will have a significant effect on a couple's discretionary income as parents limit their careers for childcare and eventually face the cost of education. This is where your prior savings are important as they provide a buffer against the decline in discretionary income.

Investment Strategies

Over time, you probably will also want to change the allocation of your investments. With a long time horizon when you are younger, it is reasonable to invest primarily in indexed, no-load mutual funds. As you approach retirement, you may want to move more of those funds into fixed income securities like bonds. These decisions will be affected by the type of pension that you acquired. If you have the less common defined benefit retirement plan that promises you a stream of income based on a formula—with it potentially being indexed for inflation—then you can afford to take more risks with your other investments. If you have the more common defined contribution plans in which you invested funds, you need to be more careful. One way to create a more predictable income stream in the future is to buy bonds that will mature at different periods during your retirement. You will receive interest on the bonds and then the return of its face value when it matures.

In conclusion, your income should reflect your employment opportunities and the types of commodities that your family prefers. By being a careful consumer, you can increase your family's welfare, while reducing the pressure to devote time to income earning.

SKILLS

The last resource over which you have some control is your skills. These skills affect the productivity of your time. We have already discussed improving your income earnings skills through education and on-the-job training. Now, we need to consider increasing your skills in other areas. Improving those skills can require the use of those valuable resources, time and money. You need to consider a balance between the skills that you use for producing different commodities. Normally, people become more productive at an activity as they do it more frequently. This is especially true for the shared commodities that are often critical for a family's welfare. We would expect people to become better cooks as they cook more often. In a similar way, people become better gardeners and plumbers.

You are not just concerned with shared commodities as improving your skills in producing private commodities probably continues to be an important component of your welfare. You may want to become a better golfer or painter. A family is a group of individuals with particular interests and needs. The welfare of the family is the welfare of the individuals in it. So, private commodities will still be important and time devoted to improving their quality may be important for the welfare of individuals.

An important skill that you probably need to develop is being a better parent. Even in primitive societies many children have survived, so being a good parent should not be that difficult. Still, as in so many other areas, the range of choices has increased dramatically. In traditional societies, the interaction of parents with their children was determined by social norms. These norms determined the allowable activities for children and the skills that parents were expected to teach them. When a parent worked in the home, the interaction between at least one parent and young children was almost constant. Since children were expected to participate in the household chores, they were gradually exposed to their parents' skills both in the home and at work. Now parents have less interaction with their children and yet the children face the more challenging world that is the subject of this book. Developing your skills as parents is discussed in more depth in Chapter 7.

CONCLUSION

Many of you might consider stopping reading at this point. You should have found your partner and the two of you have developed a plan for using your resources to produce the commodities that are most likely to make marriage attractive to both of you. But you might still benefit from some additional insights from business. The money inputs are important in your production process, but you want to acquire those inputs in the most efficient manner. In most cases, you are going to have to devote time and energy to that process. In the next chapter, we will discuss how you can make the income-generating process as enjoyable and rewarding as possible. The production of children—who bring enjoyment and complexity into your lives—has occupied an important role in this book. You might benefit from additional insights about that process, so we will also discuss it in a subsequent chapter. We will conclude the book with chapters for people that are less fortunate, dealing with divorce and remarriage.

THINGS TO REMEMBER

- While businesses attempt to maximize their profits, your goal should be to maximize your welfare—not your income.
- This welfare follows from the commodities produced by your family.
- Businesses and families can increase their welfare by encouraging specialization of labor, economies of scale, and insurance.
- Families produce three types of commodities: private commodities, shared commodities, and gifts.
- A credible commitment is important for your success in both business and marriage.
- In the short run, you face significant constraints on your decisions with those constraints becoming less limiting in the long run.
- While making your long-term plans, it is important to attempt to place yourself in a position to judge your decisions retrospectively—looking backwards.

Income as a Production Input

Now we turn to how you are going to generate that important input for your production of commodities: money. Earning an income is not a goal in itself, as you need to keep in mind that the money that it generates is just one of the inputs in your family's production process; the others are your time and skills. Decisions about your careers should be based on weighing the benefits and costs of alternatives. The benefits are the commodities that can be produced with the money that you earn and the costs are the sacrifices necessary to earn it. The more highly your family values money-intensive commodities the greater the benefits of the income earned through employment. The primary cost of employment is the commodities that could be produced with the time allocated to it, although it is also influenced by psychological aspects. Some jobs are more pleasant and rewarding than others. Some jobs you might do if you were independently wealthy and others you would quit tomorrow—or never consider—if you had some other source of income. More enjoyable jobs are less costly to you than unpleasant ones.

While making your career decisions, the Experience Trap has to be a concern. The increase in educational attainment has expanded the occupational choices of most people. Few today follow in their parents' footsteps as was often common in the past. The percentage of people twenty-five years and over with at least a bachelor's degree has increased from five percent in 1940 to 25 percent in 2000.[1] The most dramatic change was among women for whom the percentage increased from less than four to 23. With this additional education, people have far more options than in the past.

Your challenge is to find the careers that will assist you in increasing your family's welfare.

YOUR GOAL FROM EMPLOYMENT

Your goal from employment should be to increase the net gain from your career, which is the difference between the income that you can earn and effort necessary to earn it. Stated differently it is the difference between what you are paid and the minimum amount necessary to attract you to the job. Jeff Opdyke, who writes a column on Love & Money for the *Wall Street Journal*, illustrated this very important goal with his own experience.[2] He left the *Wall Street Journal* in the mid-1990s for a higher paying job. When he discovered that he was more competent and happier in his prior job at the *Journal*, he was fortunate that he was able to return to it. He notes that others that he knows have been less fortunate when they discovered that their net gain from employment had fallen when they accepted a higher paying position and they could not return to their prior position.

The income that people earn is a reflection of the fundamental market forces of supply and demand. As the wages increase for a given occupation in a particular location, the supply of people with the appropriate skills who are willing to work there increases. More people are interested in becoming bank tellers or hazardous materials removal workers in Omaha at $25,000 than at $15,000 per year. Meanwhile, the number of people that employers demand falls as the wages of those workers increase. If the salaries of bank tellers and hazardous materials removal workers increased from $15,000 to $25,000 per year, employers would attempt to reduce their work force by replacing some of them with machines or assign some tasks to less qualified individuals. The amount that people earn is a reflection of these two forces. Therefore, you would prefer to be in a field in which the demand is high and the supply low. The result would be a higher income.

A higher income is not the only consideration when you are looking at employment options as you should be interested in the net gain from employment rather than just the income. One of the earliest insights in economics was that wages vary with the characteristics of jobs such as ease or hardship, cleanliness or dirtiness, and respected and despised.[3] The characteristics of jobs affect the number of people willing to work at a given wage. More people are interested in easy, clean and respected jobs than those that are hard, dirty and despised. Given their level of education, bank tellers tend to make less than hazardous materials removal workers, for example.[4] There are jobs that are relatively high paying given the skills required because they are commonly recognized to be unpleasant. People who work on oil rigs in the Gulf of Mexico are well paid, but those high wages are necessary to attract people to those positions. Since the net gain is the difference between what you are paid and what is necessary to attract you to a job, a key lesson is that you are a fortunate person if you enjoy or can tolerate jobs that others find unattractive.

DETERMINING THE PREFERRED SKILLS

In making a decision about your career, you will have much more control over the markets into which you supply your labor than the demand for your services in those markets. The demand for labor tends to be based on forces over which you will have no control. These forces include the businesses' production process and the prices of its products. Demand for labor tends to be higher when a production process uses more productive workers—often due to the support of capital equipment—and the company's products have a higher price. You have no control over those factors. However, you have substantial control over the markets into which you are willing to supply your labor. The supply of workers to a particular profession depends on the people who have acquired the skills demanded by employers there. By selecting the skills that you acquire, you will have substantial control over the number of people against whom you have to compete.

Even if you think that you know the career that you want to pursue, it is worthwhile exploring other alternatives. A valuable place to start is with the United States Bureau of Labor Statistics' *Occupational Outlook Handbook* that describes the nature of the work in different fields, the working conditions, the necessary training and qualifications, the employment opportunities, the job outlook and earnings.[5] Someone might be indifferent about becoming a lawyer or an accountant and assumes that both will require approximately the same investment of time, money and effort.[6] This *Handbook* could then be very valuable as it notes that the median—half made more and half made less—annual earnings of all lawyers in 2004 were $94,930, while accountants earned $50,770. It would appear that being a lawyer would be the more appropriate career for this person.

Another valuable resource is the Bureau of Labor Statistics' *Occupational Employment Statistics* that provide more detailed data on earnings in different industries and locations.[7] In May 2005, it reports that the mean annual earnings of lawyers were $110,520, which was slightly higher than their median annual earnings of $98,930. However, there is substantial variation among industries and locations. People in legal services made on average $116,310, while those in state government made only $73,970. There are some surprises among the metropolitan areas with the highest earnings, as Blacksburg, Virginia, and Longview, Texas, are among the top five.

People can be too casual when making career decisions and yet there is wide variation in the earnings for different occupations and locations for people with similar abilities. As I reflect back on my career decisions, I was lucky—but not particularly systematic. At one time I thought about going to graduate school in history, a field that attracts numerous people often because of the enjoyable courses that they had as undergraduates. However, I eventually rejected that idea because my ultimate goal was to get a Ph.D. and become a college professor. Since history covered the past, I assumed that most of the good dissertation topics had already been explored. Having rejected history, I turned to economics—a field that people often find less attractive as undergraduates—but I thought that it might be interesting based on my limited exposure to it. Later, I found out two fortunate things. First, I enjoyed economics and, second, economists were paid much better and had more control of their employment opportunities than historians. Let me emphasize what I stated above: You can increase your net gain from employment by finding something that others cannot or do not want to do that you enjoy doing.

HUMAN CAPITAL

The acquisition of skills is fundamental to increasing your income.[8] These skills have two important effects. First, they increase the demand for your services because you are perceived to be more productive and, second, they reduce the number of people against whom you have to compete for jobs. Just like people invest in their businesses, they are also invested in themselves. The production of commodities requires the inputs of time, money and skills and the same inputs are necessary for a successful investment in individuals.

The ability of individuals to earn an income is described as their human capital. Investments in human capital are made by a variety of parties. Early in life it is made by parents primarily through the time devoted to teaching their children basic language skills and values. With the start of formal education, society augments the contributions of the parents with the taxes used to support public schools. Throughout this process, the time of the student is a major contribution. Eventually, students can be expected to start to absorb more of the financial cost of their education. Especially when people can earn an income, one—if not the most important—cost of education is the sacrificed income associated with the time required for it. People who have more ability to benefit from education will tend to find it easier and more rewarding, so they will be inclined to pursue more of it.

THE ROLE OF EDUCATION

By providing you with general skills, your formal education provides an important foundation for other future investments in human capital. Still, it is important to recognize the difference between the C word and the I word as applied to education. The C word is consumption and the I word is investment. Consumption occurs when you are involved in an activity that you enjoy and your experience results in only a limited increase in your marketable skills. Investment on the other hand is an experience that enhances the income that you can receive in the future.

Consumption is what life is all about, so I am not saying that it is a bad thing. However, it is regrettable when people confuse the two. This is especially true when some people think that they are investing when they are actually consuming. This can happen, for example, when someone acquires a bachelor's degree in theater arts.[9] This person may eventually find it difficult to find a well paying job and, therefore, the experience may have been enjoyable but it was not necessarily income enhancing. This is a particular tragedy when people end up with substantial debts and a degree with limited market value. You are fortunate when you enjoy education, viewing it as a pleasant—almost consumptive—experience when you are acquiring skills for which others will eventually pay you. In that case, the experience was an investment.

Another important aspect of education is that it can be viewed as a "signal." The acquisition of information is a costly and potentially unreliable process. Consider the process that employers have to go through when considering prospective employees. Most applicants for a job want to emphasize that they are intelligent and hard working, but how can an employer determine if they actually have those qualities? Given the suspicion of employers about the tendency for prospective employees to exaggerate their qualifications, prospective employees have to develop a method for convincing employers that they actually have the attributes they advertise. If it is a common perception that it is more difficult to get a degree in engineering than in the humanities, then one way to signal that you are more intelligent and ambitious is to major in engineering rather than English. One of the most fundamental signals of your intelligence and motivation to prospective employers is to graduate from high school.

Because of limited information about salaries, people may not recognize the increase in the income that follows from education. Past experience may not alert people to how education can increase their income. Much of an undergraduate education consists of classes that do not appear to have the ability to increase your income. What exactly does a survey of American history or music appreciation have to do with earning more? Educators suggest that even those classes help you think more clearly. But, it is true that often a bachelor's degree is just a requirement for an advanced degree that has the ability to increase your income.

At one time, when the number of people receiving undergraduate degrees was smaller, just having one was an important signal to employers about individuals' intelligent and diligence. Now that undergraduate degrees have become more common, it is important to have more convincing evidence of your skills. That can come from an undergraduate degree that is recognized as including marketable skills such as engineering or business, or by acquiring those skills in graduate school. The master in business administration—a program that I have taught in for thirty years— is a common pursuit for people who find their job prospects or promotions limited by their prior degrees. While there is valuable content in a graduate business degree, acquiring it also is a signal that you have qualities for which employers are looking—intelligence and ambition.

It has become popular to suggest that it no longer pays to pursue additional education. Nothing could be further from the truth. In 2003, among people in the United States over twenty-five years old, the median income of high school graduates was $25,935.[10] That figure increased to $41,800 for college graduates with a bachelor's degree and $51,244 for someone with a master's degree. Even when the time and money necessary to obtain these degrees is considered, education is still a good investment for most people.

Having discussed the importance of education in providing you with a higher income and probably more interesting jobs, it is also important to consider the costs of financing it. Higher education can be expensive as tuition costs have increased more rapidly than inflation.[11] Still, similar degrees can be acquired at very different costs with the primary difference being private versus public schools.[12] With the exception of a few highly selective colleges, there is no evidence that going to a private college results in a higher income than going to a public one.[13] Far more important than where you go is what you study there. Therefore, public colleges and universities are probably a much better investment for you. Because of their availability and initial low cost, it can be attractive to augment consumption during your education with student loans. The degree should increase your income later, but excessive student loans can also be a major burden later.

THE ROLE OF ON-THE-JOB TRAINING AND EXPERIENCE

The acquisition of human capital does not stop with formal education as on-the-job training and experience also serve an important role in enhancing individuals' human capital and, therefore, their incomes.[14] Businesses are more likely to invest in workers who have already demonstrated the desire and ability to acquire new skills. There are two types of skills acquired through education and experience—general and specific skills. General skills are those that can be used in many different positions such as learning basic language and mathematical skills. Meanwhile, the specific ones apply often to just one employer such as learning the organization of a corporation and the people within the organization that can solve particular problems.

It is important that you understand that the investment process for these two types of skills varies. Businesses would hesitate to fund the first and you would probably hesitate to fund the latter. Therefore, general skills are often acquired in an educational institution or by your accepting a below market salary as is common among interns. On the other hand, you would not be willing to accept a below market wage to acquire skills that may only have value in one business. While acquiring these specific skills, companies have to pay you as much as you can receive elsewhere, although you may not yet be very productive at your new job. Eventually, the businesses recognize that your increased productivity will justify the salary that they are paying you.

Because the experience of working in most companies provides opportunities for acquiring both general and specific skills, it is important to make sure that you avail yourself of all those opportunities. Make it clear to your employer that you are willing to accept new challenges. Your earnings will more likely increase because you are perceived to be more productive because of the skills that you have acquired than due just to your having been around longer.

In conclusion, you can get paid for how hard you work, for what you know or a combination of the two. Still for any amount of effort you get paid more if you know more—you have more human capital. Because the costs of education in terms of time, money and effort are near term, while the benefits of income and job alternatives are later, there can be a tendency to underinvest in education. Do not make that mistake. Ideally, you will choose—or have chosen—an occupation for which you are paid substantially more than is necessary to attract you into it. This is most likely to occur if you enjoy an occupation that others cannot do or do not want to do.

DOES THE FAMILY HAVE A PRIMARY INCOME EARNER?

An initial consideration for a married couple may be to determine if their family has a primary income earner (PIE). This person is the spouse who is most likely to make a commitment to full-time employment until retirement. Comparative advantage suggests that few families are able to or will benefit from both spouses making equal financial contributions over the duration of the marriage. Even though people tend to marry those with similar backgrounds—including education—one spouse will tend to be more productive at earning an income than the other. The PIE should be the person who is able to generate the larger net gain from employment subject to both spouses being able to earn some minimum amount. At least some income is required to cover necessities. This determination can be especially important for couples who anticipate being parents. With parenthood, the welfare of the family may be enhanced by the PIE's continuing to emphasize employment while the secondary income earner (SIE) adjusts career choices to accommodate childcare.

A decision about who is going to be the PIE is important because of the effect of placing an emphasis on that person's career. With limited resources, placing an emphasis on one spouse's career can be important for investments in education, the family's location and the effort that person can devote to the career. Initially, there will be the importance of investments in that person's career with education being particularly important. Making these investments may require the other family members to forego investments in their own careers. The position with the highest net gain for a spouse may also be located somewhere else, which may require the family to move. Even if the couple does not relocate, the family may benefit from one spouse being in a position to accept unanticipated overtime and travel that again may be important for that person's career. Having decided on the spouse who is the PIE makes challenging decisions such as these less stressful.

Making this determination may have little effect initially. Let's consider two high school teachers who are currently earning the same amount. The husband is already becoming disillusioned with teaching and anticipates a time when he may no longer enjoy it. Meanwhile, his wife continues to enjoy her profession and does not anticipate that her view of it will change. Their school district has a flexible parent leave program, so they know that the mother could easily return to work after a leave due to the births of their children. For this couple, the wife would appear to be the best candidate for being the PIE. Because pay scales are based on education level, investments in her education should initially be emphasized. With a stronger attachment to teaching, the return to an investment in her career would be higher than one in his.

INVESTING IN THE PIE

If there is an obvious person who is the PIE when a couple marries, an initial concern is whether there has been an adequate investment in that person's human capital. The PIE should initially have a priority for investments in human capital because of the expectation of a stronger commitment to the work force. With that attachment, the PIE also can afford to develop more general skills. Meanwhile, someone who plans on irregular employment would want more clearly defined skills that facilitate the job search process. PIEs can afford to get general degrees such as one in human resource management. That degree would permit them to obtain good entry level jobs. Their careers will be enhanced by experience and on-the-job training. These skills and the person's reputation will be the key to having a successful, prosperous career as a manager.

THE ROLE OF THE SECONDARY INCOME EARNER

If a couple decides that one spouse is the PIE, a logical conclusion is that the other is the secondary income earner (SIE). This is not meant to denigrate the importance of that person so much as to reflect the role in the production of commodities. The SIE's comparative advantage is in providing the other important inputs into the family's production process rather than emphasizing income. While the SIE will often be the wife that has become less common.[15] Not only do wives often earn more than their husbands, it has become more likely for the husband to relocate in response to a job opportunity for the wife.[16]

Motherhood has traditionally been the primary reason why women have tended to be SIEs. Some of the reasons women give for dropping out of the work force after childbirth are the desire to nurture babies in their first year, poor quality or availability of childcare, high cost of acceptable childcare, lack of extended maternity leave, lack of flexible return to work options, and decisions to switch to a more family friendly career.[17] Most mothers who leave the work force after a child's birth do not return for one to three years. It is easier for a SIE to limit employment when the PIE has a higher income. The biggest percentage decline in work force participation of mothers was among those with a bachelor's degree—who probably married men with a similar level of education—and those with husbands in the top 20 percent of earners.

Being a SIE will influence the types and timing on investments in that person. Initially, the priority within the family should be to increase the marketable skills of the PIE. If investments continue to be made in the SIE, it can be important to find investments that depreciate less with time. Being a "manager" is a broad and potentially vague career that may not leave someone particularly marketable after leaving the labor force or limiting participation in it for an extended period. Meanwhile, professions that rely on certification are much less vulnerable to this depreciation in value. Some obvious examples are teaching, nursing, medicine, and accounting. Those who are certified in these fields can leave the work force and as long as they maintain their certification, they can more easily return because their skills are validated through their certification. The validation of these skills can be important if the SIE is seeking employment after relocating or returning to full employment after emphasizing work in the home.

Initially, both spouses will probably be employed. But their circumstances can change with the result that the SIE may consider part-time employment or leaving the work force. In some cases, a couple can feel comfortable that their welfare would be improved by the SIE working part time. In 2004, approximately 25 percent of women and 10 percent of men were working part-time.[18] This decision can occur for a variety of reasons with childcare being one of the major causes. Then it helps to have chosen your employer carefully. Choosing your employer can be important because many firms have a formal policy that makes it easier to shift to part-time employment.[19] When approaching your supervisors to suggest that you cut back on your hours, it is important to emphasize the benefits to the company rather than the benefits to you.[20]

When the benefit of employment does not exceed the cost—there are no net gains—then the SIE should leave the work force. This frequently occurs when infant care is required. Because the benefit of parental attention to the child at the time is high, the cost of employment is also high. Meanwhile, employment would also require additional costs such as childcare. At least temporarily, it may be attractive for the SIE to leave the work force.

There are numerous productive activities that can occur while the SIE is working in the home, as that time period can provide a SIE with the opportunity to enhance old skills or learn new ones. Distance education has become an important process in the United States as universities offer numerous programs on the Internet.[21] According to the Alfred P. Sloan Foundation, 51 percent of public colleges offered online degree programs in business, for example, in fall 2003.[22] Childcare and other domestic obligations do not have to be a full-time commitment of the SIE, so that person should consider taking classes or developing new skills through part-time employment. As a couple's children grow up, the SIE should have more opportunities to increase the time devoted to employment, recreation or improving skills.

RETURNING TO WORK

It is common for SIEs, who have reduced their employment, to increase their employment later. There are a number of issues that have to be addressed at that time. If you were happy in your prior career, how do you return to it? If your career could be enhanced with more education or you want to change your career, were you able to acquire those skills? How much of a commitment do you want to make to the work force?

This transition will depend on a weighing of benefits and costs based on a variety of factors such as employment opportunities and domestic obligations. The better the employment opportunities and the more flexible the domestic obligations the more quickly SIEs can increase their commitment to employment. The benefits of employment will be influenced by the income level and the flexibility. In some cases, people who worked overtime and traveled frequently before becoming parents have been able to find office jobs with regular hours and no travel with the same employers.[23] Other employers give employees the flexibility to work from their homes or reduce their hours.[24] Some of the major costs of employment will continue to be access to childcare providers and commuting time.

The transition may be easier if the spouse has maintained a relationship with a prior employer or has recognizable credentials such as those associated with some professional degrees. Some employers have made it particularly attractive to return to work after an extended leave. Often these are for people who have the types of credentials that do not depreciate and they have been the beneficiary of investments in on-the-job training by their employers.

The trend toward permitting or encouraging leaves appears to be particularly popular among accounting firms.[25] Both Deloitte & Touche and KPMG permit some employees to take leaves as long as five years. During that period the employees have to maintain contact, but they do not have any other obligations. Other types of businesses such as IBM permit leaves as long as three years. Credentials that establish the individual's competence are important if a SIE is looking for employment with a new employer.

Because the general skills associated with being a "manager" can be viewed as having depreciated during any period out of the work force, business schools have started programs to help people—especially women—reenter the work force. These programs aim to help students overcome the big gaps in their resumes with job seeking strategies as well as to bring them up to date on changes in their fields.[26] Normally, these are short courses lasting only a few weeks.

For SIEs who stay out of the work force for as many as ten years, a new industry has developed to assist them in reentering the work force.[27] Part of what these businesses offer is hand holding and confidence building as people reestablish their careers. Some of their other advice is more practical as it focuses on establishing a network and contacting smaller firms who may appreciate the entrepreneurial skills that you developed working at home. One strategy is to take some of the time out of the work force to develop new skills with a focus on rapidly growing occupations. Recently, many of those opportunities have been in health or medicine such as being a physician assistant, physical therapist or audiologist.[28]

CHANGING ROLES

The opportunity for the person who was the SIE to return to the work force may provide an opportunity for the spouses to reconsider their careers. What is the state of the PIE's career? Again, here we have lots of possibilities. They range from the PIE being burned out and looking forward to shifting more time to the production of commodities in the home to this person being so financially successful and enjoying their career so much that there is no additional need for money to produce the commodities that the family prefers. With a higher income from the PIE the most valuable use of the SIE's time may be to continue to emphasize domestic production that might reflect a shift of time from childrearing to other domestic activities.

Alternatively, more of the income-earning responsibilities may shift to the person who had been the SIE. One strong influence may be diminishing returns. Careers like most other experiences can eventually experience diminishing returns—you enjoy it less the longer you do it.[29] When you start a career there are at least two things that make it interesting and rewarding other than getting paid. First, it is a new challenge, and, second, there is the excitement associated with your prospects for promotion. Eventually, both of these can dissipate as your work becomes more predictable and you get a clearer idea of your career potential. Of course, you can avoid diminishing returns by confronting new challenges and advancing through your organization. PIEs may want to alter their career when they no longer find their current position interesting and rewarding.

The SIE may be interested in new opportunities due to diminishing returns also applying to working in the home. Also, as the children grow up the value of the commodities produced in the home may decrease with the spouse who emphasized their production looking for new challenges. Their enthusiasm for employment may be increasing at the time that the enthusiasm of the initial PIE for it is waning.

CAREER FLEXIBILITY

Both PIE and SIE have to continually consider the career choices that they have made. The decisions that people have made early in life may no longer be attractive. People are often forced to make career choices before they have a clear understanding of the nature of these careers. In addition, we have already noted the effect of diminishing returns on even good choices. If the dissatisfaction with career choices is not addressed, the result can be depression associated with a mid-life crisis.[30] A study of 37 year old female college graduates found that 34 percent of Radcliffe graduates and 61 percent of those from Michigan expressed regrets of some kind about their life course.[31]

With improved employment opportunities for women, couples have more flexibility to consider alternative career choices. In middle age, people can start to evaluate their lives. The people who decide that they are unhappy and do nothing about it are the ones who will be even less happy later. If you are less than satisfied with the choices that you have made, this is the time to consider alternatives. That is not to say that you will make changes, because there may not be better alternatives, but at least you consider your situation. Maybe recognizing that there are no better alternatives will make your current situation more acceptable. In my twenties, I made the choice that so many young people make: I went to law school for a year. Even at that age, I considered alternatives and decided that there had to be something better than law. That is one of the best decisions that I ever made. Later an opportunity opened up for me to complete my law degree. Eventually, being an economist with a law degree has been very valuable for my career.[32]

FRINGE BENEFITS

When considering careers, let's not forget about the fringe benefits provided by different employers. Some fringe benefits come in the form of income such as for paid vacations and your employer's match to your 401(k) defined contribution pension plan. Matching that maximum amount being made by your employer should be automatic—even if you have to borrow the money from your parents.

Other types of fringe benefits are not part of your income. These non-pay fringe benefits can be important, consisting of pensions and insurance. In 2005, the average worker had non-pay fringe benefits that were

26 percent of the amount that they were paid.[33] Fringe benefits are particularly attractive because they permit you to shift purchases to before-tax dollars. The income that you receive in your paycheck is going to be subjected to a variety of taxes starting with social security and Medicare contributions and ending with a variety of state and federal income and sales taxes. It is not difficult to have a marginal tax rate of 35 percent. For example, if you have a taxable income of $50,000 in New Mexico, the taxes on the next $100 is 34.5 percent.[34] Then any purchases are subjected to a gross receipts tax that pushed the tax burden over 40 percent. So it is attractive to shift purchases to before tax. If you would normally buy health insurance, for example, you would prefer to have your employer purchase most of it for you. Fringe benefits vary among jobs, from being as low as the legally required ones of social security, unemployment compensation and workers' compensation of 10 percent to some union jobs for which the fringe benefits are almost 50 percent of paid compensation. White collar jobs tend to have a higher amount of fringe benefits than do blue collar jobs.

Never think of these fringe benefits as a gift as they are part of your compensation from the perspective of your employer. In fact, they would rather pay you in the form of health insurance than as income because they have to make social security and Medicare contributions on the income but not on the health insurance.

WHERE YOU LIVE

Where you decide to live will have a major impact on your ability to produce commodities because of the cost of housing and commuting. These costs are inter-related so they cannot be addressed individually. Studies have shown that the total cost of housing and transportation in many metropolitan areas remains fairly constant no matter where people live within those areas.[35] If people attempt to economize on housing, those neighborhoods are often more remote, requiring them to spend more on commuting. Low housing costs are often associated with higher transportation costs.

A cost to you of a job is not just the time that you spend there but also the time that it takes for you to get there. Commuting can be costly.[36] One of your goals might be to adjust your living and employment situations to control the time necessary for commuting as this time varies across the country. A study showed that people in Cascade County, Montana, that includes Great Falls, had the shortest commute in the country at 14 minutes, while residents in New York City's Staten Island had the longest at 42 minutes.[37] No surprise that the shortest commutes are in smaller communities and the longer ones in large metropolitan areas. In a number of states—New York, New Jersey, Maryland, Illinois and California—approximately 10 percent of workers commuted for more than 60 minutes and commutes of over 90 minutes were typical in all those states.[38] As a response to these costs, there has been a slight shift of people from metropolitan areas to non-metropolitan areas.

At both of my teaching jobs, I have had a short commute. At my first job at a small college in Florida, my office was downstairs from our on-campus apartment. When we moved to Albuquerque, we made it a priority to find a house within walking distance of campus. Both of our houses here have had that characteristic and I have not had a parking permit during my thirty years here. Walking to work became even more enjoyable with the availability of portable music players.

One of the main pressures on families to have both spouses work full time is the cost of housing.[39] Housing and other costs vary more across the country than do salaries. Therefore, living in a high housing cost area without a commensurately high income can restrict the ability of the family to produce the commodities that are likely to increase its welfare. About 80 percent of low and middle income households spend more than half of their income on housing in 2001.[40] Traditionally, lenders believed that homeowners should not spend more than 28 percent of their income on mortgage payments to reduce the risks of delinquency and default. You want to avoid states that have a high percentage of household incomes going to monthly housing costs. The top five of these states are California, Nevada, New Jersey, Florida and Hawaii.[41]

When considering a job prospect, it is worthwhile to consider the change in costs that you will experience if you relocate. There are a number of web sites that provide comparisons of the cost of living between different locations. While housing costs are particularly important in these comparisons, there are other factors such as taxes and utility bills. Just as an example, I considered what it would be like if I moved from Albuquerque, New Mexico, to San Diego, California. The salary comparison calculator on CNNMoney.com figured that I needed a salary increase of 40 percent to maintain the same standard of living. Most of the difference was based on the over 100 percent increase in the cost of housing.

The primary reason that housing costs in certain communities are particularly high is that people want to live there (demand) and the supply has been unable to adjust. If you want to live in one of the high cost communities, you will at least initially be housing poor—there will be less for other things. Often the only way to reduce these costs is to live outside of a major metropolitan area. Just as your net gain from employment is increased by enjoying what others don't, the same strategy works with housing so that you are better off if you prefer—and can be employed in—locations that are less attractive to others.

CONCLUSION

Your careers are not an end in themselves. They are means by which you acquire the income and money to produce the commodities that ultimately increase your welfare. You want to acquire a job that has the largest net gain subject to some minimum income to cover necessities. Because salaries are determined by the forces of supply and demand, you would like to find a career where demand is high and supply is low. Education serves an important role in accomplishing that goal as it increases the demand for your services while reducing the number of people with whom you have to compete. The largest net gain from employment is likely to occur if you can find an occupation that others find unattractive and yet it is one that you enjoy. In a similar fashion, finding employment in a place that others find less attractive can reduce your cost of living and pressure on you to earn an income. Most couples will probably benefit from determining the spouse who is the primary income earner and emphasizing that individual's career.

THINGS TO REMEMBER

- Your career is a means rather than an end.
- Do not think in terms of what you can earn but rather in terms of the commodities that your income will permit you to produce.
- For most couples, a decision has to be made about the spouse who will be the primary income earner.
- Designating a primary income earner will reduce deliberations about investments in human capital, relocations and career accommodations.
- Being the secondary income earner just means that that person's comparative advantage is not in income earning and, therefore, it is in some other facet of domestic production.
- It is desirable to find employment that limits commuting and housing costs.

Producing Happy, Well-Adjusted Children

Among the commodities that families produce, happy, well-adjusted children have to be at the top of most couples' list. Amy questioned the title of this chapter feeling that some of you would not agree with just happy and well adjusted as the goals that you have for your children. What kind of children do you want? When I reflect on our goals as parents, I think that these are the best adjectives for describing what we were attempting to accomplish. We wanted our children to be a source of joy rather than frustration. To accomplish that goal, we felt that it was important for our children to develop a positive attitude toward life and be comfortable with themselves. More specifically, we view a successful marriage and rewarding careers as central to their ability to obtain those goals.

You may have different goals. Recent surveys of young adults indicate that their primary goals are to be rich and famous.[1] One would have to assume that a significant influence on why they developed these goals was their parents. The accomplishments of children have become more important to parents and these may be the values that they instilled in them. Alternatively, the influence may not have been direct as constantly complaining about their financial condition may have encouraged their children to be more concerned about their finances.

No matter how these young adults arrived at these goals, their focus on being rich and famous is probably a poor plan for at least two reasons. First, becoming rich and famous is risky and unpredictable, so your children may be disappointed. Second, even if those goals are obtainable, they will inevitably require the sacrifice of other alternatives. While being financially rewarding, obtaining these goals may be very costly. The most predictable way to become rich is to work very hard both in school and at a job. In addition, it helps to find things to do that others do not want to do or cannot do. This is a good strategy if people enjoy doing those things, but if being rich is their goal they would be inclined to do them even if they did not enjoy them. Being rich is certainly preferable to being poor, but as we have suggested before: The benefits of additional income tend to experience diminishing returns. Earning $50,000 more per year might make people somewhat happier, but it may take substantially more effort to earn it.

Being famous is even more challenging. While we are all aware of the visibility and incomes of famous movie stars, the typical actor is very poorly paid, earning less than $25,000 per year.[2] The road to fame—at least in the entertainment industry—is a long, hard and unpredictable one as noted in the *Occupational Outlook Handbook*, "Actors endure long periods of unemployment, intense competition for roles, and frequent rejections in auditions." Therefore, it is important to keep your goals for your children realistic because their accomplishments are going to have a central role in your welfare.

PRODUCING QUALITY CHILDREN

Just like your pizzeria will be a success if you produce a high quality pizza at a reasonable price, your marriage is more likely to be a success if you produce high quality children. And, yes, the operative word here is produce. You can pay others to participate in the process by buying daycare services, music lessons and summer camp; but ultimately it is your time, money and skills that will probably be the most important inputs into this production process. In this chapter, we want to investigate that process.

THE MAKE OR BUY DECISION

An initial consideration, although not normally a pressing one, is whether to conceive your own children or to acquire them from some other source. This process is similar to a "make or buy" decision for a business as it considers how to acquire inputs for its production process. Consider your pizza dough. You can either make it yourself or buy it from someone else. Like most pizzerias, you will probably decide to produce your own as it is not difficult to make and its quality is essential to the success of your business. Most couples approach parenthood in a similar manner. They are capable of conceiving their own children and they know that their genes are an important ingredient in the children that they want.

Other couples may be less fortunate as they are unable to conceive the children that they want.[3] These couples have to consider alternatives such as adoption or surrogate motherhood. Of these, adoption continues to be the more popular choice.[4] However, it can be very frustrating. There is a very limited supply of the types of children that many people want such as infants with similar ethnicity and no pre-natal problems. Therefore, people who want to adopt domestically have to turn to less attractive alternatives such as older children and those of a different ethnic background. An approach that has become increasingly attractive is to adopt from abroad, which involves significant logistical problems. While some of you will have to consider those alternatives, they are sufficiently varied that the remainder of this chapter will focus on being able to conceive your own children.

YOUR OWN CHILDREN

If you want to be parents—and most couples do—then you have to ask yourself what type of children do you want and how are you going to produce them. Like so many of the decisions discussed in this book, you want to avoid the Experience Trap. Producing the types of children that will increase your welfare has become more difficult than in the past for two reasons. First, you probably have higher expectations of what you want to accomplish as parents than prior generations. Throughout most of history, parents often invested less time and effort in raising their children and, therefore, they were less concerned with their children's accomplishments. As recently as the eighteenth century, the chances were that one in three children would die in the first year of life and only one in every two would reach the age of twenty-one.[5] Because of the high infant mortality rate, parents tended to be indifferent toward their children.[6] As the children grew up, most families could not afford to support unproductive children, so children had to be productive within the family or find employment elsewhere. By ages fifteen to nineteen, three quarters of children had already left the home with the boys finding employment and the girls marrying.

Now, it is highly likely that your children will outlive you, so you will experience them throughout your lives. Their being able to increase your family's production is no longer the reason for having them, so you should be concerned about the other reasons. For most people, the reason that they have children is the enjoyment that they expect from them so that places pressure on parents to become more involved in their children's lives.

Second, the process for producing the kind of children that you probably want has become more complicated as illustrated by the discussion so far in this book. Instincts and society provide less guidance for how to raise children. For much of history, the parents worked near their home permitting regular interaction with their children. Even with the industrial revolution, a parent—usually the mother—continued to work in the home interacting with the children. Now parents have less time to devote to parenting which reduces their interaction with their children—and increases the interaction between their children and others. Your children have to address the issues presented in this book. They will have less guidance about marriage and parenting than people had in the past. Because of your other obligations, parents have to develop a more systematic parenting plan. However, little of our prior experience trains us to be parents.

Not only have individual children become more important in their parents' lives and the process of producing quality children has become more complicated, people now have to consider how many children they are going to have. In the past many people had large families, often approaching the maximum possible. It is helpful to consider why families are smaller today and why you will probably decide to have only a couple of children.

THE BENEFITS AND COSTS OF CHILDREN

The number of children that people have is a result of the inevitable interaction of benefits and costs, with people having children so long as the incremental benefits exceed the incremental costs. The benefits and costs of having children have changed. In the past, the primary benefits of children were the labor that they supplied to the family enterprise and old age support for their parents. The costs were the food, clothing and shelter associated with supporting them. Little time was devoted by the parents specifically to childcare. This is no longer the case. The benefits have become psychological rather than financial and the costs have expanded to include parental time and educational expenses.

THE BENEFITS OF PARENTHOOD

Most of us no longer expect our children to increase the family's production. This may have reduced the perceived benefits of being parents or at least of having large families. Now it is more appropriate to describe children as a form of consumption because raising them uses resources that could be used to produce other commodities. People have them because of the enjoyment that they expect from them. With the ready availability of contraceptives and abortions, it can be assumed that the vast majority of children are the result of intentional acts of their parents. The recent reduction in the number of children in families also illustrates that people have substantial control over how many children they have.

Your children's experiences will become your experiences. Children are a shared commodity, so staying married is important so that you can both share the enjoyment from your children rather than interacting with them independently. The benefits that you place on having them will probably be influenced by diminishing returns—their value falls as you have more. Let me remind you that this does not mean that you value subsequent children less—I was the middle one of three—so much as you value the ones that you did not have less than they would have cost.

THE COSTS OF PARENTHOOD

The costs of children are the sacrifices that you have to make on their behalf. These costs have increased over the last century due to the improvement in the earnings and employment opportunities of women and the expansion in educational expectations. When women had limited opportunities outside the home, the opportunity cost of their time devoted to domestic work including childcare was low. I am not saying that their work was not valuable but instead that it did not impose a large cost on the family due to foregone income. Now, the opportunity cost of either parent limiting a career to work in the home has become a concern for parents. Still, parenthood usually requires at least one parent to alter his or her career with a reduction in the family's income or an increase in inconvenience and expenditures to accommodate daycare. In addition, the education of your children has become more important for their success and in some cases that education has become very expensive. For the 2004–2005 academic year, the average cost of undergraduate tuition, fees, and room and board was $11,441 at a public four-year institution and $26,489 at a private one.[7]

When considering the financial cost of children, there are good news and bad news. It is always good to start with the good news and those are that there are economies of scale in raising children. As you have more children, their incremental cost tends to fall. According to the United States Department of Agriculture, a second child is only 81 percent as expensive as your first one and additional children are 77 percent of the cost of that first child.[8] Regrettably, the bad news is that it will cost a middle-income family over $250,000 to raise a child born in 2005 to age 17. This estimate is based on actual expenditures by families, so by spending your money wisely you can reduce the cost of your children.

This financial figure is a conservative estimate of the cost of a child because it ignored three additional costs that most couples incur due to being parents. First is the reduced income if the parents alter their careers to provide childcare, especially if the income loss is more than the daycare expense saved. Second are the costs incurred after age seventeen, predominantly higher education. Last is the cost of the time that has to be devoted to raising your children even if you have not altered your careers. The key conclusion is that children are expensive.

Couples obviously do not calculate these benefits and costs, but our experience confirms that they are aware of them and especially the fact that for some people the benefits of children have fallen and the costs have increased. The result has been fewer children for most couples. In the past most couples who could have children had them and they often had many of them. As recently as the eighteenth century, women conceived between ten to twenty times in their fertile years.[9] In response to these changes in the benefits and costs of children, people are now having fewer—and in some cases no—children. Between 1976 and 2004, the percentage of women at the end of their fertile years—forty to forty-four years old—who never had a child increased from 10 to 19.[10] Over the same period, the percentage of those women who had five or more children fell from 20 to three. Most relevant to us here is that among married couples in 2004, 19 percent did not have any children. Still, after weighing the benefits and costs of parenthood, a large percentage of married couples continue to have children.

How Many Children Do You Want?

A number of factors will determine the number of children that you have. Initially, let's consider why you might decide to have none. This will occur if you perceive the benefits to be small and the costs high. Since the benefits now are based on the psychological enjoyment that you expect from them, that estimate is up to you. The costs will be high if children conflict with other highly valued activities. If both of you have expensive tastes and high-income jobs, then you may prefer to produce money-intensive commodities rather than to have children. Alternatively, you may enjoy time-intensive commodities such as outdoor activities with which children would conflict. If you decide to have no children you should be prepared for criticism by others who view having no children as selfish.[11] Of course, you should understand that is not a valid criticism as most decisions are based on self-interest. Self-interest is only bad when there is an inadequate consideration of others. You have no obligation to your parents, friends or society to have children. If you do not think that children will increase your welfare—don't have them.

Since most people want children, we need to consider the number that they have. Among women who reached the end of their childbearing years in 2004, the most common number of children was two with those having three being just slightly more numerous than those having one.[12] You need to weigh children incrementally. Having the first one suggests that you viewed the benefits of that child to exceed the costs. What about one more? To provide a playmate for the first child or to cover your bet on children in general—diversify your portfolio—there may not be much of a change in the incremental benefits of children and the incremental cost may actually decrease. Therefore, many couples decide to have a second child.

Then things start to change. The novelty and miracle of being parents may start to lose its value. Also your time is starting to have the reverse effect of diminishing returns. Normally, we have observed that the incremental value of something tends to fall as we have more of it. Well, the reverse is also true. As you have less of something, its incremental value tends to increase. With additional children, the period of your life that will remain after your children become independent is getting smaller and, therefore, its value is increasing. You may look forward to camping with your children, but you are also considering vacations together in Hawaii after the children have left. That third child is going to restrict even more of that "open nest" period. Weighing the benefits and costs, many couples elect to stop at two and of those who continue to have children most stop at three.[13] The decisions about how many children that you are going to have will not be done at one time and will extend over the early years of your marriage. But, even with the first child, you have to address how you are going to produce the type of children that you desire.

Producing Welfare-Enhancing Children

In contrast to markets in which the consumers and producers are separate parties, we have become familiar with the idea that family members produce commodities for their own consumption. Just as we emphasized that your career is not an end itself, the same can be said about your children. You should not have children for some vague, undefined reason. Your children should be part of your attempt to increase your welfare. You have children because of their effect on your welfare. It is probably easier to define what you want than to describe how to obtain it. Having happy, well-adjusted children seems like a reasonable general goal, but you may have other aspirations for your children.

If those goals seem reasonable to you, the next question is, How are you going to produce children capable of obtaining those goals? Just as your goal for your pizzeria is to produce the type of pizza that attracts a large clientele, one of the goals for most couples is to produce welfare-enhancing children. Just like with your pizzeria, it is important to think in terms of production. Success in any endeavor does not just occur. It takes planning and effort to produce a quality product.

The first important step in this production process is to recognize that it will be easier and probably more successful if you stay married to each other. Child rearing is easier for married couples because children, especially when they are infants, require a substantial time commitment. By sharing these responsibilities, the burden on each parent is reduced. Staying together is also important for your success as parents. Being raised by their biological parents is a far greater indicator for children's success than any other arrangement. Children who grow up with only one biological parent are worse off on average than children who grow up with both of their biological parents.[14] Growing up with both parents is more likely to help children avoid experiencing a wide range of cognitive, emotional and social problems not only during childhood but also when they become adults.[15] The poor quality of outcomes of children if they grow up with a single parent does not improve if that parent remarries.[16] Children who have been exposed to living in a stepfamily have elevated risks of a range of psychosocial outcomes by age eighteen. Therefore, fundamental to the production of the type of children that you probably want is critically evaluating your marriage to assure yourselves of its durability before you become parents.

The next consideration with regard to your production process is your roles in this process. Comparative advantage should influence the roles of parents and potentially outside providers. Is there a lower cost provider of the services that these children are going to require? This could be a parent, a relative or a daycare provider. Each source has benefits—the service provided—and a cost—what is given up to provide the service. While the quality of service may be a concern of any provider, the cost is often a driving force. The cost for a parent is primarily the lost income, while for an outside provider it is the price and potentially the inconvenience. When considering a parent providing childcare, the criteria should be the net gain from employment—which in this case is a cost—in contrast to the net gain from domestic activities including childcare—which is a benefit. There is always the constraint of having to earn or have saved an amount to cover necessities. But, with those expenses covered, the preferred parent is the one with the highest benefit to cost ratio. This will often be the secondary income earner described in the prior chapter. Still, it is hard to escape that there are sacrifices associated with parenthood and one of them may be a reduction in the family's income.

Comparative advantage may suggest that you buy some childcare services from others. When weighing the benefits and costs of daycare, you now have to also consider those of the parents as well as the children. When considering daycare, the cost of it being provided by a parent is not that person's gross or net income, but the income after taxes and job-related expenses including childcare. When a child is an infant, many couples conclude that the benefits of a parent providing childcare are very high relative to the costs. At least one parent can find the challenges at that time very rewarding and the consensus is that this is an important time for a quality interaction between the child and others. Many parents feel that they are in the best position to provide that interaction. Over time, the parents may conclude that the benefits of parental-supplied childcare for both the provider and the child will tend to decline. It may become less rewarding for the parent and the child will have already received most of the important stimulation and attachment. Meanwhile, the costs of parental childcare may increase as that provider starts to lose access to employment opportunities. As the benefits fall and the costs increase, the couple may eventually decide that the family is better off using an outside source for daycare. Still, daycare can be very expensive and inconvenient. Also, daycare costs vary across the United States with it being more expensive in the cities than in rural areas.[17]

When considering parenthood, it is important to avoid the Unilateral Divorce Trap. You fall into this trap when you place too much emphasis on maintaining your career over the best interests of your family. Even if you avoided altering your career until you became a parent, at least one of you then is going to probably have to make an adjustment for the best interests of the family. The parents may have to subordinate their personal preferences for those choices that will be in the best interest of the family. You are most likely to avoid the Unilateral Divorce Trap if you are comfortable that your marriage is going to last.

PARENTING

It is important to understand that the development of quality children does not just occur. Most children, especially when they are young, benefit from a major commitment of their parents' time that usually requires at least one parent to modify a career. The evidence from psychologists would suggest that the interaction with caregivers is extremely important for the development of young children.[18] These caregivers do not necessarily have to be parents, but others are less likely to provide the quality of interaction provided by a parent. Infants respond to a variety of stimulations in the development of their body, the mind, the person, and the brain.

Here we have another example of the Experience Trap as this stimulation in the past often occurred without a plan when at least one parent was in close proximity to an infant doing normal domestic activities. With attractive employment opportunities for both parents outside the home, a conscientious effort has to be made to make the choices that result in someone providing this stimulation. This is a critical time and you may not be able to buy your way out of this obligation. As Ross Thompson, a noted researcher on early childhood development, states, "Sensitive parenting—not educational toys or Mozart CDs—provides the essential catalysts for early intellectual growth."[19]

Now parents have less time to devote to child rearing and yet the world that their children have to face is much more complicated. You want to help your children minimize their exposure to the Experience Trap that may have frustrated you. Professionals suggest that the three most important areas in which parents need to help their children develop skills are with regard to discipline, education and finances.[20]

DISCIPLINE

Developing discipline is important because children are inherently impulsive and yet good decision making requires contemplative choices. Discipline can be defined as a process to help people learn appropriate behaviors and make good choices. One of the most important ways to teach discipline is through the example of the parents' actions. By making decisions in a deliberate manner with a concern for social norms and laws, the parents convey to their children appropriate behavior. Often parents will be required to force their children to do things that the children would prefer not to do. You may always enjoy being a parent, but not always enjoy parenting.

Parents need to learn how to vary the discretion that they permit their children as they grow. The appropriate activities for an infant will be different from those of a teenager. Teaching your child discipline will have important long-term consequences as making the preferred educational and career choices requires the discipline of a longer-term perspective. People who have not developed the self-control associated with discipline are tempted to choose short-term gratification over longer-term objectives. It takes discipline to appreciate the value of education and moderation when dealing with the people with whom you work.

Learning discipline can be important for avoiding the Self-Interest and Emotions Traps. A sense of discipline causes people to be aware of their actions on others. People fall into the Self-Interest Trap when they do not have an adequate concern for the impact of their actions on others and how those other people will react. Many of the patterns of acceptable social behavior have developed to facilitate the interactions among people. Discipline can be important for gaining the ability to control our emotions. Discipline can help people make the types of instinctive decisions that are less likely to alienate others.

EDUCATION

Learning how to assist the education of your children is the second skill that you need to develop. We often forget that up until a century ago, parents were the primary source of education for their children. Now people tend to delegate to the public education system the responsibility for teaching their children all the normal academic subjects as well as sex education and values. Parents continue to have an important role as they are still the primary source for educating their children about values, while encouraging them to see the value in formal education.

Because students have to usually forego full-time employment to go to college, they may be tempted to seek employment if they see few benefits in higher education. Parents need to rebut arguments such as those by academics such as Paul Krugman who argue that college-educated workers are not sharing in the nation's recent prosperity.[21] Parents need to remind their children that there tends to be a high rate of return for most people from pursuing additional education. Parents usually have to address an additional problem facing their children which is the high cost of education. Between 1986/1987 and 2004/2005, the cost of tuition, fees, room and board at public universities increased by 176 percent and at private universities by 164 percent.[22] These increases were much more than prices in general, which increased by 72 percent over the same period.[23] While financial aid is available, students from middle-income families will often have to incur all of the costs of their education. Without the financial and moral support of their parents, they may be reluctant to go into debt for an education that promises vague benefits at some future date.

FINANCES

The last set of skills that parents need to develop for their children is an understanding of money and how it is earned and spent. Parents have already been forced to allocate their limited money and recognize the tradeoffs present in all transactions. Initially, children will not have the same knowledge. Developing a sense of financial discipline can be important for your children's welfare later.

After dropping his daughter off at college, Jonathan Clements, who writes a column on money management for the *Wall Street Journal*, wrote a column entitled, "Advice I'll Pass Along to My Daughter."[24] In that column, he made some suggestions about money management that parallel comments made in this book. Some of his suggestions are made for the benefit of his daughter as a consumer. Being able to buy more things is less important than how you handle your money. Some people work hard to earn a living and then they use poor judgment when they spend their income. They buy sports club memberships and then seldom go there. The pay for HBO and never watch it. Forget about appearances when you are making decisions as your values are far more important than those of others. Whole Foods is a place to shop when you are rich. Start out shopping at Wal-Mart. The key to financial success is to spend less than you earn. Unless you are in a position—such as the last year of your medical residency—that you expect a dramatic increase in your income in the near future, it is probably poor judgment to spend more than your current income. Our sons do not listen to me, but I emphasize that beer is much cheaper at home than at a bar.

Other parts of his advice deal with how to manage your savings. He suggests that you become your own financial adviser to avoid fees that often have little value—and I would add: Put your retirement savings initially in indexed no-load mutual funds. Savings can be important for providing you with career options in the future. When it comes to your investments, it is best to invest for the long run rather than trading stocks frequently. Unless you have valuable sources of information, by trading frequently all you are doing is incurring trading expenses without necessarily increasing the value of your portfolio. Usually, the result is a decrease in the value of your portfolio. Last, know yourself and be humble when it comes to investing. In other words, do not take on more risk than you are willing to accept later. Do not invest in a friend's business and then regret that decision later. Just like Clements planned on passing on these thoughts to his daughter, you would be well advised to pass them on to your children.

CHILDREN AND MARITAL QUALITY

Before we leave our discussion of children, it may be important to consider their effect on marital quality. People marry because they are in love and most couples plan on being parents. A surprising result is that parenthood can be one of the most destructive influences on the success of a marriage. Researchers have noted that the transition to parenthood is one of the family's most difficult adjustments.[25] During this transition there is a dramatic decrease in positive marital interchanges, a dramatic increase in marital conflict, and a precipitous decline in marital satisfaction. These findings are particularly pronounced for wives.

Few couples can anticipate how challenging parenting will be. That is why it has been suggested that couples make sure that their marriage is durable before they become parents. Parenting is not likely to draw dissatisfied couples closer together. Because wives are the ones who are most likely to become dissatisfied with the marriage during this period, researchers have investigated the steps that husbands can take to reduce their wives' frustration.[26] It is most important for the fathers to show fondness for the mothers and to be aware of their relationship. The most destructive situations occur when spouses express disappointment with their marriage and their lives are chaotic. Some people have suggested that when couples find increased marital conflict at the time that they become parents that it may be a good time to become involved in parenting groups to observe the frustration of others.[27]

CONCLUSION

Children can be the ultimate accomplishment and frustration of marriage. You have to make decisions about how many you are going to have—if any at all—and how you will produce the quality that you desire. The number that you have will be influenced by how you view the benefits and costs associated with them. Parenting is going to be a challenge as there are so many demands on your time. Still, you are going to observe the accomplishments of your children during the rest of your life, so it is important to do a good job of parenting. It is constructive to view parenting as a production process. You take inputs of time, money and skills by both parents and their children to ultimately produce a person with important skills and abilities.

THINGS TO REMEMBER

- High-quality children do not just occur as they are produced.
- The primary inputs into this production process are your time, money and skills.
- A weighing of the benefits and costs of additional children will determine how many you have.
- The most important skills that you can pass on to your children are an appreciation for the importance of discipline, education, and financial responsibility.
- As important as children will probably be in your life you will have to be prepared to make adjustments to your relationship when you become parents.

The Bankrupt Marriage: Divorce

Not all marriages will continue to be viewed as a success, so at some point you may consider divorce. In contrast to the joint decision to marry, either of you can obtain a divorce even if one of you is opposed to it.[1] Considering a divorce is similar to the process that businesses go through when they are considering bankruptcy or dissolution. The costs associated with the business continuing exceed its benefits. Bankruptcy is a special case that occurs when a firm lacks sufficient capital to cover its obligations. In a similar fashion, you might consider a divorce if the costs of continuing the marriage appear to exceed the benefits.

It is important to read this chapter long before you ever consider a divorce. You should read it before you marry or at least when your marriage seems to be in great shape as it attempts to help you make the types of decisions that will not make divorce attractive. Much of the earlier chapters were about what you should do to make your marriage a success. The primary emphasis here is on what you should not do.

WHY DO SOME BUSINESSES AND MARRIAGES FAIL?

There are parallels between why businesses fail and why marriages end in divorce. Even though approximately 50 percent of marriages end in divorce,[2] it is a far more successful enterprise than most new small businesses.[3] Of course, not all businesses that fail end in bankruptcy, but any business failure has a financial and emotional toll on its owners. In both cases of divorce and business failure, the cause comes down to poor decisions. Some of those decisions could be improved with better information, while others are unfortunately poor because of unforeseen events.

While experts offer a variety of reasons why new small businesses fail, it usually comes down to a short list consisting of planning, money and management.[4] Problems associated with poor planning include a lack of experience and choosing the wrong location and business associates. When you start a new business, you will not have very much room for error. If you do not plan for some of your potential problems, you may not be in a position to avoid them. The next problem area is money if a new business starts with inadequate capital or does not spend what it has wisely. A particular problem exists when businesses have to rely on too much credit. Debt payments may result in fixed monthly obligations that are difficult to meet. Last is the management of employees, suppliers and customers. Alienating any of these groups will jeopardize the potential success of your business.

A marriage can fall victim to the same three problems.[5] Your planning should have consisted of choosing the type of person that you were going to marry and then considering the roles that you were going to assume during marriage. If you chose the wrong type of person or now discover that there is a conflict in the roles that you want to assume during marriage, then your marriage is going to be vulnerable. Conflicts over money—or the lack of it—is one of the primary reasons that marriages fail. Most young couples are working very hard and it is easy for them to conclude that they have a right to the material benefits of success. Not only do they commit their income to these purchases, but they can also commit their future income through debt. This expenditure pattern places constraints on their careers, leisure and other expenditures that can result in conflict and frustration later. The last concern is how you deal with other people, especially your spouse. One of the major causes of divorce is the poor quality of the interaction between the spouses.[6] They do not develop key communication and problem-solving skills. Rather than confronting problems, they ignore them or stonewall solving them. Poor communication often compounds other marital problems.[7]

THE IMPORTANCE OF AVOIDING FAILURE

While both divorce and bankruptcy may appear to be ways to escape undesirable situations, they have to be viewed as a last resort. People considering bankruptcy may view their current situation as so unattractive that any alternative is preferable. Still, they have made a significant investment of time and effort in their business that they would lose if they were to dissolve it. It took time to develop a customer base and find reliable suppliers. Moreover, a bankruptcy leaves individuals with a blemished credit record that can inhibit their ability to start another enterprise later. The bankruptcy process will also absorb time, energy and money that could have been used to help the business survive. So it is often worth considering creative ways to keep the business going.

For similar reasons you should attempt to avoid divorce. It can be easy to fall into another Experience Trap. It is easy to overestimate the positive attributes of the situation that you will be in after a divorce. Finding your spouse and then adjusting to each other required substantial time and effort. Going through that process again can be very costly. If you are divorced—especially if you have children—that is going to make it more difficult to establish a new relationship.[8] As you date new people, there can be the issue of why you failed in your past relationships that may make you less attractive to new partners. The logistics of parenthood also may make it difficult to meet and develop a relationship with others. Last, a divorce can be very costly as the legal process can be expensive, time consuming and emotionally draining. Do not view divorce as an easy solution to any frustration that you have with your marriage.

DISSOLVING A VIABLE ENTERPRISE

A discussion of divorce also benefits from a consideration of situations in which a business is not in financial difficulty but a partner no longer wants to be involved. The business has been a success—it is making a reasonable profit. However, a partner may conclude that the business is no longer viable or wants to pursue other activities such as a new business opportunity. Without an agreement to the contrary, just one partner can dissolve the partnership. Now that alone would not dissolve the business, but with the loss of the benefits of the partnership, such as specialization of labor, economies of scale and insurance, the other partner may not be able to continue to operate the business. One way to avoid this problem is by having a partnership agreement that commits both of you to this enterprise for a specific period.

A marriage has an interesting parallel to this potentially viable business except that you cannot draft a marital agreement prohibiting its dissolution by one party. With unilateral divorce, one spouse can conclude that a marriage is no longer the best long-term arrangement and so pursue a divorce. Just like the business may not be viable if one partner leaves, the marriage will certainly not survive the departure of a spouse. The dissolution of this marriage can occur even though at least one spouse feels that the marriage is a good, durable one.

THE DECISION TO DIVORCE

You have to carefully weigh the benefits and costs of this decision, only divorcing when the benefits exceed the costs. The decision to divorce can be a very emotional one and yet you do not want to fall into the Emotion Trap. One place to start this evaluation is to reflect on why your initial optimism about this marriage could be wrong. A common case of the Emotion Trap is when you have been caught up in the excitement of a wedding and are now taking a closer look at your marriage. This is not a time to compare your marriage to some idealized standard and then want to dissolve it because it fails to meet that standard.

THE ROLE OF INFORMATION

The decision to divorce can be the result of having had imperfect information at the time you married.[9] Given the information that you possessed prior to your wedding, you were convinced that your marriage was going to be a success; it was going to be a better relationship than any other that you could imagine. Your decision to marry was the result of a search process in which you married when you decided that the benefits of additional search did not warrant the additional cost. The benefits of course were to find someone better, while the costs would be those associated with finding that person.

The key question now is, why might you change your mind? There are two types of new information that influence that decision: what you could not have known and what was potentially available then but that you ignored. The first is unexpected events that you could not have anticipated such as either of you finding someone that you feel is superior to your current spouse or a change in your health or financial situation. Infidelity—or more broadly someone else—is one of the primary causes of divorce.[10] In addition, both of you assumed that you would have certain health and financial levels before marriage. Poor health or financial reversals can place pressure on a marriage.

The second type of information is that which may have been available at the time that you married, but you did not know it or ignored what you should have known. Better information at that time might have changed your decision to marry. The casual drinking that you observed during courtship turns out to be a major case of alcoholism later. With this "new" information, you might conclude that your initial enthusiasm was misguided.

Both for your current marriage and, if you decide to divorce, in any subsequent marriage, a key issue is why you chose to use the information that you used in choosing your spouse. Normally, it is not acceptable to place all the blame for the failure of your marriage on the other person. Certainly, there are cases in which people make fundamental changes in their behavior and preferences after marriage that no longer make it attractive to be married. However, with many marriages occurring when people are solidly into their twenties or older, this transformation would appear to be much less likely. So why do you no longer want to be married to this person that you initially loved? By asking that question you may be able to find reasons to work harder to make this marriage work. Alternatively, if there were flaws in your evaluation of this person prior to marriage, you should use that insight to improve your decision making in the future. Even though your spouse is not exactly the person that you thought, is your spouse really worse than realistic alternatives?

During the first few years of marriage couples accumulate more information about their spouse and if some of it conflicts with their prior evaluation, they may decide that they are better off dissolving the marriage. That is why many divorces occur in the first few years of marriage.[11] Alternatively, as the duration of marriage increases, the likelihood of divorce falls for two reasons: new information can confirm the initial information that made you optimistic about your marriage and you have invested in your marriage. Some of those investments will be the ones discussed in Chapter 5 as you made sacrifices to increase your family's welfare. Maintaining your marriage is important for gaining a return on that investment. The other investments can be more subtle as the two of you have adjusted to each other and those investments will not have very much value in any other relationships.

Because only one spouse has to make the decision to divorce, the following discussion is from the perspective of those who want to leave. For those spouses who do not want to divorce, the following discussion should assist them in making sure that this decision is made within an appropriate framework. Like all decisions, you will only want a divorce when you conclude that the benefits of divorce exceed the costs. Because of the Emotion Trap, it can be too easy to overestimate the benefits and underestimate the costs of divorce.

THE BENEFITS OF DIVORCE

The benefits consist of the alternative living arrangements that you envision. As you consider the benefits of divorce, you can also fall into the Experience Trap. While you have been single before, your return to that state may be complicated by a divorce. This transition is going to be particularly difficult if you are a parent. More than half of divorces involve children under the age of eighteen.[12] Just as you never had an experience similar to marriage before you were married, you probably also have never experienced being a single parent before—even if you do not have primary custody, you will still be a single parent. This will reduce the time and energy that you have for finding other arrangements. You may also be in a new situation even if you are not a parent. Having dated others is seldom detrimental to finding a spouse. However, having been married places you in a slightly different situation. You made a commitment to someone else and then concluded that that commitment was not a good idea. Will you make that mistake again? Being concerned about that possibility may deter others from wanting to make a commitment to you.

People frequently find the benefits that they expect from divorce are not realized. Numerous studies have shown that divorced individuals in contrast to married individuals tend to have lower levels of psychological well-being, more symptoms of psychological distress, and poorer self-concept.[13] This literature cautions whether these results are caused by a divorce or perhaps the individuals who divorce are predisposed to being less well adjusted. One study shows that two out of three married couples who were unhappy with their marriage but avoided divorce or separation ended up happily married five years later.[14] Of course, it is no surprise that the people who initiated a divorce are more likely to be happier after a divorce than spouses who did not want the divorce.[15] In either case, people often do not feel better off after a divorce and they probably do not feel that they are better off than they felt when they married.

THE COSTS OF DIVORCE

The costs consist of what you are giving up, the steps that you have to take to establish your new arrangements and the financial arrangements at divorce.[16] While the benefits of divorce are primarily psychological, the costs are much more tangible. An initial cost will be finding a new living arrangement and, if you continue to have the goal of a successful marriage, the challenge is to find an acceptable person. An ongoing cost of divorce is the reduction in the specialization of labor, economies of scale, and insurance that existed during marriage. The most obvious problem is that the two of you are going to have to pay for two residences. Researchers have found that both fathers' and mothers' incomes plus or minus any court awards fell after divorce with the income of the mothers falling substantially more than that of the fathers.[17] After adjustment for family size, they conclude that the fathers' incomes decreased by 15 percent even three years after the divorce, while the mothers' incomes fell by 35 percent. This was frequently due to support payments being a small percentage of the mothers' post-divorce income.

A special concern has to be the effect of the divorce on any children. A divorce can be very costly for the children involved. This book has not placed much importance on altruism as a primary source of motivation for people. The exception to this exclusion is the bond between parents—especially mothers—and their children. While being concerned about your children's welfare, you may attempt to rationalize that they will be better off due to the divorce. That may be true if you made a poor choice of a spouse, but it is more likely that the divorce will have an adverse effect on their welfare. Children from divorced families have poor outcomes in a variety of areas including academic achievement, conduct, psychological adjustment, self-concept, and social competence.[18] Not only is the quality of their lives diminished, so is your interaction with them. While sharing them with the other parent, both of you will see less of them than if you were continuing to live together.

A last consideration about the costs of divorce is the resources that have to be used to obtain it. The most obvious of these is the financial outlays required and they can be considerable. A truly uncontested divorce that requires very little time with a lawyer can be obtained for as low as $200 plus the filing fees.[19] However, the costs can increase rapidly if there are continuous issues such as custody and property allocation. Then the costs can run as high as hundreds of thousands of dollars.[20] In addition to these financial outlays, there will be the time and emotional costs. In other words, do not anticipate that it will be a quick, low-cost process.

As an economist, I do not expect people who are thinking about a divorce to adequately consider the costs of it to others. Still, it may be difficult to avoid some of those costs. If you are a normal person, it may be hard to escape observing the welfare loss to your children and your interaction with them. For a variety of reasons, only one of which is children, it may be difficult to avoid an interaction with your ex-spouse—someone about whom you cared deeply at one point. If your spouse is less happy than would have been the case had you remained married, you may be forced to recognize the cost of the divorce to your ex.

As we conclude our discussion of the costs and benefits of divorce, please be aware that divorces often occur in low-conflict marriages.[21] Many people find after a divorce that they made the wrong decision in not working harder to make their marriage work. In other words, they continue to fall into traps by overestimating the benefits and underestimating the costs of divorce. Are there things that you can do to salvage your marriage? This chapter exposed you to the benefits and costs of divorce, encouraging you to work harder to make the decisions that will increase the likelihood that your marriage will be a success.

THE ROLE OF UNILATERAL DIVORCE

While both of you had to agree to marry, your marriage can be dissolved unilaterally by either of you because of no-fault divorce. The result can be divorces that reduce social welfare—the costs to all affected parties exceed the benefits. This can occur because the people making the decision are probably only relying on the costs and benefits to themselves—the Self-Interest Trap. Being aware of the perverse incentives created by unilateral divorce can help you avoid making the mistakes that increase the likelihood that either of you will seriously consider divorce.

During marriage and when considering divorce, you have to consider the subtle, but perverse, incentives created by unilateral, no-fault divorce. While the current divorce laws are often presented as no-fault, the more appropriate adjectives—as noted so often in this book—should be easy and unilateral. That being the case, it makes it easy to dissolve your marriage when you are not happy with it. Seldom—ok, never—will a marriage continue to be as perfect as it was on your wedding day. There will be good times and bad times and often those periods will not be brief. During the down periods, it is important to keep your focus on your ultimate goal of a successful marriage. Unilateral divorce makes it too easy for one person to conclude that the solution to a marriage that is less than satisfactory is to end it. You may know that you are currently unhappy in this marriage and it may be easy to see the future through rose-colored glasses, concluding that there are more attractive alternatives out there.

Unilateral divorce has a number of subtle influences that increase the probability of divorce. You may need to take steps to neutralize those influences. Even when deciding to marry, the prospect of an easy divorce may discourage you from making as strong a commitment to your marriage or to evaluate your prospective spouse as carefully as you should. This could leave your marriage vulnerable to future events.

After you marry, unilateral divorce may reduce the incentives for you to invest in your marriage. The Unilateral Divorce and Self-Interest Traps are inter-related here. Given the vulnerability of marriage, people have an incentive to continue to give their narrowly defined self-interest a priority. The most obvious example is when both spouses emphasize their careers to the detriment of their parenting and domestic activities. People are most likely to view a consideration of the best interests of all family members as being in their self-interest, if they view their marriage as a solid long-term commitment by both spouses. To the extent that they question this commitment—especially by their spouse—they will reduce their focus on their family's welfare.[22] The likelihood of divorce increases.

An important reason to guard against these influences is that divorces under unilateral divorce are often inefficient. Because people who want a divorce will often only consider their costs and benefits, divorces can be inefficient because the costs to all affected parties exceed the benefits. In other words, the perceived benefits to the spouse initiating it are less than the cost to the other spouse and the children. In a perfect world, if the costs of a decision to one group are more than the benefits to another, the losers should be able to seek compensation, which might change the initial decision. Consider a numerical example. Burning leaves—for which you have a legal right—is worth $10 to you, while it imposes a cost of $20 on me. Therefore, by my paying you $15 to not burn your leaves, we are both better off by $5. So when negotiations are easy and both parties have a common frame of reference—money in our example—they should be able to negotiate the outcome that maximizes their collective welfares.

This process does not work when considering divorce for the simple reason that couples are not negotiating using a common frame of reference. The wife may want out of the marriage because of the poor communication skills of the husband. Meanwhile, he is incapable of making that change, but he still loves her and is willing to offer her a larger share of the family income if she stays. Although there may be a net loss for all parties from the divorce—the benefits to her are less than the costs to him, the husband cannot induce his wife to stay.

Because a divorce under unilateral divorce can be inefficient, it is important to take steps to minimize the likelihood that it will occur. An important strategy to reduce the potential adverse effects of unilateral divorce is evaluation in the early stages to avoid self-centered decisions that can threaten your marriage. Is your spouse still the person that you wanted to marry? If so, are there decisions that either of you are making that are straining the marriage? Is your spouse complaining about working long hours, while you see few benefits now or later from her commitment to that job? Did your spouse decide that a long-distance commuting marriage was what he wanted when you got the attractive offer to move to your new and distant position? If you want to make your marriage work, then you need to address whether both of your decisions are focused on increasing your family's welfare rather than giving too much emphasis to your narrowly defined self-interest.

This early evaluation is important to avoid future problems, but also because the potential costs of divorce to you increase with the duration of the marriage as spouses make career adjustments or couples become parents. Early in marriage, if you have the careers that you had before marriage and no children, a divorce can be emotionally draining, but there are few long-term costs. That situation changes over time. You give up an attractive position to relocate with your spouse. Someone has to devote time to raising your children. Then, divorce becomes much more costly for everyone involved. It may be worthwhile to use anniversaries to celebrate your success, but also potentially to evaluate your marriage. It is like a business having an annual meeting and considering its future.

So You Are Going To Do It

If you have gotten to the point that you have concluded the benefits of a divorce exceed the costs, you will want to move ahead. The key here is to obtain your divorce in the least costly manner. An uncontested divorce can be obtained in many jurisdictions for only slightly more than the filing fees. Essentially, any money that you pay above that amount is potentially a waste of resources. One of you may not be happy with the prospect of a divorce, but both of you should be aware that any funds spent on the divorce are funds that will not be available later. This is not the time for revenge. If it is possible for the two of you to interact in a civil manner, then the more planning that you do without an attorney the better you will be.

There are a number of specific steps that you can take to reduce your expenditures. A first step is to educate yourself about the law in your state. Often there are web sites that provide basic information about the process.[23] It is important to avoid litigation at all costs as it is very time intensive and, therefore, very expensive. You should make a list of all the things about which you agree such as how to deal with pension plans and custody of any children. You also should not sign up with an attorney at a particular hourly rate without putting limits on how much the lawyer can charge you. There may be the need to do a cost-benefit analysis of the issues being addressed. It is not worth $2,000 in legal fees to attempt to get a $1,000 television set as part of the property settlement. When considering custody, remember that children do much better under joint physical custody rather than sole custody by either the mother or father.[24]

CONCLUSION

If you did the things suggested in the early chapters, it is less likely that you will even consider divorce—but you may. Even if it enters your mind, think long and hard as the costs of divorce are substantial. Divorce can be viewed as an easy—although not pleasant—decision when you find yourself in a situation similar to a company considering bankruptcy. The costs of continuing appear to exceed the benefits. New information causes you to conclude that you are better off in another arrangement. However, research has shown that people often use divorce to escape from a temporary reduction in the quality of their marriage. Later, they are no better off—and often worse off—than they would have been if they had stayed in their marriage. People who want to avoid divorce often have to overcome the perverse incentives created by unilateral divorce. If a divorce becomes inevitable, then it is important to approach it as a business proposition, attempting to minimize its costs.

THINGS TO REMEMBER

- Divorce is like bankruptcy when the benefits of continuing the enterprise no longer exceed the costs.
- Because of unilateral divorce, it can occur when the costs to all affected parties exceed the benefits.
- The likelihood of divorce is reduced when you discuss key decisions to make sure that spouses recognize the effect of their decisions on other family members.
- It is important to avoid the Emotion Trap and critically evaluate both the costs and benefits of divorce.
- If you decide to divorce, then it is important to limit the cost.

Merging Families: Remarriage

So you want to try again? Since a successful marriage is such an important goal for most people, those who divorce usually want to remarry. In 2001, of the people over age twenty-five who have ever divorced, 55 percent of men and 44 percent of women were currently remarried.[1] If creating a Smart Marriage was difficult before for these people, it has now become much more complicated. If you become one of these people, then it is essential for you to explore why your earlier marriage failed. Into which of the Traps did you fall and how are you going to avoid them in the future? There are new challenges in a subsequent marriage due to ex-spouses and children of prior relationships that can make it difficult to make the best decisions.[2]

CHALLENGES

Let's consider the challenges that you face. Remarriage by at least one spouse has become much more common. Almost half of marriages consist of at least one person who was married before.[3] However, second marriages tend to be less successful than first ones. The probability that a second marriage will be disrupted by separation or divorce within the first ten years is higher for remarriages than for first marriages.[4] In addition to the usual complications associated with careers and recreational preferences, subsequent marriages are complicated by the presence of ex-spouses and children from prior relationships. A marriage disruption is much more likely for women who remarry with children than those who have none at that time.[5]

Children can be a source of conflict for a variety of reasons, especially if the remarried couple eventually has children of their own. Approximately half of women who remarry while in their childbearing years give birth to a child in that marriage and a majority of these births occur within the first two years of the second marriage.[6] While these couples may feel that having a child is an important confirmation of their relationship, it tends to increase the stress in that relationship. There are not only the childcare obligations, but there can be financial strains due to the new limits on the mothers' employment.[7] Often because of children, remarried spouses are observed to more openly express criticism, anger, and irritation than do spouses in first marriages. These disagreements generally focus on issues related to stepchildren such as discipline, rules for children, and the distribution of resources to children.[8]

If you are a parent, you are undoubtedly concerned about your children's welfare. Living with a stepparent is often not a good situation for children. Stepchildren do not function as well in school as children living with both parents based on grades earned in school and scores on achievement tests.[9] Moreover, compared with children in first marriage families, stepchildren show more behavioral problems and are more at risk for having emotional problems.

This data is not meant to impress on you that you are doomed to failure, so much as to confront you with the challenges ahead. You are going to have to work harder to make the best decisions. Start off by reviewing your first marriage. What went wrong and how can you improve your decision making? Then you need to look ahead. You should review the materials in prior chapters on the type of person that you should consider, on how you can find that person and convince that person to marry you, and then how the two of you should interact during marriage. A special concern now has to be to make sure that the preferred investments are made in your children. Stepparents do not have the same incentives to invest in stepchildren as do their biological parents, so biological parents are going to have to be especially attentive to the needs of their children.

You are heading into uncharted territory. Even if you can identify the mistakes that you made in your first marriage by choosing the wrong person or making the wrong decisions during it, a remarriage presents new challenges. How can you escape the Traps? A particular concern as it has often been in the past is the Experience Trap. Blended families that occur with a remarriage are probably different from your past experiences. A valuable source of guidance for a successful remarriage is available in the literature on successful business mergers. Remarriage is similar to a merger between two existing firms with all the associated assimilation problems.

A SUCCESSFUL BUSINESS MERGER

Creating a successful business merger is not an easy task. The vast majority of mergers are unsuccessful as judged by their ability to benefit the owners—usually shareholders. A recent study by the global accounting and consulting firm, KPMG, concluded that 83 percent of mergers were unsuccessful in producing any benefits for the shareholders, who are most interested in the effect of the merger on the price of the company's stock.[10] If so many mergers fail, what are the characteristics of those that succeed? A number of studies have identified the factors that are associated with success.[11] One way to look at successful mergers is by dividing these factors into Hard Keys that affected the production side of the merged business and Soft Keys that reflected the personal and cultural side of the mergers.

THE HARD KEYS

There were three Hard Keys: synergy evaluation, integration of project planning and due diligence. Synergy occurs when two enterprises are more profitable together rather than apart. This can occur because its revenues increase more than its costs—or alternatively its revenues fall less than any reduction in costs. For a merger to be a success there must be opportunities for synergies, and the management of the combined company must be able to implement practices that capture them. Some mergers may be considered that do not encompass any synergy, but there is the hope of increasing the combined firm's market power. That additional power may be difficult to establish and would certainly be frowned upon by the antitrust authorities. Therefore, most successful mergers look for opportunities for synergy between the components of the merger. The integration of project planning within the combined firm is essential for capturing the available opportunities for synergy. Last is the need for due diligence. This diligence can include market reviews, risk assessments, and an assessment of management competencies. Many of the failed mergers can be traced to not having adequately investigated the existing state of the companies. All of the Hard Keys are inter-related as this due diligence should also consider the opportunities for synergies and the ability to capture them.

SOFT KEYS

The Soft Keys consist of selecting the management team, resolving cultural issues, and communications. It is important to quickly establish the management team that is going to implement the changes necessary to integrate the two businesses. These individuals can come from both businesses, although more will come from the acquiring company if a motive for the merger is the perception of poor management in the acquired company, for example. To the extent possible, it is helpful to use at least some managers from both organizations, so the acquired company's employees feel that they have a say in any reorganization. A common problem in mergers is integrating people from different corporate cultures. Some businesses emphasize a collegial and structured atmosphere, while others can be individualistic and informal. It would appear that a company increases its chances of success if it uses reward systems, such as compensation, to stimulate cultural integration rather than to rely on more informal methods. The last of the Soft Keys is communication. Mergers can create anxiety among employees as a common method for realizing synergy is to reduce the work force. It is important to communicate the merged company's plan to its employees and keep them informed as the process progresses. Faced with uncertainty, some of the more marketable of the acquired company's employees may be tempted to leave. Increased clarity may keep them on board. In KPMG's survey, just nine companies addressed all three soft keys and carried out an integration of project planning.[12] All nine were successful in increasing the value of the company's stock.

PLANNING YOUR MERGER

These insights from businesses provide a framework for making your remarriage a success. Let's consider them in order. Many of them are essentially the issues that you should have addressed in your first marriage.

SYNERGY

Synergy is important for all marriages as it is a process by which people working together increase their ability to produce commodities. They are better off together than apart. This usually occurs because of specialization of labor and economies of scale, for example. Starting a first marriage, you can often initially ignore synergy—although it will eventually become important for your marital success. That is usually not going to be the case with a second marriage. Second marriages potentially have more challenges than first marriages, so it is even more important to consider how you are going to produce the commodities that leave both spouses feeling better off in your marriage than in any other relationship. This is going to require you to assume roles different from when you were single and often different from the ones that you assumed in a prior marriage. If both of you want to continue to emphasize your careers or work in the home, you will have less synergy than if each of you has different preferences for the type of work that you want to emphasize.

YOUR INTEGRATION PLAN

The potential for synergy is not enough. You need a plan for using its potential to increase your welfare. Often that plan in a second marriage will focus on children. If you already have them, how are you going to accommodate childcare? Their ages will influence the distribution of responsibilities between parents and daycare providers with the importance of the latter increasing with age. If you do not have children, you have to address the usual questions of how many children to have, and when to have them. There are still the usual issues of how you are going to produce the commodities that will increase your welfare. Since some of those commodities are often time intensive—even without children—someone has to produce them. How are both of you going to balance your careers and work in the home? These issues should be addressed in your integration plan.

DUE DILIGENCE

Due diligence and the collection of relevant information is important for making essentially all decisions. The collection of information is especially important when considering marriage to someone who is divorced. Too often divorce is associated with bad luck. It has been suggested here that bad luck is often associated with poor decision making. It is hard to escape that someone who is divorced made some poor decisions either about the person they chose to marry or the actions they took after marriage. You have probably failed due diligence if you accept their position that they were victimized by their prior spouse. You have to dig deeper and ask more questions. Alternatively, do the responses suggest that similar conflicts will occur in your relationship? If the complaint is that his spouse was too committed to a job, that could be a problem if you are committed to yours. In that case, you should be looking for someone who is willing to accommodate your career.

The financial situation of your spouse is also a consideration for due diligence. Since you are now older than when you married for the first time, you are more likely to encounter people with more assets—and potentially more liabilities. While it might be a pleasant surprise to find out that someone you love and who loves you has more wealth than you anticipated, you do not want to be surprised about outstanding debts.

THE MANAGEMENT TEAM

You are right—you and your spouse are the management team. With all of your responsibilities, it is important for you to assign them. What are the commodities that will increase your family's welfare and how are you going to produce them? The clearer your responsibilities are, the less likely there is going to be conflicts. With the complexity created by children, you may have to make many more adjustments than when you married the first time. In addition to the allocation of your incomes and who is going to cook dinner, you have to determine how you are going to interact with your children.

Because of blended families, you may have a variety of new responsibilities. How are you going to make sure that all the children are being treated equally? What is an acceptable custody arrangement for any children? How are you going to deal with your ex-spouse(s)? The management of your relationship has to address these issues and they probably need to be addressed early in the new relationship. Often they need to be addressed even before the wedding.

CULTURAL ISSUES

Not a lot has changed here since your first marriage. You and your spouse have to be compatible, and fundamental to that are similar cultural values. Culture is a broad concern including specific preferences such as religion, but also numerous personal traits such as cleanliness and punctuality. Similar cultures are important in business mergers and they are equally important in marriage. Physical attraction cannot often overcome differences in fundamental values. If conflicting values were a problem in your first marriage, it should not be one in your second.

COMMUNICATION

Clear communication is an essential component of success in all phases of life. We can see its importance in successful business mergers, and in earlier chapters we saw its importance in making families function more smoothly. All marriages start with people who love each other and want to make their marriage a success. Since many divorces occur in marriages in which there is very little conflict, one has to wonder what went wrong. One of the central problems is a lack of clear communication. Without clear communication, it is easy to distort each other's actions. Decisions that are perceived to be selfish can cause a selfish response. The situation can deteriorate from there unless the couple reaches an understanding of their motives. This communication has to start before a wedding as you are confronting the challenges of remarriage.

MANAGING MERGED FAMILIES

Now that you have merged your families, you are confronted with the need to manage this more complex organization. Most of the decisions about the roles that the two of you will assume in the production of your family's commodities have not changed from those concerns in your first marriage. However, decisions about children and money have potentially become more complex. In many cases, you will not have the opportunity to gradually adapt to each other and eventually to parenthood. Parenthood is often already part of your life. Not only will you have to adapt to each other but you may also have to adjust to each other's children. Income is potentially coming from more sources and expenditures are going out to more.

CHILDREN

It is important that all children within the family are treated equally. Because of child support, there may be different amounts of money attributable to each child. However, that should not influence how much is spent on each one. It is instinctive to be more concerned about your own children than those of others such as those of your new spouse. You need to recognize when you are acting in a biased fashion. There will inevitably be conflicts between the children that you are asked to mediate. Treating your children different from those of your spouse is likely to lead to conflicts between the two of you. A concern about communication between parents and children is especially important because families often have so little time together. Dinner can provide a good opportunity to discuss family concerns.

Managing Money

The effective management of money is critical for marital success and that is especially true in a subsequent marriage. I think that it is important for you to start off having a joint checking account. Marriage is a team effort and separate checking accounts detract from that emphasis. More-over, separate checking accounts place too much emphasis on the income-earning capacities of the spouses and their other sources of income such as child support. If you did not believe that you were receiving equivalent value from marrying your spouse, you should not have married. You brought different attributes to your marriage of which income earning is only one. Although you have a joint account, it is probably wise to have only one person writing checks against it. Meanwhile, it would be reasona-ble to have separate credit cards with an understanding of how much each of you should spend during any period of time. This will probably not be equal because of different expenditure patterns and obligations. One career may require more meals and travel expenses, for example.

With a remarriage, especially when there are children involved, it is prob-ably going to be important to discuss the variety of income and expendi-ture flows that are occurring. There can be child support either coming in or going out.[13] When the non-custodial parents are not living up to their obligations that can create friction between custodial parents and their new spouse. The potential financial obligations that the new spouse is going to incur should be discussed before marriage.

Eventually, there may be concerns about paying for post-secondary educa-tion. While many states have laws that give courts the authority to order a non-custodial parent to pay for a college education, there is still the problem of collecting it. Even if the custodial parent assumes a significant responsibil-ity for these expenses, the funds are coming from those that normally would be available to the family. Conflict can arise when a stepfather feels that he is being asked to sacrifice to pay for the education of a stepchild because that child's father is unwilling to make an adequate contribution.[14]

Prenuptial Agreement

With remarriage, a prenuptial agreement may become much more important than it was prior to a first marriage. This agreement can address the allocation of preexisting assets and liabilities as well as considering issues affecting any children. The commingling of preexisting assets and liabilities with those acquired after marriage can convert them into marital assets and liabilities. Therefore, you will probably want to be specific about preexisting assets and liabilities. While I think that it is important to have a joint checking account, it would probably be wise to place preexisting assets in a separate account so that there is no confusion about their origin. It would also be wise to have a plan for eliminating some of any preexiting liabilities, since any future payments would probably have to come from those that otherwise would be available to the family for other purposes.

This recognition of preexisting assets can also be important for protecting the children of the earlier marriage, especially at your death. In a premarital agreement, one spouse can give up the right to claim a share of the other's property at death in exchange for an agreed amount of property.[15]

A prenuptial agreement can be used to recognize and provide compensation for potential sacrifices of the spouses. The sacrifices that marriage may require will probably be much more visible in a subsequent marriage than they were prior to a first marriage. Who is going to limit a career to provide childcare? If one spouse is particularly financially successful, the couple may decide that they are better off with the other spouse limiting a career even if there are no children. The spouses may be living in different locations, so the marriage may require one of them to relocate. Often, the adjustments due to marriage will be substantial. However, having been exposed to a failed marriage before and the associated costs might encourage the couple to be more specific about any compensation—especially to a spouse who is limiting a career—if the marriage is dissolved.

By this point you should not be alienated by the use of a business perspective on marriage, but some people may still view marriage as too romantic and emotional to permit a prenuptial agreement. Businesses frequently draft contracts not with the intention of using them for litigation so much as to force them to be specific about their arrangements. They can serve the same role for a couple establishing the assets and liabilities of the spouses and any special concerns during marriage as well as protecting your children. They can be a valuable planning tool.

CONCLUSION

The challenges facing spouses in a subsequent marriage are similar to those of two businesses considering a merger. To justify the merger, the combined company has to be more profitable than the separate entities. To accomplish that goal, companies have to address where there is synergy between the businesses, form an integration plan to realize that synergy, and perform due diligence to confirm that synergy is possible. The success of the merger is dependent on the people involved, so it has been shown to be important to establish a management team that can implement the consolidation. This team will have to be capable of resolving any cultural issues and communicating effectively with employees to minimize anxiety. As in all marriages, for this marriage to succeed it has to improve the welfare of the spouses relative to any other living arrangement. To accomplish that goal, the spouses have to consider the factors that increase the likelihood that a business merger will be a success. The special concerns in a subsequent marriage are handling blended families and money.

THINGS TO REMEMBER

- A successful subsequent marriage for either spouse will often have to meet the requirement of a profitable business merger in which established companies have to integrate their activities.
- A successful business merger requires synergy between the companies, an integration plan to realize the synergy and due diligence to confirm that synergy is possible.
- In addition, to get the employees functioning smoothly together, the acquiring company has to establish a management team that is capable of resolving any cultural issues and communicating effectively with employees to minimize anxiety. A successful subsequent marriage requires the same ingredients.
- The major challenges facing this new family are treating the children fairly and managing income and expenditures when there are various sources and obligations.

Conclusion

So let's tie this process all together. Making the best decisions about marriage is hard work as you cannot rely on your instincts or society for guidance. Your instincts tend to encourage you to focus decisions too narrowly on yourself. Historically, society established norms and expectations that forced people to consider the welfare of others when making decisions about marriage. Social norms no longer provide guidance for the complex decisions that you have to make. Adults have never had the freedom that they have today to make decisions about a range of choices including careers, leisure activities, partners, and children.

THE TRAPS

Because of this freedom, it is too easy to fall into traps and make poor decisions. While the high divorce rate has been attributed to a variety of forces, it has been suggested here that the primary cause of failed marriages is poor decisions. People enter marriage optimistically that theirs will be a success. A significant number of people eventually conclude that they were wrong. How can that be? Bad luck alone cannot explain those people's frustration. Ultimately, we have to realize that people make decisions and when they are disappointed about the outcome that often means that they made bad ones. Therefore, to improve the likelihood of marital success people have to learn how to make better decisions. Better decisions will assist people in avoiding a number of traps that can result in poor decisions.

The Experience Trap

The first trap is the Experience Trap that occurs because people's prior experiences do not adequately prepare them for making the best decisions about marriage. Historically, people had a limited range of choices when they married. They often waited until men were able to support a family and then they married someone from a limited social and geographic pool. Having married, they assumed predictable roles that were dictated by society but were often based on necessity. Men did the things that men did and women had their own responsibilities. Children were important as a source of labor and old age support, so couples had numerous children. Having numerous children was important because so few of them survived past infancy.

All of this has changed. People have become much more geographically mobile and they are marrying when they are older. As a result, they have been exposed to a much broader range of potential mates. The biggest change in the roles available to adults has been the increase in employment opportunities for women, so that they are less dependent on men for financial support. People also have more options about whether they will have children, how many they will have and when they will have them. Dating and even living together have not adequately prepared people for the decisions that they have to make as a married couple. The Experience Trap occurs when people make poor decisions that reduce the potential welfare that they should expect from marriage. The impact of this Trap can be minimized by seriously considering the type of person that you should marry and what you hope to accomplish during marriage. A careful identification of the benefits and costs of alternatives is central to making better decisions.

The Emotion Trap

The second trap is the Emotion Trap as the decisions about marriage—especially your choice of a spouse—is more likely to be influenced by your emotions than other decisions. This occurs because you will often be less aware of the costs associated with those choices. This was seldom a problem in the past in most societies, because choosing a spouse was usually viewed as too important to be left exclusively to the parties involved. Choices were made or strongly influenced by parents and other members of society.

Without those constraints, people are usually able to make their own choices relying on a variety of factors with love and physical attraction having a central role. This decision is different from most that we make as it can ignore or minimize the associated costs. The cost of choosing one person is the sacrifice of all others, which may seem insignificant to someone in love. Most other decisions require the use of our limited resources of time or money that will normally corral our emotions. Going on vacation in Mexico is going to require time and money that could be used to remodel your house. You can minimize the effect of the Emotion Trap by carefully weighing the benefits and costs of decisions.

THE SELF-INTEREST TRAP

The next trap is the Self-Interest Trap that can cause people to focus their decisions too narrowly on themselves. A substantial literature demonstrates that the primary motivating force behind people's decisions is their perception of their self-interest. Given the interactions that occur among people this may appear to be a destructive force. Society has historically placed restrictions on individual actions to limit its adverse effects.

People have more freedom today and as a result self-interest can induce people into making decisions that do not improve their welfare. This can occur when they are not adequately sensitive to the effect of their actions on others. Our welfare is usually enhanced by our interaction with others. We want to love and to be loved. Because the importance of reciprocity can be subtle, without social constraints people may be inclined to overlook it. This can be particularly destructive when it comes to marriage. It is not necessary to become altruistic to avoid the Self-Interest Trap. All you have to do is recognize that your welfare is dependent on the actions of others, so keeping them happy dealing with you is important to you.

THE UNILATERAL DIVORCE TRAP

The last trap is the Unilateral Divorce Trap as it discourages you from making the decisions that historically have been important for marital success. While love is probably the most common concept currently associated with a successful marriage, the most important in the past was probably commitment. People expected to be better off in a number of very tangible ways if they married, so they married. They married with the expectation that it was going to last as long as their joint lives. With that expectation, they really did not have any choice other than to make a commitment to it. That commitment has become weaker for many couples. Marriage is perceived as having become less important for increasing people's material well-being. Divorce has become more common.

The introduction of no-fault divorce laws that usually permit either spouse to dissolve a marriage unilaterally has significantly weakened the commitment that some people make to their marriage. Unilateral divorce coupled with limited compensation for sacrifices made on behalf of a marriage have discouraged some people from making those sacrifices and the associated commitment to their marriage. Because of the ease with which a marriage can be dissolved—even when one spouse strongly disagrees—people can be discouraged from making the necessary commitment to it. Hard times can lead to divorce rather than an increased commitment to make a loving relationship work. The way to avoid the Unilateral Divorce Trap is to question the choices that you make when there is a conflict between your and your family's welfares. Are your career choices improving the welfare of your family or are they primarily in your best interest, especially if you are divorced? It is easiest to avoid this trap if you chose your spouse wisely and continue to believe that both of you are committed to the success of your marriage.

AVOIDING THE TRAPS

The key to avoiding these traps is to make better decisions, and guidance for those decisions can come from using a business framework. This framework has its roots in economics, which is the study of choice and how people can improve their decision making. Choices have to be made all of the time because of scarcity—wants exceed resources. People improve their welfare by making the choices for which the benefits exceed the costs. These choices are made by people acting as consumers and workers as well as by businesses. A focus on business decision making can help us improve our decision making as individuals.

Families and many businesses are more similar than you might think. People voluntarily agree to enter into a joint venture in both cases. They anticipate that by working together they will be better off than they would be working on their own. In both cases, they convert inputs into outputs with the goal of improving their welfare. For a business, this occurs as it converts raw materials into products with the goal of making a profit. In a similar fashion, a family takes the time, money and skills available to it and uses them to produce a variety of commodities with the goal of increasing its welfare. Just like a business does not survive if it is not profitable, families do not survive if they do not increase their participants' welfare.

WHO SHOULD YOU MARRY?

So the key decisions leading to a successful marriage have to focus on increasing a family's welfare. This process starts with finding the type of person who will work with you to accomplish that goal. This person will have important characteristics that go beyond being someone to whom you are physically attracted. The key characteristics of this person should be commitment to your marriage, compatibility with you and complementary skills and aspirations. A clear and unambiguous commitment is essential for marital success. This happens when you have done a conscientious search for a spouse and are now comfortable with your choice. Commitment is so important because it encourages personal sacrifices, while helping you to weather any down periods in your relationship. Compatibility should be obvious including values as well as activities. Less obvious is complementarity especially when people are misled into believing that love is the only important ingredient in a successful marriage. Complementarity is important for improving the family's productivity. People stay married because they feel better off in it than in any alternative arrangement. This improved welfare is the result of the production that occurs in families, with the commodities produced ranging from meals to peace of mind. This production is often enhanced by the spouses assuming more specialized roles.

Finding people with the characteristics that you prefer can be frustrating. In the past, people often found their spouse in their neighborhood or in school. Potential spouses were numerous and readily available. Having now rejected those venues, some people find the process to be much more difficult. You have to think more about marketing yourself. Also, long-term relationships have become more common and so—if you are looking for something more permanent—you have to address the ultimate challenge for a marketer: closing the deal.

THE PRODUCTIVE FAMILY

Your next challenge is creating a productive family. This does not just happen; it has to be appreciated and planned. Families use their resources of money, time and skills to produce commodities. Families that do this efficiently will prosper and persist. This production benefits from specialization of labor based on comparative advantage. With only so much time in the day, no one is even remotely capable of doing everything. Jobs and responsibilities have to be allocated. Some important commodities are money intensive such as a meal at an expensive restaurant, while others are more dependent on time input such as an afternoon at the beach. One advantage that families have is the ability to produce shared commodities that benefit a number of people simultaneously. Marriage encourages critical investments that enhance a family's productive capacity.

GENERATING MONEY INPUTS

Since money is just one of the resources that are used to produce commodities, earning it should not be a goal in itself. Moreover, people should consider the net gain from employment rather than just the income earned. The net gain also takes into consideration the costs incurred in earning the income. If you have to accept a stressful and unpleasant job to earn a high income, it is probably time to consider how you can cut back on expenditures to permit you to consider lower paying—but more attractive—jobs. Education continues to be the key to finding jobs that have the potential for a substantial net gain.

THE ROLE OF CHILDREN

Probably the most important commodities produced in most families are children. There is no other reason for having children than the enjoyment that you expect from them. You will have them so long as the benefits exceed the costs. The investments that you make in your children are going to strongly influence the enjoyment that you receive from them. This investment will often require one parent to adjust a career to accommodate childcare. This adjustment does not have to be complete or lifelong.

Avoiding Bankruptcy

You may not always conclude that your marriage is a success. With unilateral divorce, dissolving your marriage may become appealing at that time. All of the Traps can mislead you at that point. Due to a lack of experience, you may attribute too many benefits to being single again. Frustration with your marriage may encourage you to respond emotionally without an adequate consideration of the benefits and cost. Thinking primarily about your concerns may lead you to ignore those of others and yet their concerns—especially your children—may result in substantial costs for you later. Last, unilateral divorce may have encouraged you to limit your investment in your marriage and then when that relationship's quality suffered, it encouraged you to dissolve the marriage. If you made an even remotely good choice of a spouse, seldom is divorce going to dramatically improve your welfare.

Merging Families

A remarriage is going to present even more challenges as you attempt to integrate two families. It is similar to two businesses merging. The presence of children from prior relationships as well as new children is one of the primary reasons that couples find adjusting to a subsequent marriage difficult. A remarriage is likely to be more successful if people critically evaluate the decisions associated with their first marriage, recognizing the areas in which they made poor choices.

Conclusion

So there you have it. There are significant benefits from approaching marriage as you would a new business. It is important to recognize that being pragmatic about your decisions is not a contradiction to your romantic goals of tender moments and great sex. You are more likely to have those experiences if you have made good decisions about your spouse and activities during marriage. These are probably the most important decisions that you make, so make them carefully.

Things to Remember

- It has become more difficult to make the best decisions about marriage.
- Help in making better decisions can come from viewing marriage from a business perspective.
- You can make better decisions by carefully weighing the benefits and costs of alternatives.
- A credible commitment is essential for marital success.
- While people marry because they are in love, they stay married because they feel better off in their marriage than in any other arrangement.

Notes

CHAPTER 1: INTRODUCTION

1. Norval D. Glenn, "Values, Attitudes, and the State of American Marriage," in David Popenoe, Jean Bethke Elshtain, and David Blankenhorn, eds., *Promises to Keep* (Lanham, MD: Rowman and Littlefield, 1996), pp. 15–34.

2. Linda J. Waite and Maggie Gallagher, *The Case for Marriage* (New York: Doubleday, 2000).

3. U. S. Census Bureau, *Statistical Abstract of the United States, 2007*, Table 55, p. 51.

4. Constance Ahrons, *The Good Divorce* (New York: HarperCollins, 1998).

5. The divorce rate peaked at 5.3 per 1,000 total population in 1981 before declining to 3.6 in 2005. Still, both these figures are substantially higher than the 2.0 that the United States experienced in 1940. National Center for Health Statistics, *Births, Marriages, Divorces, and Deaths: Provisional Data for 2005*, July 21, 2006. Table A, p. 1.

6. See Glenn, "Values."

7. Bob Dole, Elizabeth Dole, and Richard Norton Smith, *Unlimited Partners* (New York: Simon and Schuster, 2001).

8. Mia Farrow, *What Falls Away* (New York: Bantam, 1997).

CHAPTER 2: THE FOUR TRAPS

1. In a survey of high school students, almost 60 percent responded that they felt that they were unprepared for marriage. See Paige D. Martin, Gerald Specter, Don Martin, and Maggie Martin, "Expressed Attitudes of Adolescents Toward Marriage and Family Life," *Adolescence*, 38(150), Summer 2003, pp. 359–367.

2. Lois Smith Brady, "State of the Unions: Susan Molinari and Bill Paxon," *New York Times*, November 9, 2003, Styles, p. 14.

3. The Oprah Winfrey Show, January 16, 2002.

4. Carole Hyatt and Linda Gottlieb, *When Smart People Fail: Rebuilding Yourself for Success* (New York: Penguin, 1993).

5. Carole Hyatt, *Women and Work* (New York: M. Evans, 1980).

6. Shirley Glass, *NOT "Just Friends": Rebuilding Trust and Recovering Your Sanity After Infidelity* (New York: Free Press, 2004).

7. William J. Bennett, *The Broken Hearth: Reversing the Moral Collapse of the American Family* (New York: Doubleday, 2001).

8. Frank F. Furstenberg and Andrew Cherlin, *Divided Families: What Happens to Children When Parents Part* (Cambridge, MA: Harvard, 1991), p. 100.

9. For a history and impact of no-fault divorce, see Allen M. Parkman, *Good Intentions Gone Awry: No-Fault Divorce and the American Family* (Lanham, MD: Rowman and Littlefield, 2000).

10. Lia Macko and Kerry Rubin, *Midlife Crisis at 30: How the Stakes Have Changed for a New Generation—And What to Do About It* (New York: Rodale Press, 2004).

11. See Allen M. Parkman, "Unilateral Divorce and the Labor-Force Participation Rate of Married Women, Revisited," *American Economic Review*, 82(3), June 1992, pp. 671–678; and Allen M. Parkman, "Why Are Married Women Working So Hard?," *International Review of Law and Economics*, 18(1), Winter 1998, pp. 41–49.

CHAPTER 3: WHY DO YOU NEED A BUSINESS PARTNER?

1. For a history of marriage, see Edward Shorter, *The Making of the Modern Family* (New York: Basic Books, 1975).

2. According to the National Federation of Independent Businesses, 27 percent of the privately held small businesses in 2004 had two owners.

3. "Who's Your Type?" *American Demographics*, February 2000, p. 12.

4. Commitment is so obvious that it is often ignored. Compatibility and complementarity have been identified as the most important attributes of successful marriage as researchers have noted that in successful marriages the couple has similar leisure interests and expectations about the roles that they expect to assume during marriage. Renate M. Houts, Elliot Robins, and Ted L. Huston, "Compatibility and the Development of Premarital Relationships," *Journal of Marriage and the Family*, 58(1), February 1996, pp. 7–20.

5. Mat Boggs and Jason Miller interviewed 200 couples who had been married more than forty years and they concluded that the most frequent explanation for their success was the couples' commitment to each other and to their marriage. Chrissie Thompson, "Mastering Marriage," *The Washingon Times*, October 5, 2006.

6. David G. Blanchflower and Andrew J. Oswald, "Well-being Over Time in Britain and the USA," *Journal of Public Economics*, 88 (2004), pp. 1359–1386.

7. Approximately half of single mothers with children are divorced or separated. US Census Bureau, *America's Families and Living Arrangements: 2003*, November 2004, Table 4, p. 9.

8. Linda J. Waite and Maggie Gallagher, *The Case for Marriage* (New York: Doubleday, 2000), p. 148.

9. John T. Molloy, *Why Men Marry Some Women and Not Others* (New York: Warner Books, 2004), p. xv.

10. Ibid., 110.

11. Eve Tahmincioglu, "Friends Don't Always Make Good Partners," *The New York Times*, September 7, 2006, p. 6.

12. Some people take the idea of a soul mate to the extreme by assuming that there is a unique person out there for them. It is more realistic to assume that becoming soul mates is something that develops over time through the couple's communication and empathy. See Karen S. Peterson, "Search for a Soul Mate, or Love the One You're With?" *USA Today*, May 29, 2003, p. 12D.

13. Compatibility between spouses based on similar interests and values is enhanced if they have developed constructive communication and problem-solving skills. Mari L. Clements, Scott M. Stanley, and Howard J. Markman, "Before They Said 'I Do': Discriminating Among Marital Outcomes Over 13 Years," *Journal of Marriage and Family*, 66, August 2004, pp. 613–626.

14. Of course, this is one of the most fundamental ideas in economics going back to Adam Smith. It is discussed in the first chapter of his *Wealth of Nations* (New York: The Modern Library, 1937), pp. 3–12. This is obvious in large corporations with numerous specialized divisions, but it is also true for small businesses.

15. Tahmincioglu, "Friends."

16. For a discussion of the economic approach to marriage and more specifically the gains from specialization of labor, see Gary S. Becker, *A Treatise on the Family, Enl Ed.* (Cambridge, MA: Harvard University Press, 1991).

17. For a discussion of the effect of unilateral divorce on decisions before and during marriage, see Allen M. Parkman, *Good Intentions Gone Awry: No-Fault Divorce and the American Family* (Lanham, MD: Rowman & Littlefield, 2000).

18. For an example of a discussion of concerns about cash flow in the trucking business, see Milton Zall, "Starting and Operating a Small Business," *Fleet Equipment*, August 1999, pp. 5–8.

19. An analysis of the causes of divorce can be very complicated as many of the factors are inter-related. However, studies have shown that the most consistent predictors of divorce are jealousy, infidelity, spending money foolishly, and drug or alcohol use. See Paul R. Amato and Stacy Rogers, "A Longitudinal Study of Marital Problems and Subsequent Divorce," *Journal of Marriage and the Family*, 59(3), August 1997, pp. 612–624.

20. Tahmincioglu, "Friends."

Chapter 4: Acquiring Your Partner

1. Edward Frazelle, *Supply Chain Strategy: The Logistics of Supply Chain Management* (New York: McGraw-Hill, 2002).

2. Dave Nelson, Patricia E. Moody, Jonathan Stegner, *The Purchasing Machine* (New York: The Free Press, 2001).

3. For a discussion of supply professions, see "Purchasing Managers, Buyers, and Purchasing Agents" in the Bureau of Labor Statistics, *Occupational Outlook Handbook*, which is available at http://www.bls.gov/oco/ocos023.htm.

4. Approximately a third of couples met through friends. "So, Where'd You Meet?" *Men's Health*, 21(5), June 2006, p. 50.

5. Todd Outcalt, *Before You Say "I Do": Important Questions for Couples to Ask Before Marriage* (New York: Perigee Book, 1998) and Susan Piver, *The Hard Questions: 100 Essential Questions to Ask Before You Say I Do* (New York: Penguin, 2004).

6. Beverly Rodgers and Thomas A. Rodgers, *Soul-Healing Love: Ten Practical, Easy-To-Learn Techniques for Couples in Crisis* (San Jose, CA: Resource Publications, 1998).

7. John T. Molloy, *Why Men Marry Some Women and Not Others* (New York: Warner Books, 2003).

8. Molloy, *Why*, p. 16.

9. Barbara Dafoe Whitehead, *Why There Are No Good Men Left* (New York: Broadway Books, 2003).

10. Molloy, *Why*, p. 13.

11. Ibid., p. 11.

12. Ibid., p. 3.

13. Ibid.

14. In 2003, the typical woman earned $17,259, while the typical man earned $29,931. U. S. Census Bureau, *Statistical Abstract of the United States: 2006*, Table 684, p. 465.

15. In 1960, approximately two thirds of degrees were conferred on men with the percentage going to men being even higher for advanced degrees. By 1985, men were receiving less than 50 percent of degrees with that percentage falling to 42 percent in 2003. Ibid., Table 286, p. 186.

16. Ibid., Table 291, p. 189.

17. See Allen M. Parkman, "Bargaining Over Housework: The Frustrating Situation of Secondary Wage Earners," *American Journal of Economics and Sociology*, 63(4), October 2004, pp. 765–794.

18. "So, Where'd You Meet?" *Men's Health*, June 2006, p. 50.

19. According to the Pew Internet & American Life Project, 38 percent of people in serious long-term relationships or married met their partner at work or in school. Lee Rainie and Mary Madden, *Not Looking for Love: Romance in America*, Pew Internet & American Life Project, February 13, 2006.

20. Sue Shellenbarger, "Office Romance: The Challenges of Mixing Business and Pleasure," *Wall Street Journal*, February 19, 2004, p. D1.

21. In 2005, people spent half a billion dollars on online dating sites. Dennie Hughes, "8 Simple Rules for Dating," *USA Weekend*, February 13, 2005.

22. Ellen Gamerman, "Mismatched.com," *Wall Street Journal*, April 1, 2006, p. D1.

23. Evan Marc Katz, *I Can't Believe I'm Buying This Book: A Commonsense Guide to Successful Internet Dating* (Berkeley, CA: Ten Speed Press, 2004).

24. http://www.itsjustlunch.com.

25. http://www.8minutedating.com.

26. HurryDate promises as many as 25 three-minute dates in a single evening. The result is the ability to determine whether you are physically attracted without any clear idea of whether you would actually enjoy having dinner with the person. Eleena de Lisser, "Cranky Consumer: Hitting the Speed Dating Circuit," *Wall Street Journal*, February 10, 2004, p. D2.

27. Robert Kurzban and Jason Weeden, "HurryDate: Mate Preference in Action," *Evolution and Human Behavior*, 26, 2005, pp. 227–244.

28. Janis Spindel Serious Martchmaking Incorporated's fees, for example, begin at $20,000 for an initiation fee, plus $1,000 for a one-year membership that includes twelve dates. Melanie Thernstrom, "The New Arranged Marriage," *The New York Times Magazine*, February 13, 2005.

29. Gary Armstrong and Phillip Kotler, *Marketing: An Introduction, 7th Edition* (Upper Saddle River, NJ: Pearson/Prentice Hall, 2005).

30. Ibid., p. 57.

31. Ibid., p. 183.

32. B. Joseph Pine II and James H. Gilmore, *The Experience Economy* (Cambridge, MA: Harvard Business School Press, 1999).

33. Armstrong and Kolter, *Marketing*, p. 160.

34. Normal Li, J. Michael Bailey, Douglas Kenrick, and Joan Linsenmeier, "The Necessities and Luxuries of Mate Preference: Testing the Tradeoffs," *Journal of Personality and Social Psychology*, 82(6), 2002, pp. 947–955.

35. Physical attractiveness does not just mean gorgeous or sexy, but instead researchers have shown that conveying a sense that someone is upbeat and positive can actually be more important. Among physical attributes, being slender is particularly important. See Molloy, *Why*, p. 69.

36. Molloy, p. 26.

37. Kate White, "9 Ways to Meet a Man," MSN Dating & Personals, http://msn.match.com/msn/print.aspx?articleid=6617.

38. In her advice to women, Giuliana DePandi suggests that women should act more like men by avoiding discussions of fears and insecurities and the desire to be a stay at home mom. See Giuliana DePandi, *Think Like a Guy* (New York: St. Martin's Press, 2006).

39. Combining a career and finding a husband can require a delicate balance for women. It would appear that men like the financial resources that come with a successful woman, but they do not like the inconveniences that come with a demanding career. Men are increasingly finding women who are good financial prospects attractive. See David M. Buss, Todd K. Shackelford, Lee A. Kirkpatrick, and Randy J. Larsen, "A Half Century of Mate Preferences: The Cultural Evolution of Values," *Journal of Marriage and Family*, 63, May 2001, pp. 491–503. However, some men find successful women unattractive because of the higher probability of divorce, cheating and being childless. See Michael Noer, "Don't Marry Career Women," *Forbes.com*, August 23, 2006.

40. Zhenchao Quian, Daniel T. Lichter, and Leanna M. Mellorr, "Out-of-Wedlock Childbearing, Marital Prospects and Mate Selection," *Social Forces*, 84(1), September 2005, pp. 473–491.

41. Jeffrey Gitomer, *The Little Red Book of Selling: 12.5 Principles of Sales Greatness* (Austin, TX: Bard Press, 2004).

42. Rachel Greenwald, *Find a Husband After 35* (New York: Ballantine Books, 2003).

43. Liz H. Kelly, "10 Winning Profile Tips," Boston.com Personals, http://boston.personals.yahoo.com/us/statis/dating-advice-perfect-profile.

44. Molloy, *Why*, p. 35.

45. Both sexes are becoming more concerned about physical appearance and financial prospects in a mate. David M. Buss, Todd K. Shackelford, Lee A. Kirkpatrick, and Randy J. Larsen, "A Half Century of Mate Preferences: The Cultural Evolution of Values," *Journal of Marriage and Family*, 63, May 2001, pp. 491–503.

46. Erich Goode, "Gender and Courtship Entitlement: Responses to Personal Ads," *Sex Roles*, 34(3/4), pp. 141–169.

47. Ibid.

48. Ibid., 116.

49. Ibid., 128.

50. Bradly Gerstman, Christopher Rizzo and Rich Seldes, *Marry Me* (New York: William Morrow, 2000).

51. Research has shown that the women who got married insisted on a commitment early in their relationship. Molloy, *Why*, p. 12.

52. Richard Kirshenbaum and Daniel Rosenberg, *Closing the Deal: Two Married Guys Take You From Single Miss to Wedded Bliss* (New York: Collins, 2006).

53. Jay Teachman, "Premarital Sex, Premarital Cohabitation, and the Risk of Subsequent Marital Dissolution Among Women," *Journal of Marriage and Family*, 65, May 2003, pp. 444–455.

54. Paul R. Amato and Stacy J. Rogers, "A Longitudinal Study of Marital Problems and Subsequent Divorce," *Journal of Marriage and the Family*, 59(3), August 1997, pp. 612–624.

CHAPTER 5: THE FAMILY AS A BUSINESS

1. The idea that individuals do not receive welfare just from goods and services but also from commodities that result from the combining of goods and services with time was developed in Gary S. Becker, "A Theory of the Allocation of Time," *Economic Journal* 75, September 1965, pp. 493–517 and Kevin Lancaster, "A New Approach to Consumer Theory," *Journal of Political Economy* 74, April 1966, pp. 132–157.

2. Shopping, which requires time, can also be viewed as a source of enjoyment for some people.

3. In a survey of people's most enjoyable activities, intimate relations, socializing and relaxing were the three most enjoyable activities. See Daniel Kahneman, Alan B. Krueger, David A. Schkade, Norbert Schwarz, and Arthur A. Stone, "A Survey Method for Characterizing Daily Life Experience: The Day Reconstruction Method," *Science*, 306, December 3, 2004, pp. 1776–1780.

4. In a Pew Research Center poll, a majority of young people said that getting rich was their main goal rather than being happy or any other more subjective accomplishment. See Pew Research Center, *How Young People View Their Lives, Futures and Politics*, January 9, 2007.

5. According to data from the General Social Survey, the percentage of people who respond that they are very happy increases from 22.2 percent among those with family incomes less than $20,000 to 41.9 percent for those with family incomes between $50,000 and $89,999. However, having an income above $90,000 only increases the response rate to 42.9 percent. See Daniel Kahneman, Alan B. Krueger, David Schkade, Norbert Schwarz, and Arthur A. Stone, "Would You Be Happier If You Were Richer: A Focusing Illusion," *Science*, 312, June 30, 2006, pp. 1908–1910.

6. Some have argued that the legalization of abortion and the increased availability of contraception to unmarried women in the United States led to the erosion in the custom of shotgun marriages. See George A. Akerloff, Janet L. Yellen, and Michael L. Katz, "An Analysis of Out-of-Wedlock Childbearing in the United States," *Quarterly Journal of Economics* 111(2), May 1996, pp. 277–317.

7. Among the 4.6 million unmarried couples in 2003, more than 2.7 million did not have any children under age eighteen. U.S. Bureau of the Census, *America's Families and Living Arrangements: 2003*, November 2004, Figure 7, p. 17.

8. This section benefits from the discussion in Allen M. Parkman, *Good Intentions Gone Awry* (Lanham, MD: Rowman & Littlefield, 2000).

9. The standard economic discussion of the gains from specialization within a relationship, assumed to be marriage, is contained in Gary S. Becker, *A Treatise on the Family, Enl. Ed.* (Cambridge, MA: Harvard, 1991), pp. 30–53. For a thorough review of the sociological perspective on the division of labor within households, see Sarah Fenstermaker Berk, *The Gender Factory: The Apportionment of Work in American Households* (New York: Plenum Press, 1985).

10. For an introduction to economics as applied to the family, see Francine D. Blau, Marianne A. Ferber, and Anne E. Winkler, *The Economics of Women, Men and Work, 3rd Ed.* (Upper Saddle River, NJ: Prentice Hall, 1998). A central theme in economics is diminishing returns as the incremental gains from consumption and production tend to decline as the quality increases. While one person might initially find cooking less tedious, if not more enjoyable, than their partner, that situation could change with the amount of cooking. As one did more of the cooking, it might become more tedious, thereby creating an opportunity for the couple to increase their overall welfare by the initially reluctant partner assuming some of the cooking responsibilities. In a similar manner, one person may have a comparative advantage at earning income, but finds earning income beyond a certain level extremely unpleasant. The partner who had assumed primary responsibility for domestic activities might be able to earn comparable income on a part-time basis and at a lower opportunity cost to the couple. This is especially true because diminishing returns probably resulted in some of the time spent working in the home having a low value to the couple.

11. N. Gregory Mankiw, *Principles of Economics, 4th Ed.* (Mason, OH: Thomson Higher Education, 2007), p. 600.

12. It is much more likely that both partners who live together will be employed than among married couples. Also, married men tend to earn much more than their wives than do unmarried men relative to their partners. See US Census Bureau, *America's Families and Living Arrangements: 2003*, P20–553, November 2004.

13. The idea that marriage is based on the gains from specialization is often ignored. Individuals can usually find members of the opposite sex whom they find attractive and with whom they can acquire the additional commodities available through marriage. In that environment, the focus is usually on the individual mate rather than the gains from marriage. In other situations, for example on the American frontier, marriages were arranged without the parties knowing each other because of the gains that the parties expected from a marriage to essentially anyone. See Ray Allen Billington, *America's Frontier Heritage* (Albuquerque: University of New Mexico Press, 1974), p. 215.

14. Among couples in which at least one spouse is employed, in couples with children under age eighteen it is more likely that the father is the only parent employed and less likely that the mother is the only parent employed. The percentage of couples with both employed is similar for those without children at home. See US Census Bureau, *America's Families and Living Arrangements: 2003*, P20–553, November 2004.

15. Twenty percent of married fathers with employed wives were the primary provider of childcare to children under five years of age in 2002. See US Census Bureau, *Who's Minding the Kids? Child Care Arrangements: Winter 2002*, P70–101, October 2005, p. 19.

16. Of course, those traveling are not just men. According to the Travel Industry Association, 43 percent of business travelers in 2004 were women. Lisa W. Foderaro, "Working Mothers Find Some Peace on the Road," *New York Times*, November 1, 2006.

17. My research has shown that married women were more likely to be employed in unilateral, no-fault divorce states. If the decision to be employed was based on the best interest of the family, the law in the state should not effect the decision. See Allen M. Parkman, "Unilateral Divorce and the Labor-Force Participation Rate of Married Women, Revisited," *American Economic Review*, 82(3), June 1992, pp. 671–678.

18. Marriage provides insurance, if one accepts the element of the marriage vow in which the parties agree to fulfill their duty "for rich or for poor, in sickness and in health." See Lloyd Cohen, "Marriage, Divorce, and Quasi Rents: or 'I Gave Him the Best Years of Life,'" *Journal of Legal Studies*, 16(2), 1987, pp. 267–304. It also can provide insurance against risks originating from random events outside the family's control. See Murray Brown, "Optimal Marriage Contracts," *Journal of Human Resources* 27(3), Summer 1992, pp. 534–550.

19. Without children, there are usually fewer incentives for a couple to marry. There still can be incentives to take advantage of filing a joint tax return, receive employer provided fringe benefits such as health insurance, or have marriage provide psychological benefits due to the commitment that it represents.

20. Marriage can be viewed as an institution that provides couples with the confidence to make long-term investments in their relationship. See Robert Rowthorn, "Marriage and Trust: Some Lessons From Economics," *Cambridge Journal of Economics*, 23(5), September 1999, pp. 661–691.

21. See Robert H. Lauer, Jeanette C. Lauer, and Sarah T. Kerr, "The Long Term Marriage: Perceptions of Stability and Satisfaction," *International Journal of Aging and Human Development* 31(1), 1990, pp. 189–195.

22. For a more detailed discussion of the importance of gifts for a successful marriage, see Allen M. Parkman, "The Importance of Gifts in Marriage," *Economic Inquiry*, 42(3), July 2004, pp. 483–495.

23. Children born to cohabiting parents may spend about a quarter of their childhood years with a single parent, a quarter with a cohabiting parent and less than half with married parents. In contrast, children born to married parents spend the vast majority (84 percent) of their childhood in two-parent families. See Larry Bumpass and Hsien-Hen Lu, "Trends in Cohabitation and Implications for Children's Family Contexts in the United States," *Population Studies*, 54, 2000, pp. 29–41.

24. The outcomes that children who have grown up with their biological parents experience are much better than those who grow up either with a single parent or in a stepfamily. See Sara McLanahan and Gary Sandefur, *Growing Up With a Single Parent* (Cambridge, MA: Harvard, 1994).

25. Of course, effective communication is important in all phases of marriage. Here we are discussing making decisions. However, there are other important areas that are affected by effective communication. One early challenge for many marriages is the decline in perceived quality associated with being parents. Couples with good communication before and after being parents handle these changes best. See Alyson Fearnley Shapiro, John M. Gottman, and Sybil Carrere, " The Baby and the Marriage: Identifying Factors that Buffer Against Decline in Marital Satisfaction After the First Baby Arrives," *Journal of Family Psychology*, 14(1), 2000, pp. 59–70.

26. Clear communication has been shown to be the most important attribute identified by couples who are very satisfied with their marriage. See Mark R. Nielsen, "Couples Making It Happen: Marital Satisfaction and What Works for Highly Satisfied Couples," in Barbara Schneider and Linda J. Waite, eds., *Being Together, Working Apart: Dual-Career Families and the Work-Life Balance* (Cambridge, UK: Cambridge University Press, 2005), pp. 196–216.

27. The frequency of family dinner has been shown to be an important process for encouraging positive outcomes such as self-confidence and discouraging negative outcomes such as high-risk behavior. See Jayne A. Fulkerson, Mary Story, Alison Mellin, Nancy Leffert, Dianne Neumark-Sztainer, and Simone A. French, "Family Dinner Meal Frequency and Adolescent Development: Relationships with Developmental Assets and High-Risk Behaviors," *Journal of Adolescent Health*, 39, 2006, pp. 337–345.

28. The Coalition for Marriage, Families and Couples Education has a web site that provides valuable information for couples. See http://www.smartmarriages.com.

29. See Arlene Dubin, *Prenups for Lovers: A Romantic Guide to Prenuptial Agreements* (New York: Villard, 2001).

30. See US Bureau of Labor Statistics, *100 Years of U. S. Consumer Spending*, May 2006, p. 65.

31. Half of married couples keep separate bank accounts with a concern about divorce being one of the driving forces. See Sue Shellenbarger, "For Richer or for Poorer, but Only If We Have Separate Checking Account," *Wall Street Journal*, February 24, 2005, D1.

32. According to Global Financial Data, stocks outperformed U.S. government bonds by more than 5 percent per year over the period 1951 to 2001. Its analysis is available at http://www.globalfinancialdata.com/index.php3?action=gfd_research.

33. Kahneman, et al., "A Survey," 1777.

34. Between 1970 and 2002, the percentage of food expenditures that was spent on food away from home increased from 26 to 42 percent. US Bureau of Labor Statistics, *100 Years*, 66.

35. Jonathan Clements, "Why You Should Think Twice About Investing in Real Estate," *Wall Street Journal*, January 24, 2007, D1.

36. Because of the fixed costs associated with buying and selling a house, it will be less attractive if you anticipate relocating in the near future. Also, because of the supply of rental properties, it may be attractive to rent in some markets.

37. See Kahneman, et al., "A Survey."

38. US Census Bureau, *Number, Timing, and Duration of Marriages and Divorces: 2001*, P70–97, February 2005.

39. As early as 1957, researchers identified the transition to parenthood as one of the family's most difficult adjustments. See E. E. Lemasters, "Parenthood as a Crises," *Marriage and Family Living*, 19, pp. 352–355. For a more recent discussion, see Shapiro, et al., "The Baby."

40. The birth rate in the United States declined most during the last hundred years. The birth rate per 1,000 people declined from 32.3 in 1900 to 14.1 in 2003. See US Census Bureau, *Statistical Abstract of the United States, 2007*, Table 78, p. 64 and US Bureau of the Census, *Historical Statistics of the United States: Colonial Times to 1970*, Volume 1 (Washington, DC: USGPO, 1975), Series B 5–10, p. 49.

41. Sue Shellenbarger, "Reasons to Hold Out Hope for Balancing Work and Home," *Wall Street Journal*, January 10, 2007, p. D1.

42. Years of education have been shown to be correlated with not smoking and controlling one's weight. See Gina Kolata, "A Surprising Secret to a Long Life: Stay in School," *New York Times*, January 3, 2007, p. A1.

43. While it is easier than ever to earn a comfortable income, most people work just as much as their ancestors. Moreover, even with the additional income, they are no more satisfied with their lives than were their ancestors. See Gregg Easterbrook, *The Progress Paradox* (New York: Random House, 2003).

44. In 2003, the average earnings of male high school graduates were $38,331, while that of males with a bachelor's degree or more were $81,007. See US Census Bureau, *Statistical Abstract of the United States, 2007*, Table 684, p. 453.

45. See Kahneman, et al., "A Survey."

46. Parkman, *Good Intentions*, 120.

47. Sperling's Best Places' web site (http://www.bestplaces.net/col/) provides comparisons between different communities. For example, it suggests that someone making $50,000 in Mobile, Alabama would have to make $122,000 to maintain the same standard of living in San Francisco, CA.

48. See Claudia Goldin, *Understanding the Gender Gap* (New York: Oxford University Press, 1990).

49. See Arlie Russell Hochschild, *The Time Bind: When Work Becomes Home and Home Becomes Work* (New York: Metropolitan Books, 1997).

50. In 2003, 17 percent of wives earned at least $5,000 more than their husbands and another 25 percent earned about the same as their husbands. See US Census Bureau, *America's Families and Living Arrangements: 2003*, P20–553, November 2004.

51. See Allen M. Parkman, "Bargaining Over Housework: The Frustrating Situation of Secondary Wage Earners," *American Journal of Economics and Sociology*, 63(4), October 2004, pp. 765–794.

52. See Parkman, "Gifts."

53. A 1990 poll of U.S. pediatricians conducted by the Thomas Jefferson School of Medicine in Philadelphia showed that 77 percent believed infants six months or younger ought to be cared for only at home. A different survey of 1,100 baby doctors carried out that same year by the American Academy of Pediatrics reported that a substantial majority of physicians consider full-time daycare harmful for children under age four. See Karl Zinsmeister, "Longstanding Warnings From Experts," *The American Enterprise*, 9(3), May/June 1998, pp. 34–35.

54. Early childhood is a unique developmental period that serves as a foundation for behavior, well-being and success later in life. See Lynn A. Karolym, *Investing in Our Children* (Santa Monica, CA: Rand, 1998), p. 106.

55. The Cost, Quality and Child Outcomes in Child Care Centers study conducted in 1993–1994 examined 401 childcare centers in four states and concluded that 86 percent of the centers provided mediocre or poor quality services. There was not much variation, on average, between fees for mediocre and good care, but parents frequently do not make the best choice for their child. Parents may be more concerned about the location, hours, and dependability of childcare arrangements than they are about aspects of quality considered important by child development professionals. See Suzanne W. Helburn, ed., *Cost, Quality, and Child Outcomes in Child Care Centers: Technical Report* (Denver, CO: Department of Economics, Center for Research in Economic and Social Policy, University of Colorado, 1995).

56. In the 1970s, it was more likely that a married woman would be working in a unilateral, no-fault divorce state that provided protection for marital sacrifices than in fault divorce states that provided some protection for those sacrifices. See Parkman, "Unilateral Divorce."

57. See Allen M. Parkman, "The Contractual Alternative to Marriage," *Northern Kentucky Law Review*, 32(1), 2005, pp. 125–155.

58. The average age at retirement has been declining for the last few decades. It declined from 65 years of age for both men and women during the period 1960–1965 to approximately 62.5 years of age during the period 1995–2000. See Murray Gendell, "Retirement Age Declines Again in 1990s," *Monthly Labor Review*, 124(10), October 2001, pp. 12–21.

59. Christopher Conkey, "Credit-Card Issuers on the Spot," *Wall Street Journal*, January 25, 2007, A4.

60. It has been pointed out that adjusted by the consumer price index that hourly earnings are currently less than they were in the early 1970s. See President's Council of Economic Advisers, *Economic Report of the President 2006*, Table B-47, p. 338. However, economists have concluded that the consumer price index overstates actual inflation by about one percent, so most workers are substantially better off now than they were decades ago.

CHAPTER 6: INCOME AS A PRODUCTION INPUT

1. US Census Bureau, Census 2000 PHC-T-41: *A Half Century of Learning: Historical Statistics on Educational Attainment in the United States, 1940 to 2000.*

2. Jeff D. Opdyke, "Love & Money: Money Can't Buy You Job Happiness," *Wall Street Journal*, April 17, 2005, p. 2.

3. Adam Smith, *Wealth of Nations* (New York: The Modern Library, 1937), p. 100.

4. Although bank tellers tend to have more education that hazardous materials removal workers, their median annual earnings in 2004 were $21,120, while the median annual earnings of hazardous materials removal workers was $33,321 in 2004. US Bureau of Labor Statistics, *Occupational Outlook Handbook, 2006–07 Edition* that is available at http://www.bls.gov/oco/home.htm.

5. Ibid.

6. This is just assumed for simplicity as law school generally takes more time and money than that required to be qualified as an accountant.

7. See http://www.bls.gov/oes/home.htm.

8. A thorough presentation of human capital is contained in Gary S. Becker, *Human Capital, 3rd Ed.* (Chicago: University of Chicago Press, 1993).

9. In an article on student debt in *USA Today*, one of the examples is a woman who acquired over $20,000 in loans to get a degree in theater. Having gotten it, she noted that she would have been better off with a degree in something more lucrative, an investment, and minored in theater, consumption. Mary Beth Marklein and Ryan Holeywell, "How Can Collegians Shoulder Their Debt?" *USA Today*, January 31, 2007, p. 6D.

10. US Census Bureau, *Current Population Survey, 2004 Annual Social and Economic Supplement*, Table PINC-03.

11. Between 1986–7 and 2004–5, the cost of tuition, fees, room and board at public universities increased by 176 percent and at private universities by 164 percent. US Department of Education, National Center for Education Statistics, *Digest*

of Education Statistics 2005, Table 312. These increases were much more than prices in general that increased by 72 percent over the same period. US President's Council of Economic Advisers, *Economic Report of the President*, February 2006, Table B-60, p. 351.

12. For the 2004–5 academic year, the average cost of undergraduate tuition, fees, and room and board was $11,441 at a public four-year institution and $26,489 at a private one. US Department of Education, National Center for Education Statistics, *Digest of Education Statistics 2005*, Table 312.

13. See Estelle James, Nabeel Alsalam, Joseph C. Conaty, and Duc-Le To, "College Quality and Future Earnings: Where Should You Send Your Child to College?" *American Economic Review*, 79(2), May 1989, pp. 247–252 and Scott Imberman, "Are There Returns to Attending a Private College or University?" University of Maryland Working Paper, July 26, 2006.

14. An age-earnings profile illustrates the relationship between the earnings of workers and their age. This relationship is much steeper for higher educated people in contrast to those with less education. Not only do people with more education start at higher salaries, their incomes increase more rapidly over time. Becker, *Human Capital*, 233.

15. In 25 percent of the families in which both the husband and wife have earnings, the wife earns more than the husband. In 32 percent of all families in which the wife has earnings, but the husband may not have any earnings, the wife earns more than the husband. See Bureau of Labor Statistics, *Women in the Labor Force: A Databook*, Report 985, May 2005, Table 25.

16. Jeff Opdyke left a job with the Wall Street Journal to move to Louisiana, where his wife had a higher paying position. From Louisiana, he continued to write a column for the Wall Street, but at a lower compensation level than when he was a reporter. Jeff D. Opdyke, "Love & Money: As Amy Hunts for a Job, What's My Role?" *Wall Street Journal*, May 8, 2005, p. 2.

17. Sue Shellenbarger, "More New Mothers are Staying Home Even When It Causes Financial Pain," *Wall Street Journal*, November 30, 2006, D1.

18. Bureau of Labor Statistics, "Women at Work: A Visual Essay," *Monthly Labor Review*, October 2003, pp. 45–50.

19. In a 2005 survey by the Society for Human Resource Management, 33 percent of the respondents said that they had a formal policy allowing part-time work for professionals. See Lynn Berger, *The Savvy Part Time Professional: How to Land, Create and Negotiate the Part Time Job of Your Dreams* (Sterling, VA: Capital Books, 2006).

20. Erin White, "Build a Case Before Asking To Work Less," *Wall Street Journal*, October 24, 2006, D1.

21. Numerous colleges and universities offer distance education programs leading to highly marketable degrees—and a few that are just fun. For example, see a selection of programs offered by Penn State University at http://www.worldcampus.psu.edu/.

22. Daniel Golden, "Degrees@StateU.edu," *Wall Street Journal*, May 9, 2006, B1.

23. Sue Shellenbarger, "The Mommy Drain: Employers Beef Up Perks to Lure New Mothers Back to Work," *Wall Street Journal*, September 28, 2006, D1.

24. A valuable web site for those considering more flexible employment options is www.workoptions.com. Also, see Jaclyne Badal, "To Retain Valued Women

Employees, Companies Pitch Flextime as Macho," *Wall Street Journal*, December 11, 2006, B1.

25. While most of these programs are aimed at women, they are usually also available to men. Anne Marie Chaker, "Luring Moms Back to Work; to Fight Female Flight, Some Companies Overhaul Leave Programs; a Five Year Break," *Wall Street Journal*, December 30, 2003, D1.

26. Anne Marie Chaker, "Business Schools Target At-Home Moms," *Wall Street Journal*, May 10, 2006, D1.

27. Hilary Stout and Anne Marie Chaker, "Mom for Hire: Industry Springs Up Around Mothers Returning to Work," *Wall Street Journal*, May 6, 2004, D1.

28. See Sue Shellenbarger, "The Secrets of Sequencing: How Moms Can Set the Stage for a Return to Work," *Wall Street Journal*, July 24, 2003, D1.

29. For example, a study of nurses found that their work satisfaction diminished over time. See Asa Sand, "Nurses' Personalities, Nurse-Related Qualities and Work Satisfaction: a 10 Year Perspective," *Journal of Clinical Nursing*, 12, 2003, pp. 177–187.

30. See Marco Piccinelli and Greg Wilinson, "Gender Differences in Depression: Critical Review," *British Journal of Psychiatry*, 177, 2000, pp. 486–492.

31. Sue Shellenbarger, "How to Tell If You're a Candidate for a Midlife Crisis," *Wall Street Journal*, April 7, 2005, D1.

32. I have used the combination of law and economics as a basis for most of my research and having those degrees helped me obtain a position as a Senior Economist on the staff of the President's Council of Economic Advisers in Washington, DC, during the first year of the Reagan Administration.

33. US Census Bureau, *Statistical Abstract of the United States 2006*, Table 635, p. 418.

34. These taxes consist of social security and Medicare contributions of 7.65 percent, a federal income tax rate of 15 percent, a New Mexico income tax rate of 5 percent and finally a sales tax of 6.875 percent on any in-state purchases.

35. Nationally, for every dollar a working family saves on housing costs, it spends 77 cents more on transportation. While the total amount varies among metropolitan areas, it is fairly constant within each metropolitan area. Center for Housing Policy, *The Combining Housing and Transportation Burdens of Working Families*, October 2006.

36. See Daniel Kahneman, Alan B. Krueger, David A. Schkade, Norbert Schwarz, and Arthur A. Stone, "A Survey Method for Characterizing Daily Life Experience: The Day Reconstruction Method," *Science*, 306, December 3, 2004, pp. 1776–1780.

37. Erika Lovley, "America, Up Close and Personal," *Wall Street Journal*, October 26, 2006, D1.

38. Alan Pisarski, *Commuting in America III*, Transportation Research Board, October 16, 2006.

39. Elizabeth Warren and Amelia Warren Tyagi, *The Two-Income Trap: Why Middle-Class Mothers and Fathers are Going Broke* (New York: Basic Books, 2003).

40. Janny Scott, "New York Homeowners Paying a Record Share for Housing," *New York Times*, December 10, 2002.

41. The United States Conference of Mayors, *Metro Economies Report: Housing and Energy Outlook*, October 2006.

CHAPTER 7: PRODUCING HAPPY, WELL-ADJUSTED CHILDREN

1. Eighty-one percent of the 18 to 25 year olds who were surveyed in a Pew Research Center poll responded that getting rich is their generation's most important or second most important life goal. Fifty-one percent responded that being famous was also one of their most important goals. Sharon Jayson, "Generation Y's Goal? Wealth and Fame," *USA Today,* January 10, 2007, D1.

2. US Bureau of Labor Statistics, "Actors, Producers, and Directors," *Occupational Outlook Handbook,* available online at http://www.bls.gov/search/ooh.asp?ct=OOH.

3. There have been divergent patterns in the ability of women to give birth over the past two decades. Between 1982 and 2002, the percentage of married women 15–44 who had impaired fecundity, which is the ability to become pregnant and take a child to term increased from 12 to 15 percent while the percentage who were infertile and, therefore, could not become pregnant fell from 8 to 7. See Anjani Chandra, Gladys M. Martinez, William D. Mosher, Joyce C. Abma, and Jo Jones, *Fertility, Family Planning and Reproductive Health of the U. S. Women: Data From the 2002 National Survey of Family Growth,* US Centers for Disease Control and Prevention, Series 23, Number 25, December 2005, p. 1.

4. The source of adopted children can consist of public agencies, private agencies, independent adoption and inter-country adoptions. In 2001, there were 127,407 adoptions with 46 percent being private agencies, independent, kinship and tribal; 39 percent being public agencies, and 15 percent being inter-country. See U. S. Health and Human Services, *How Many Children Were Adopted in 2000 and 2001?* August 2004. In 2004, there were 36,760 live births ad 49,458 infants as a result of assisted reproduction in the United States. See U. S. Department of Health and Human Services, *2004 Assisted Reproduction Technology Success Rates,* December 2006.

5. Edward Shorter, *The Making of the Modern Family* (New York: Basic Books, 1975), p. 26.

6. Ibid., p. 168.

7. US Department of Education, National Center for Education Statistics, *Digest of Education Statistics 2005,* Table 312.

8. US Department of Agriculture, *Expenditures on Children by Families, 2005,* Table ES1, p. 11.

9. There were not that many actual births because of miscarriages. Shorter, p. 26.

10. US Census Bureau, *Fertility of American Women: June 2004,* December 2005, Table 6, p. 11.

11. Numerous studies have shown that childfree women are often stigmatized. See Karla A. Mueller and Janice D. Yoder, "Stigmatization of Non-Normative Family Size Status," *Sex Roles,* 41(11/12), 1999, pp. 901–919.

12. The percentages for one, two and three children were 17.4, 34.5, and 18.1, respectively. On average these women had only 1.9 children per woman, which is not enough to maintain the current national population without immigration. US Census Bureau, *Fertility of American Women: June 2004,* December 2005, Table 6, p. 11.

13. Ibid. Only 11 percent of women in 2004 who were 40 to 44 years old had more than three children.

14. Sara McLanahan and Gary Sandefur, *Growing Up with a Single Parent* (Cambridge, MA: Harvard, 1994), p. 1.

15. Paul R. Amato, "The Impact of Family Formation Change on the Cognitive, Social and Emotional Well-Being of the Next Generation," *The Future of Children*, 15(2), Fall 2005, pp. 75–96.

16. These elevated risks consist of juvenile offending, nicotine dependence, abuse or dependence on illicit substances, leaving school without graduation, early onset of sexual activity and multiple sexual partners. See Jan M. Nicholson, David M. Fergusson, and L. John Horwood, "Effects on Later Adjustment of Living in a Stepfamily During Childhood and Adolescence," *Journal of Child Psychology*, 40(3), 1999, pp. 405–416 and Marilyn Coleman, Lawrence Ganong, and Mark Fine, "Reinvestigating Remarriage: Another Decade of Progress," *Journal of Marriage and the Family*, 62, November 2000, pp. 1288–1397.

17. In 2004, daycare expenses for a three year old child in a profit center, 8 hours a day, 5 days a week ranged from $339.44 in Baton Rouge, Louisiana, to $1,057.83 in New York City. See Runzheimer International, "Runzheimer Analyses Daycare Costs Nationwide," January 20, 2004.

18. Ross A. Thompson, "Development in the First Years of Life," *The Future of Children*, 11(1), Spring/Summer 2001, pp. 20–33.

19. Ibid., 23.

20. The Internet is a valuable source of information on parenting skills. One important source is http://www.allaboutparenting.org.

21. Antony P. Carnevale, "Hitting the Books Still Pays Off," *Business Week*, July 17, 2006.

22. US Department of Education, National Center for Education Statistics, *Digest of Education Statistics 2005*, Table 312.

23. US President's Council of Economic Advisers, *Economic Report of the President*, February 2006, Table B-60, p. 351.

24. Jonathan Clements, "Advice I'll Pass Along to My Daughter," *Wall Street Journal*, December 10, 2006.

25. Jay Belsky and John Kelly, *The Transition to Parenthood: How a First Child Changes a Marriage. Why Some Couples Grow Closer and Others Apart* (New York: Dell, 1994).

26. Alyson Fearnley Shapiro, John M. Gottman, and Sybil Carrere, "The Baby and the Marriage: Identifying Factors that Buffer Against Decline in Marital Satisfaction After the First Baby Arrives," *Journal of Family Psychology*, 14(1), 2000, pp. 59–70.

27. "Couples education" during marriage is not very different from it before marriage, placing a strong emphasis on developing communications skills. See W. Kim Halford, Howard J. Markham, Galena H. Kline, and Scott M. Stanley, "Best Practice in Couple Relationship Education," *Journal of Marital and Family Therapy*, 29(3), July 2003, pp. 385–406.

CHAPTER 8: THE BANKRUPT MARRIAGE: DIVORCE

1. For example, using data for couples who divorced between 1988 and 1992 from the National Survey of Families and Households, I found that less than 10 percent agreed that they both wanted the divorce equally. Approximately a third agreed that they did not want the divorce or their spouse wanted it more than

them. See Allen M. Parkman, "The Importance of Gifts in Marriage," *Economic Inquiry*, 42(3), July 2004, 483–495, Table 1, p. 491.

2. The probability of divorce in the United States remained constant at about half of marriages during the last two decades of the twentieth century. However, there are large differentials by race, age at marriage and education. The probability of divorce is higher for blacks, people married when they were young and those with less education. R. Kelly Raley and Larry Bumpass, "The Topography of the Divorce Plateau: Levels and Trends in Union Stability in the United States after 1980," *Demographic Research*, 8, April 2003, pp. 245–260.

3. Only about half of new small firms survive longer than four years. Not all of them, of course, go bankrupt as they can close for a variety of reasons such as not living up to the expectations of the owners. See Brian Headd, "Redefining Business Success: Distinguishing Between Closure and Failure," *Small Business Economics*, 21, 2003, pp. 51–61.

4. Research has shown that the primary causes of bankruptcy are undercapitalization, capital structure, breadth of knowledge, depth of knowledge, financial planning and control, and product pricing strategy. See Stewart Thornhill and Raphael Amit, "Learning About Failure: Bankruptcy, Firm Age, and the Resource-Based View," *Organization Science*, 14(5), September-October 2003, pp. 497–509. Marriage and bankruptcy have one important variable in common in that they are more likely with young participants. See C. Mirjam van Praag, "Business Survival and Success of Young Small Business Owners," *Small Business Economics*, 21, 2003, pp. 1–17.

5. To be more specific, the top five reasons that marriages fail are infidelity, no longer in love, emotional problems, financial problems and sexual problems. See David H. Olson and John DeFrain, *Marriage and Families: Intimacy, Diversity and Strength*, 5th Ed. (Columbus, OH: McGraw-Hill, 2005).

6. Most of this work has been done by psychologists who have evaluated the interactions between successful couples and those that are less successful. See John M. Gottman and Nan Silver, *The Seven Principles for Making Marriage Work* (New York: Three Rivers Press, 1999). However, other disciplines such as economics have also considered the quality of those interactions including my work on the importance of the intangible aspects of marriage such as empathy and understanding. See Parkman, "Gifts."

7. See American Academy of Matrimonial Lawyers, *Making Marriage Last: A Guide to Preventing Divorce* that is available at http://aaml.org/Marriage_Last/MarriageMain.htm.

8. Five years after their divorce, many women are still single. Only 58 percent of white women, 44 percent of Hispanic women, and 32 percent of black women have remarried. The probability of remarriage after a divorce has declined over recent decades. See Matthew D. Bramlett and William D. Mosher, *Cohabitation, Marriage, Divorce and Remarriage in the United States*, National Center for Health Statistics, 2002, pp. 1–32.

9. The seminal work on the economics of divorce is by Gary S. Becker and is summarized in Gary S. Becker, *A Treatise on the Family, Enl. Ed.* (Cambridge, MA: Harvard University Press, 1991), pp. 324–341.

10. Often infidelity will be the symptom of other problems in a marriage. See Matrimonial Lawyers, *Making Marriage Last*.

11. Twenty percent of marriages have been disrupted by separation or divorce within the first five years. See Bramlett and Mosher, *Cohabitation*.

12. About 40 percent of all children will experience parental divorce before they reach adulthood. Paul R. Amato, "The Consequences of Divorce for Adults and Children," *Journal of Marriage and the Family*, 62, November 2000, pp. 1269–1287.

13. Ibid., 1274. There are studies that argue that people are better off when they make the transition from marriage to divorce. See Jonathan Gardner and Andrew J. Oswald, "Do Divorcing Couples Become Happier by Breaking Up?" *Journal of the Royal Statistical Society*, 169, 2006, pp. 319–336.

14. Linda J. Waite, Don Browning, William J. Doherty, Maggie Gallagher, Ye Luo, and Scott Stanley, *Does Divorce Make People Happy?* (New York: Institute for American Values, 2002), p. 5.

15. See Megan M. Sweeney, "Remarriage and the Nature of Divorce," *Journal of Family Issues*, 23(3), April 2002, pp. 410–440.

16. The financial arrangements at divorce can be viewed as a benefit to one party and a cost to the other. The last systematic analysis of these arrangements was by the US Census in 1989. In that year, only 15 percent of ever divorced or separated women were awarded alimony and only 60 percent of mothers had been awarded any child support. In both cases, they often did not receive the amount awarded. See U. S. Census, *Child Support and Alimony, 1989*, available at http://www.census.gov/hhes/www/childsupport/cs89.html.

17. Eleanor E. Maccoby and Robert H. Mnookin, *Dividing the Child: Social and Legal Dilemmas of Custody* (Cambridge, MA: Harvard University Press, 1992), p. 260.

18. Amato, "Consequence of Divorce," 1277.

19. See http://www.divorceinfo.com/divorceline/755.htm.

20. See http://www.peace-talks.com/compare.html.

21. See Paul R. Amato and Alan Booth, *A Generation at Risk* (Cambridge, MA: Harvard University Press, 1997).

22. This statement seems like heresy. How can anyone question the commitment of spouses to each other? However, my research shows that unilateral divorce encourages women to place a much greater emphasis on their careers. While married men have increased their efforts in the home, the number of hours spent working in the home by both spouses has decreased. See Allen M. Parkman, "Unilateral Divorce and the Labor-Force Participation Rate of Married Women, Revisited," *American Economic Review*, 82 (3), June 1992, pp. 671–678; Allen M. Parkman, "Why Are Married Women Working So Hard?" *International Review of Law and Economics*, 18(1), Winter 1998, pp. 41–49; and Allen M. Parkman, "Bargaining Over Housework: The Frustrating Situation of Secondary Wage Earners," *American Journal of Economics and Sociology*, 63(4), October 2004, pp. 765–794.

23. For example, here is a web site from North Carolina: http://www.rosen.com/special_report.asp?ID=918.

24. In other words, the children are better off if the parents maintain the appearance of a cordial relationship. See Christy M. Buchanan, Eleanor E. Maccoby, and Sanford M. Dornbush, *Adolescents after Divorce* (Cambridge, MA: Harvard University Press, 1996).

CHAPTER 9: MERGING FAMILIES: REMARRIAGE

1. See Rose M. Kreider, *Number, Timing, and Duration of Marriages and Divorces: 2001*, US Census Bureau, Household Economic Studies, P70–97, February 2005, Table 4, p. 8.

2. It is much more likely that the mother has custody of the children that are affected by a remarriage. Approximately 80 percent of households consisting of a biological parent and a stepparent consist of a biological mother and a stepfather. See Rose M. Kreider and Jason Fields, *Living Arrangements of Children: 2001*, US Census Bureau, P70–104, July 2005, Table 1, p. 3.

3. Marriages consisting of never married brides and grooms fell from 69 percent in 1970 to 54 person in 1988, the last year for which data is available. In 1988, 22 percent of marriages consisted of a first marriage for one spouse and a remarriage for the other and 23 percent consisted of remarriage for both spouses. US Census Bureau, *Statistical Abstract of the United States: 2000*, Table 145, p. 101.

4. The probability of a disruption within ten years is .33 for first marriages and .39 for a second marriage. See Matthew D. Bramlett and William Mosher, *Cohabitation, Marriage, Divorce, and Remarriage in the United States*, US Department of Health and Human Services, Series 23, Number 2, July 2002, Tables 21 and 41.

5. The probability of a disruption of a remarriage within ten years is .32 when a woman has no children with the probability increasing to .41 if she has one child and to .43 if she has more than one. Ibid., Table 41.

6. See Howard Wineberg, "Childbearing after Remarriage," *Journal of Marriage and the Family*, 52(1), February 1990, pp. 31–38.

7. Ibid., p. 37.

8. Marilyn Coleman, Lawrence Ganong, and Mark Fine, "Reinvestigating Remarriage: Another Decade of Progress," *Journal of Marriage and the Family*, 62, November 2000, pp. 1288–1307, 1291.

9. Ibid., p. 1292.

10. This study collected data from 700 mergers that occurred between 1996 and 1998. See KPMG, *Unlocking Shareholder Value: The Keys to Success*, 1999, p. 2.

11. Ibid. Also see Bill Fitzgerald, "The Mechanics of Successful Merger: Seven Key Levers," *Washington Business Journal*, June 21, 2002 and Booz, Allen & Hamilton, *Merger Integration: Delivering on the Promise*, undated.

12. These nine were less than 10 percent of the respondents to the survey. Ibid., 4.

13. Receiving child support payments is a major problem for custodial parents of which 85 percent are the mothers. Only 60 percent of custodial parents have an agreement or award and less than half of those parents receive the full prescribed amount. See US Census Bureau, *Statistical Abstract of the United States: 2007*, Table 554, p. 361.

14. One study on children from divorced families found that less than 30 percent of them received college support from their parents in contrast to almost 80 percent of children from nuclear families. See Sherrie Bennett, "Paying for College," available at lawyers.com.

15. While it is probably a good idea to have separate attorneys draw up your agreement, if the property is not particularly valuable, you might consider doing it yourself using materials such as those available from Nolo Press. See Katherine E. Stoner and Shae Irving, *Prenuptial Agreements: How to Write a Fair & Lasting Contract* (Berkeley, CA: Nolo, 2005).

Index

About the Author

ALLEN M. PARKMAN is a nationally known economist specializing in marriage and family issues. Currently Regents' Professor of Management at the University of New Mexico, he served a year as Senior Staff Economist for the President's Council of Economic Advisors in Washington, D.C. Parkman holds dual doctorates, in economics and law, and served as Visiting Scholar at the Institute for Research in Social Sciences at the University of York.